Global War,
Global Catastrophe

NEW APPROACHES TO INTERNATIONAL HISTORY

Series Editor: Thomas Zeiler, Professor of American Diplomatic History, University of Colorado Boulder, USA

New Approaches to International History covers international history during the modern period and across the globe. The series incorporates new developments in the field, such as the cultural turn and transnationalism, as well as the classical high politics of state-centric policymaking and diplomatic relations. Written with upper-level undergraduate and postgraduate students in mind, texts in the series provide an accessible overview of international diplomatic and transnational issues, events and actors.

Published:
Decolonization and the Cold War, edited by Leslie James and Elisabeth Leake (2015)
Cold War Summits, Chris Tudda (2015)
The United Nations in International History, Amy Sayward (2017)
Latin American Nationalism, James F. Siekmeier (2017)
The History of United States Cultural Diplomacy, Michael L. Krenn (2017)
International Cooperation in the Early 20th Century, Daniel Gorman (2017)
Women and Gender in International History, Karen Garner (2018)
International Development, Corinna Unger (2018)
The Environment and International History, Scott Kaufman (2018)
Scandinavia and the Great Powers in the First World War, Michael Jonas (2019)
Canada and the World since 1867, Asa McKercher (2019)
The First Age of Industrial Globalization, Maartje Abbenhuis and Gordon Morrell (2019)
Europe's Cold War Relations, Federico Romero, Kiran Klaus Patel, Ulrich Krotz (2019)
United States Relations with China and Iran, Osamah F. Khalil (2019)
Public Opinion and Twentieth-Century Diplomacy, Daniel Hucker (2020)
Globalizing the US Presidency, Cyrus Schayegh (2020)
The International LGBT Rights Movement, Laura Belmonte (2021)
American-Iranian Dialogues, Matthew Shannon (2021)

Forthcoming:
Reconstructing the Postwar World, Francine McKenzie
China and the United States since 1949, Elizabeth Ingleson

Series Editor Preface

New Approaches to International History takes the entire world as its stage for exploring the history of diplomacy, broadly conceived theoretically and thematically, and writ large across the span of the globe, during the modern period. This series goes beyond the single goal of explaining encounters in the world. Our aspiration is that these books provide both an introduction for researchers new to a topic, and supplemental and essential reading in classrooms. Thus, *New Approaches* serves a dual purpose that is unique from other large-scale treatments of international history; it applies to scholarly agendas and pedagogy. In addition, it does so against the backdrop of a century of enormous change, conflict and progress that informed global history but also continues to reflect on our own times.

The series offers the old and new diplomatic history to address a range of topics that shaped the twentieth century. Engaging in international history (including but not especially focusing on global or world history), these books will appeal to a range of scholars and teachers situated in the humanities and social sciences, including those in history, international relations, cultural studies, politics and economics. We have in mind scholars, both novice and veteran, who require an entrée into a topic, trend or technique that can benefit their own research or education into a new field of study by crossing boundaries in a variety of ways.

By its broad and inclusive coverage, *New Approaches to International History* is also unique because it makes accessible to students current research, methodology and themes. Incorporating cutting-edge scholarship that reflects trends in international history, as well as addressing the classical high politics of state-centric policymaking and diplomatic relations, these books are designed to bring alive the myriad of approaches for digestion by advanced undergraduates and graduate students. In preparation for the *New Approaches* series, Bloomsbury surveyed courses and faculty around the world to gauge interest and reveal core themes of relevance for their classroom use. The polling yielded a host of topics, from war and peace to the environment; from empire to economic integration; and from migration to nuclear arms. The effort proved that there is a much-needed place for studies that connect scholars and students alike to international history, and books that are especially relevant to the teaching missions of faculty around the world.

We hope readers find this series to be appealing, challenging and thought-provoking. Whether the history is viewed through older or newer lenses, *New Approaches to International History* allows students to peer into the modern period's complex relations among nations, people and events to draw their own conclusions about the tumultuous, interconnected past.

Thomas Zeiler, University of Colorado Boulder, USA

Global War, Global Catastrophe

Neutrals, Belligerents and the Transformation of the First World War

Maartje Abbenhuis
Ismee Tames

BLOOMSBURY ACADEMIC
LONDON • NEW YORK • OXFORD • NEW DELHI • SYDNEY

BLOOMSBURY ACADEMIC
Bloomsbury Publishing Plc
50 Bedford Square, London, WC1B 3DP, UK
1385 Broadway, New York, NY 10018, USA
29 Earlsfort Terrace, Dublin 2, Ireland

BLOOMSBURY, BLOOMSBURY ACADEMIC and the Diana logo are trademarks of Bloomsbury
Publishing Plc

First published in Great Britain 2022

Cover design: Terry Woodley
Cover image: World War I British poster for the Polish Victims Relief Fund, 1915.
Homeless Polish men, women and children carry their few possessions away
from a burning village. (Photo by Universal History Archive/Getty Images)

A catalogue record for this book is available from the British Library.

Library of Congress Cataloging-in-Publication Data
Names: Abbenhuis, Maartje M., author. | Tames, Ismee, author.
Title: Global war, global catastrophe : neutrals, belligerents and the
transformations of the First World War / Maartje Abbenhuis, Ismee Tames.
Other titles: Neutrals, belligerents and the transformations of the First World War
Description: London ; New York : Bloomsbury Academic, 2021. | Series: New
approaches to international history | Includes bibliographical references and index. |
Identifiers: LCCN 2021012904 (print) | LCCN 2021012905 (ebook) | ISBN
9781474275859 (paperback) | ISBN 9781474275866 (hardback) | ISBN
9781474275873 (epub) | ISBN 9781474275880 (ebook)
Subjects: LCSH: World War, 1914–1918. | World War, 1914–1918–Influence.
Classification: LCC D521 .A23 2021 (print) | LCC D521 (ebook) | DDC 940.3–dc23
LC record available at https://lccn.loc.gov/2021012904
LC ebook record available at https://lccn.loc.gov/2021012905

ISBN: HB: 978-1-4742-7586-6
         PB: 978-1-4742-7585-9
         ePDF: 978-1-4742-7588-0
         eBook: 978-1-4742-7587-3

Series: New Approaches to International History

Typeset by Integra Software Services Pvt. Ltd.

To find out more about our authors and books visit www.bloomsbury.com
and sign up for our newsletters.

CONTENTS

List of Illustrations viii
Acknowledgements ix

Introduction: A total global tragedy 1

1   A world of war before 1914 15

2   Germany's invasion of Belgium and the expectations
    of 'civilized' war 29

3   Short-war ambitions: The global importance of Britain's
    declaration of war 43

4   Long-war realities: Economic warfare and the
    evolution of total war in 1915 61

5   The 'barbarian' next door: Total war at home
    and abroad in 1915 77

6   The test of endurance: Rethinking the war in 1916 97

7   Nothing stays the same: Revolutionary transformations
    in 1917 115

8   The end of neutrality? The global importance
    of the United States' declaration of war 135

9   Exit ... 1918–19 157

Notes 174
Select Bibliography 213
Index 226

ILLUSTRATIONS

0.1 The World at War, Chinese map, 1917 3

1.1 'The Barnum & Bailey Greatest Show on Earth', poster, 1898 20

1.2 Defensive War, German cartoon, 1914 26

2.1 'Destroy This Mad Brute', American recruitment poster, 1917 32

3.1 Sword of Damocles, Brazilian illustration, 1914 44

3.2 The Bombing of Papeete, photograph, 1914 52

3.3 Soldiers in Lemnos, photograph, 1915 59

4.1 German Women Work in the Home Army, poster, 1916 65

5.1 Indian Prisoners of War in the Ottoman Empire, 1915–16 79

5.2 *Lusitania*, 1915 87

6.1 'In the Shadow of Liberty', French cartoon, 1916 108

7.1 Alexander Kerensky, photograph, 1917 120

8.1 China in the War, Dutch cartoon, 1917 149

8.2 Greece in the War, Dutch cartoon, 1917 153

9.1 World Unrest, American cartoon, 1919 159

9.2 Women Wearing Masks, Australian photograph, 1919 162

9.3 The Spanish Flu, Dutch cartoon, 1918 163

ACKNOWLEDGEMENTS

Surely, we do not need another history of the First World War? This book is different, however. It attempts to expand the accepted narrative of the war to include a whole range of communities previously considered peripheral, including neutrals and the non-belligerent subjects of the warring empires. It is a book that began many years ago as a conversation about how to integrate neutrals and neutrality into the general history of the war. It evolved into a history of the transformations that affected so many people across the world between 1914 and 1918. We are only too acutely aware how impossible this self-assigned task actually is. As the author Nino Haratischvili notes in her superlative novel *The Eighth Life* (2019): 'You can't put the simultaneity of the world into words'. By its very nature, then, this is a book of attempted synthesis and constant questioning. By no means is it intended as a complete history of the war. Rather, we see it as a starting point to ask new kinds of questions about the inter-connected nature of global industrial warfare between 1914 and 1918. We hope it inspires numerous thought-provoking conversations.

This book would not exist without the generous support of the Netherlands Institute of Advanced Study in the Humanities and Social Sciences (NIAS) in Amsterdam. Not only did the NIAS house Maartje as a fellow-in-residence for five months in 2018, thus enabling us to work in close proximity, but it also hosted a work-in-progress seminar and workshop with other NIAS fellows and respected colleagues alike. We cannot thank the NIAS enough for their support and wish to extend a warm thank you to Peter Romijn, Remco Raben, Houssine Alloul, Uğur Üngör, Kylie Thomas and Saskia Coenen-Snijder for their enthusiasm and input in the project. We are also extremely grateful to Gordon Morrell, Samuël Kruizinga, Michael Neiberg, Bernadette How, Alex Strete, Bethany Warner, Annalise Higgins, Femke Jacobs and Mark Stevenson for their various contributions. We particularly wish to thank our editors at Bloomsbury for their patience and support across some difficult years, including Emma Goode, Maddie Holder, Abigail Lane and Dan Hutchins.

Maartje Abbenhuis (Auckland), Ismee Tames (Amsterdam)

Introduction: A total global tragedy

The First World War had profound global importance. It led to the collapse of four of the world's most powerful empires, namely those of Russia, Austria-Hungary, Germany and the Ottomans. It almost bankrupted the French and British empires. It occasioned the Russian revolutions of 1917 and brought the Soviet Union into being. It confirmed that the United States and Japan had become powerful industrial and imperial states. Historians often describe the years 1914–18 as marking an epochal transition between the 'long' nineteenth century of industrial imperialism and the 'short' twentieth century of extremes.[1] Yet when the historian Annette Becker styled the First World War as a 'total global tragedy', she was less concerned with these age-defining characteristics than she was with the conflict's transformative impact on ordinary people.[2] For the war's 'dynamic of destruction'[3] left few communities – be they belligerent or neutral – unaffected or unchanged.

In the Ugogo region of present-day Tanzania, for example, the Wagogo people experienced the First World War as a period of extreme crisis and offered their own portentous descriptor: *Mtunya* ('the scramble'). After 1915 the Wagogo suffered the 'worst famine in the area's long history of drought', this one almost entirely manufactured by human activity.[4] The German military authorities in the region confiscated food and cattle and conscripted 35,000 Wagogo as courier troops for their army in aid of their local campaigns. When the British subsequently occupied the same region in 1917, they commandeered a further 27,000 Wagogo into their Carrier Corps and sequestered all available food resources to feed their soldiers, leaving little for locals to consume or replant. Collectively, these acts caused the Wagogo social order to collapse: villages were abandoned as families looked for food, mob justice ruled, children were pawned, corpses littered the roads and reports of cannibalism circulated. Once the 1918 global influenza pandemic hit, very little was left of the Wagogo's pre-war social structures. The *Mtunya*'s long-term consequences cannot be overstated. It established decisive power differentials between the few wealthy locals who managed to hang on to their cattle and land and the impoverished masses who lost everything.[5]

The Wagogo's *Mtunya* offers a dramatic example of the First World War's destructive power. It also highlights the intense emotional ties and personal connections that ordinary people around the world had to this global conflict. Santanu Das describes this 'tumultuous world of feeling' in his recent book *India, Empire and First World War Culture*. In the book's introductory chapter, Das notes a letter sent by a Punjabi girl named Kishan Devi in February 1916 to her father stationed as part of the Indian Expeditionary Forces in Egypt. She asks, with intense anxiety and concern, 'please take leave and come to meet us. Please do come. We repeat again and again.'[6] Devi's pleas for the safe return of a beloved parent were echoed in the letters, prayers, hopes and dreams of millions of others caught up in the global maelstrom of warfare and state violence after July 1914.

By late 1917 there were few escapes from the condition of global warfare. Officially, 1.4 billion people were at war out of a total world population of 1.8 billion.[7] More than 70 million people died as a direct consequence of the conflict, of whom almost 10 million were military casualties in campaigns fought in Europe, Africa, the Middle East, across the Asia-Pacific and on the world's seas and oceans. The others were non-combatant victims of military campaigns, revolutions, civil wars, famines, plagues and influenza, and of the world's humanitarian and material resources being diverted to aid the warring powers. In the Middle East, anywhere between 2.5 and 10 million non-combatants died during the war. In the words of Mustafa Aksakal, the war 'incinerated the [Ottoman] Empire's social fabric' much as it did for the Wagogo and so many others.[8] It left behind, as Leila Tarazi Fawaz so evocatively describes, a 'land of aching hearts' and displaced communities.[9]

For many of the people who survived them, the transformations brought on by the war years were confronting. In 1916, Léon Daudet, the French editor of the monarchist publication *Action Française*, wrote a staunchly anti-German exposé entitled 'Une guerre totale: eux ou nous' ('Total war: them or us'). Reflecting on the impact of the Verdun offensives that resulted in more than 700,000 military casualties, Daudet explained that Germany had forced a total war on France. This war, fought by such extreme means, made it impossible for any German to ever be welcome in France again.[10] In 1918, he further developed his definition of 'total war' as a struggle of 'political, economic, commercial, industrial, intellectual, legal and financial domains', a war in which 'not only the armies fight but also traditions, institutions, customs, moral codes, emotions and especially the banks'.[11]

While Daudet considered total war as a phenomenon forced upon France and its allies by their principal enemy, Germany, he acknowledged that its impact extended well beyond the warring great powers. The war was carried on the winds of global commerce, finance and information exchange and was won by those who most effectively mobilized the available human

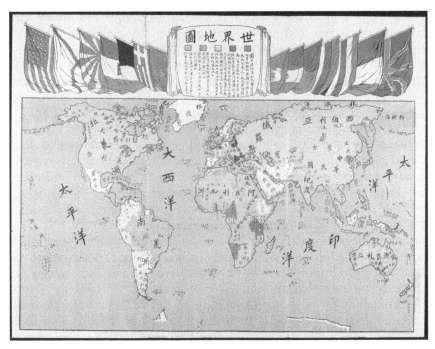

ILLUSTRATION 0.1 *This Chinese map of the world at war was published late in 1917 after China declared war on Germany. The poster celebrates China's allies in the conflict (including Britain, France, Russia, Japan and the United States), highlights all the belligerent countries involved (light shading) and marks the major military theatres of warfare (dark shading). By late 1917, there were only a very few formally neutral states left in the world (marked in white). With China's declaration of war, 1.4 billion people were officially at war out of a total world population of 1.8 billion.* Source: *Art.IWM PST 13587, Imperial War Museum, London.*

and material resources. As a result, neutral and belligerent civilians were both victims and instruments of this total global war. They certainly counted among its tens of millions of casualties.[12]

This book presents a history of the war's global dynamic of destruction and transformation much as Daudet did in 1918, namely as a product of an all-consuming industrial war fought between the world's major imperial powers.[13] It offers a wide-ranging history of the ways people, communities and states experienced, considered and behaved in response to the First World War. By necessity, it is a history that asks more questions than it answers. As such, it is not a general history but an interrogative history of what happens when the fundamental functioning of the world order unravels and what that means for people and the functioning of their own societies.[14] We take our inspiration from the wealth of scholarship undertaken during the war's centennial years (2014–18), which highlights how neutral and belligerent communities around the world were affected by and, in turn, shaped the contours of the war as it evolved into a total global reality. In integrating these myriad global faces of war – as Trevor Wilson once described them –[15] this book aims to destabilize existing war narratives, particularly those that present the conflict as 'Europe's war'.[16] The First World War may have begun in Europe, but it did not remain a singularly European venture for very long.[17]

The ensuing nine chapters describe the history of the world at war between 1914 and 1918 as it transformed into an inescapable reality. Each chapter concentrates on a global moment of transgression (of expected behaviours and norms) or transformation (of lived realities) and charts its variegated impacts on individuals and communities around the world, without aiming to emphasize one experience over another. It is a history of transformations, of shifting horizons, perspectives and choices. It is also a history of the inescapability of the war's global influences, which confronted so many at the time and subsequently. It is a history that focuses on the sinews of globalization that existed on the eve of the war and explains that the local and the global were intimately connected.[18]

Throughout the book, we turn repeatedly to Daudet's concept of *guerre totale* to describe the process by which the war's dynamic of destruction globalized. Much like Daudet, we define 'total war' as the product of a prolonged industrial war that affected 'all domains' (political, economic, commercial, industrial, intellectual, legal and financial, as well as familial, communal and cultural). It was a global reality with a multitude of local impacts. This book then recounts how 'traditions, institutions, customs, moral codes, emotions and … banks' were mobilized in response to the evolving landscape of war. To do this, each chapter is dedicated to a key theme that explains how the war globalized and affected an increasing number of states and communities, who became direct and indirect agents, victims and sometimes beneficiaries of the war's global dynamism.[19] By 1917 few people could escape the ramifications of the global war even if they lived in a neutral country, in an outpost of a neutral or belligerent empire or far away from an official military front. Nor could many of them avoid addressing the war's economic impact on their lives and livelihoods. The war altered the conduct of everyday lives, offered opportunities to exploit and affected political views and moralities. Whether they lived in German-controlled Rwanda, the neutral Dutch East Indies or on the Russian steppes, the global war presented them all with confrontational and inescapable realities, which linked, in the words of the historian Peter Gatrell, the 'epic' with the 'domestic'.[20]

Of course, the path to total war was not pre-determined and its impacts were far from uniform. The war experiences of Rwandans, Javanese or Kazakhs were in no way 'the same', but they were nevertheless interconnected. This book aims to bring out some of the ways in which 'the war' became an inescapable reality for states, communities and individuals.

It also looks to explain why the war years occasioned so many revolutionary developments. Most historians agree that the First World War ushered in the twentieth century.[21] Our book shows how the war challenged and then unmoored pre-war norms and political values at a global and local level. It does so by channelling contemporary reflections on and reactions to the transformations that occurred during the war. It shows that while it would be absurd to suggest there was a singular or universal 'war experience', most contemporaries nevertheless had some kind of war experience that they registered as important. After 1914, their lives were shaped by the contours of this evolving global war.

The term 'total war' infuses many studies of warfare and no consensus exists on its definition.[22] For some, 'total war' defines a conflict where the formal differentiations made between military personnel and civilians have eroded. For others, a total war is a conflict that witnesses the complete industrial mobilization of state and society. Yet others define total war as a state of mind or as a war conducted without limits or restraints. It can also be applied to wars that seek the unconditional surrender of an enemy or the genocidal eradication or extermination of another society.[23] The historian Stig Förster suggests that in its plethora of definitions, 'total war' risks becoming a platitude, lacking any real use or meaning.[24] Some military and strategic historians go even further by suggesting that a state of genuine total war cannot exist: only total nuclear meltdown or apocalyptic violence would suffice to meet its conditions.[25] In contrast, we agree with William Mulligan that 'total war' remains a useful concept through which to grasp how contemporaries understood the global and local contours of the First World War as it progressed.[26] The French Prime Minister Georges Clemenceau, for example, launched his ministry in November 1917 with the claim that France was now conducting a *guerre integrale* (integrated war), a policy which clearly spoke to Daudet's idea of *guerre totale*.[27] The Wagogo's *Mtunya* spoke equally powerfully to the concept of an all-encompassing war.

By focussing on contemporary experiences, agency in and conceptions of their world at war, this book argues that the label 'total war' is an apt descriptor of the First World War and that 'totalization' is a useful designator of the war's local and global transformations. Both terms give depth and meaning to the myriad human faces of the conflict. Much like Paul K. Saint-Amour, we argue that the concept of 'total war' should not be considered as a straightjacket to judge whether a war conformed to a pure definition. That the Second World War was more 'total' than the First really does not tell us much about either event after all.[28] Rather, we see 'total war' as a useful lens to ask questions of how the war evolved and how contemporaries reacted to the expansion of the war's reach and impact. For us, the First World War grew into a total war as it drew in an increasing number of belligerents and neutrals and came to affect the lives and livelihoods of an increasing number of states, societies and individuals.

In the existing historiography, the term 'total war' is usually applied only to belligerent societies, that is, to societies conducting a war. Their need for victory at any cost determines most of the discourse around what it meant to be at 'total war'. But the First World War as a 'total war' was not only shaped by the actions of belligerent governments, nor did it only affect belligerent societies.[29] A history of the war should acknowledge neutrals and the local agency of citizens and subjects in determining the course, conduct and impact of the conflict in their immediate environment. Another way to acknowledge the totality of the First World War as a transformative exercise is to highlight just how fundamental the war experience was for communities outside of Europe. For example, how Kurdish tribes interacted with the formal belligerents had an important bearing on how the war developed in the Middle East. Similarly, African Americans' military service in 1917 and 1918 helped to shape the politics of segregation in the United States, much as south Asian war experiences helped to shape the politics of independence in Mahatma Gandhi's post-war India.[30] The local and global realities of a world at war intersected in a complex web.

One of this book's ambitions, then, is to connect the international history of the war (the war as conducted by governments and states) with the experiential history of the war (the war as experienced and conducted by individuals and communities). Our definition of total war requires both an analysis of how a war fought between the great power belligerents expanded its impact and reach and an analysis of how the war was perceived as expanding by those who lived through it. Most importantly, we argue that only by integrating the roles and experiences of neutral and belligerent states and communities across the world can we truly appreciate the conflict's many metamorphoses and understand it as a 'total war' and 'global tragedy'.

In 1914, 'neutrality' was the term used to describe countries whose governments formally declared their intention of not joining a war fought between other states. After 1815, neutrality was the fall-back position of most governments when other countries went to war. In fact, across the nineteenth century, neutrality developed into a respected and useful foreign policy platform. It successfully helped to keep wars from expanding and protected the economic and imperial interests of great and small powers alike. These same powers also regulated the international laws that applied to neutral states and their subjects in time of war. The aim of these rules was to ensure that inter-state wars, when they occurred, could be geographically constrained and kept from adversely affecting the international balance of power or upsetting the international economy.[31]

This is not to suggest that the nineteenth century was peaceful. The years 1815–1914 were beset with warfare and state violence, particularly in aid of the major industrial empires' expansion.[32] Nevertheless, when wars occurred between recognized governments, the great powers purposely and collectively kept them from expanding. They did so by declaring neutrality and by recognizing the rights of neutrals to continue operating as if they were at peace. Neutrality then was an extremely useful tool of statecraft and diplomacy, a tool that sustained the industrial empires' hegemony over the rest of the world.[33] Many also considered neutrality as a powerful international norm, protecting the world from unnecessary wars.

Of course, because neutral states and subjects were by definition non-belligerent, they were not the most immediate agents of the human catastrophe that evolved after July 1914. The actions of belligerents should occupy any First World War historian. The history of warfare is, after all, the history of human-made death and destruction.[34] But if we take seriously the premise that what stood this war apart from all its predecessors was its global reach and its industrial nature, then we must do more to understand and appreciate the roles played by neutral states and neutral subjects. Neutrals were as much part of the integrated global economy and international system as any belligerent state and subject. This book thus argues for considering neutrals as agents 'in' war, rather than allocating them to an existence 'outside' or 'on the peripheries' of war.

During the war, neutrals acted as economic agents, profiteers and suppliers of arms, foodstuffs, fuels and raw materials. They served as bankers to the belligerents, as humanitarians and offered refuge for the war's victims, deserters and absconders. Neutral governments offered 'good offices' to their belligerent neighbours and provided havens of artistic and ideological exile. They could also function as hubs of revolution. Neutrals were potential belligerents. Neutral territories existed as vital geostrategic breakers and as spaces to conduct espionage. Neutral representatives could offer their diplomatic services as mediators and negotiators. Neutrals were also key witnesses and judges of the war's violence and therefore targets of the belligerents' public diplomacy campaigns. Significantly, while the nineteenth century had made neutrality a common foreign policy position for states, and many countries began the First World War in 1914 as formally declared neutrals, far fewer remained neutral by the end of the conflict in 1918. The general shift from neutrality to belligerency was one key transformation of the 1914–18 war years, which also explains why neutrals ought to be considered as important cogs in the evolution of total war.

Another key transformation occasioned by the war was the subversion of the global economy to the belligerents' need for victory at almost any cost. Where in the 'long' nineteenth century the global economy was largely protected from the military exigencies of its many local and imperial wars, the First World War ended those predictabilities. In the nineteenth century, as C.H. Stockton explained it in 1920, a 'military war' was supported by a global economy that functioned as if it was operating under a condition of a 'commercial peace'.[35] The nineteenth-century great powers (and Britain especially) took great care to protect the parameters of that 'commercial peace', not least by constraining the geographic locus of most conflicts. They also did so by codifying the rights and duties of neutrals in international law.

Significantly, all nineteenth-century wars involved more formally declared neutral states than belligerents. Thus, while the nineteenth century was an extremely violent century, it was also an age of 'limited war'. The industrializing great powers in Europe along with the United States and Japan determinedly used neutrality declarations to keep out of their imperial rivals' conflicts. In so doing, they protected their collective economic, diplomatic and military power. In the process, they were also able to impose their collective authority, their norms of 'civilization' and their claimed 'right to rule' on the rest of the world. These 'limited war' strategies helped to keep these empires in power by enabling them to suppress any opposition to their imperial rule more easily.[36]

The First World War undid the concept of 'limited war' on all fronts: military, social, political, cultural and economic. These transformations had a profound impact on belligerent societies, on their empires and on neutrals. The impact of economic deprivation occasioned by the war was acute in many parts of the world, including in Europe, across Eurasia, Africa and the Middle East. For Iranians, Libyans and Syrians, for example, the years 1915 to 1918 were years of extreme famine. One in seven Syrians died during this period, most of them civilians. In response, the Ottoman term *seferberlik* ('mobilization') remains a word that leads people in Syria to shudder, to this day.[37] In contrast, the initially neutral Americans and belligerent Japanese grew tremendously wealthy by maximizing their unfettered access to the Asia-Pacific regional economy between 1914 and 1918.[38] While Europe was at war, and the seas around Europe were militarized, the Japanese and Americans could maximize profits and heighten their global economic power, which had a fundamental impact on their governments' wartime agency and on the post-war international order.[39] Yet even the United States and Japan experienced heightened levels of social unrest in 1917 and 1918 in response to the general war situation. To call the First World War a total war, then, is to argue that the tentacles of war stretched across the globe and were shaped by a range of actors: neutral and belligerent, state and society, citizen and subject. It is to accept that the war did not begin as a total global war, although it certainly finished as such.

This history offers a patchwork of experiences that collectively help to explain how the war transformed the world. It is not a comprehensive history of the entire war. We do not spend any time on the origins of the conflict, for example, nor do we provide a narrative of any battlefronts. Jörn Leonhard's 1,087-page *Pandora's Box: A History of the First World War* and the opening volume of Hew Strachan's *First World War* clearly highlight how difficult writing a truly universal history of the war would be.[40] We have no ambitions to replicate these magisterial works nor to reinvent the collective academic power of the *Cambridge History of the First World War* and John Horne's edited *Companion to World War I*.[41] More modestly, we aim to show how the global connections at play during the war provide important context for understanding its course, conduct and legacies. If, as a result, we sometimes prioritize 'outlier' examples, we do so to underscore our argument that this was a global war with a myriad of human faces.

Each of the following chapters addresses a key global moment, which people at the time considered significant or registered as transgressive or transformative. Individually, the chapters interrogate the interactions that existed between states and communities, between people and power and between the global and the local as they dealt with the implications of each of these transformative moments. Collectively, the chapters offer a chronological account of the war as it evolved into an inescapable total global reality, which through the course of 1916, 1917 and 1918 upended the great power order that had operated during the nineteenth century. By the time the First World War formally came to a close in November 1918, the world was in complete disarray, its people desperately seeking new ways forward and new models to organize their lives and the communities and states in which they lived.

Chapter 1 begins by outlining the expectations and experiences attached to the idea of 'war' and 'peace' on the eve of the July crisis in 1914. It explains the contours of the nineteenth-century international order and the role played by warfare in that world. As such, it offers a reference point for the rest of the book, not least because it describes what contemporaries understood of war before the First World War challenged those expectations. The chapter spends some time with definitions, in terms of both what contemporaries expected of neutral and belligerent states and their people before 1914 and how they conceived of warfare and mass violence.[42] The chapter also describes global reactions to the outbreak of war on 28 July 1914, when Austria-Hungary invaded Serbia, and explains that most observers at the time did not expect that this Balkan crisis would turn into a global conflagration within the space of little more than a week.

Chapter 2 explains the enormous importance contemporaries attached to Germany's invasion of neutralized Belgium and Luxembourg on the night of 3–4 August 1914. This German act of aggression transgressed most people's expectations of how inter-state wars should be conducted. The news confronted those who encountered it, which they did all over the newspaper-reading world. Germany's actions in the first days of August 1914 effectively turned a Balkan war (fought between Austria-Hungary and Serbia) into a continental war (fought between Germany and Austria-Hungary, on the one side, and Russia, Serbia, Belgium, Luxembourg and France, on the other). In so doing, Germany ensured that the 'limited war' ethos that had operated at the heart of the European balance of power since 1815 had ended. The invasion also registered as a major transgression of the expectation that neutral countries were relatively 'safe' spaces in time of inter-state war. By invading Belgium, particularly, the German government unmoored people's expectations that wars should remain geostrategically contained. These realizations unsettled observers. They became incensed, however, when they learned that Germany's armies were massacring civilians in Belgium and northern France, acts of war that defiled all their expected norms of 'civilized' warfare and the laws of war and occupation. These acts of wanton violence became a powerful trope, which observers used to explain what they thought the war was about. From 1914, the 'rape of Belgium' motif underwrote many contemporary observations of the stakes involved in the global war.

The German invasion of Belgium, Luxembourg and France certainly made Great Britain's entry into the war more likely. Chapter 3, then, focuses on the second key moment that globalized and totalized the war, namely Britain's declaration of war on Germany on 4 August 1914. This act of belligerency was entirely out of keeping with Britain's long-term policy of adopting neutrality when other European countries went to war with each other. Britain had, in fact, not gone to war with another European power since 1856. And up until Germany's invasion of Belgium, it was highly uncertain whether Britain would go to war to aid France at all: the British cabinet prevaricated on the subject for days and a vocal neutrality movement appeared in public.

What swayed the government for war, in the end, was its fear of a German hegemon appearing in Europe which, if successful, threatened not only British imperial security but also the underlying principles of the nineteenth-century international system. The British government interpreted the German invasion as breaching the principles of 'limited war' and 'restraint' that had dominated international relations between the European states up to this time.[43] But in going to war, Britain also globalized the conflict, turning its more than 446 million imperial subjects into belligerents: altering their everyday lives, economic realities and prospects for the future in small and large ways.[44] Britain's entry in the war and the developing stalemate on the western front also ensured that the possibility of a short war 'over by Christmas' quickly evaporated. Alongside that realization, contemporaries registered that every economy and thus every society might be seriously affected by the war. The chapter describes the contours of these global reverberations and focuses on key declarations of belligerency in 1914, including by Japan and the Ottoman empire. It also highlights the consequences, both dire and opportunistic, for neutrals and belligerents as they faced the prospect of a global economy now mobilized for global war.

Another major wartime transformation, the subject of Chapter 4, came with the general realization late in 1914 that this war would not be won quickly and would require much more concerted targeting of enemy resources. After December 1914, then, the world witnessed the intensification of economic warfare. Until this point of time, the belligerents had upheld the terms of the 1909 Declaration of London and 1907 Hague Conventions, including the rights of neutrals to trade in non-contraband items with the belligerents. After December 1914, the idea that the belligerents were conducting a nineteenth-century style 'limited war' disappeared. From March 1915 onwards both sides increasingly rejected or revised neutral rights and in so doing harked back to principles of unrestricted economic warfare advanced in Europe during the early modern period. They aimed at putting their enemy under as much economic pressure as possible.

The shift to unrestricted economic warfare highlighted that if the war was to be won, it would be won by the side that was best able to mobilize the world's industrial resources and, at the same time, be able to prevent the mobilization of its enemy's human and material capacities. The consequences of the transformation were profound. For one, no neutral was left unaffected. Just as importantly, no belligerent civilian remained unaffected, however close or far away they lived to a military front. Chapter 4 thus analyses the kinds of questions and agency that evolved as the human impact of the transformation to global economic warfare became more profound through the course of 1915 and beyond. It shows how the 'politics of hunger'[45] and the belligerents' willingness to target civilians framed the politics of war at a domestic and global level in neutral and belligerent societies alike. It also shows how strong a hand greed and economic opportunism played in the politics of war.

Chapter 5 develops the conceptual and lived implications of the transformation to a war fought for and against civilians. It marks the year 1915 as the year belligerents willingly transgressed any and all restraints to achieve 'victory at any cost'. The chapter looks at the consequences of the shift by focusing both on the mobilization of civilians for war and on the consequences of targeting civilians as objects of military violence. It deals with a diverse range of subjects: from the experimentation with new forms of military armaments (such as gas, aerial bombardment and U-boat warfare) and the institutionalization of violence at the warfronts to the impact of industrial warfare on refugees, forced deportations, internment policies, occupation regimes and genocide. It explains how quickly societies at war internalized and justified violence against enemy or alien 'Others' both within and outside their own communities. It casts its lens across the world and uses examples from neutral and belligerent societies to make its case. Above all, the chapter confirms John Horne's claim that in 1915 the war became 'a world in itself' and Annette Becker's assertion that the First World War witnessed every form of mass and state violence imaginable.[46]

In Chapter 6 the focus of the book shifts to explaining the impact of this enduring total global war on communities around the world and shows how the experience of total war strained the social fabric of an increasing number of communities. It argues that the near universal experience of war weariness that set in during 1916 was a product of the seeming endlessness of the war's ever-expanding spiral of violence and economic insecurity. The chapter shows how the multiple stresses of total war led individuals, communities and governments to really question: What is this war about? What should happen next? What should my role in the war continue to be? This kind of questioning also opened up avenues for action, sometimes aimed at provoking change, at others at resisting or reconfiguring existing authorities. The chapter explains that, in large part due to the seeming endlessness of the war, it became increasingly more difficult for governments to mobilize and control the loyalties of their people. Their willingness to be at war (or to remain neutral in the war) shifted in key ways through the course of 1916. These changing loyalties made revolutionary political change within empires and states increasingly more likely. They also altered perceptions of what it meant to remain neutral. What international and intermediary functions could neutrality serve if total war had become a permanent feature of everyday life?

Chapter 7 focuses on what the historian Jay Winter calls the 'climacteric of 1917', the year that the Russian revolutions erupted and reconfigured global politics and power relations.[47] During 1917, the war truly became a 'total global tragedy', which unravelled the social and political fabric of many belligerent and neutral communities. Over the succeeding months of total war, four major powers disintegrated into revolution and civil war – Russia, Austria-Hungary, the Ottoman empire and Germany. The others – Britain, France, Japan, China and the United States – faced serious social and political crises from within. In the words of Michael Neiberg, these crises mark the year 1917 as the 'starting point of the wars that would shape the rest of the twentieth century and beyond'.[48] He might have added that these crises also mark the starting point of the twentieth-century era of decolonization.

Chapter 8 focuses on the fundamental wartime transformation that occurred in parallel to the two Russian revolutions, namely the United States' declaration of war on Germany on 2 April 1917. This act of belligerency was all important as it signalled the final collapse of the nineteenth-century international order that was predicated on the willingness and ability of individual states to declare their neutrality when others went to war. When the United States went to war in April 1917, it went to war not only against the Germans but also in aid of a new vision of an international order. That vision denied neutrality as a valid foreign policy. In so doing, the United States made it all but impossible for the world's remaining neutrals to uphold their formal neutrality, let alone to protect their neutral rights in accordance to international law. They were all astutely aware that neutrality, as an international principle steeped in nineteenth-century legal obligations, was increasingly considered an out-dated norm that needed replacing. The chapter thus also highlights that the transformations experienced by neutrals of their neutrality were as much signals of the 'climacteric' of 1917 as the violent revolutions that shook the world and undid its empires.

If anything, the final chapter of the book is not a proper conclusion. For one, it does not show how the war came to an end sometime in the aftermath of the 11 November 1918 Armistice nor in the wake of a series of peace treaties or the establishment of the League of Nations. Rather, the chapter argues that the transformations of the war years unleashed a tidal wave of largely unbridgeable and ultimately unsolvable political expectations about the shape of communities, nation-states, industrial empires and the principles and norms that ought to define international relations. All of these ideas and concepts may have originated in the nineteenth-century age of industrial globalization, but the course of the First World War enabled them to radicalize and gave them room to grow. In the aftermath of this total global tragedy, the world and its many communities and peoples would continue to struggle to define a way forward that could accommodate the needs, desires and wishes of all.

1

A world of war before 1914

Warfare and state violence beat at the heart of the nineteenth- and early twentieth-century global order. From 1815 on, a small number of increasingly powerful industrializing states and empires dominated that global order. These powers willingly used state violence to police their territories and borders, quell resistance and assert their self-proclaimed right to rule. They readily used violence or the threat of violence to acquire new lands (and economic markets), to subjugate local communities, to police dissent, to seize resources and to champion their rights as sovereign states in international law.[1] Yet while they were always willing to use warfare to protect and advance their own interests, these same states and governing elites tended to avoid going to war with rival or neighbouring countries. They understood that wars were harbingers of economic malaise, popular revolution and social unrest. As such, while only ardent pacifists argued against Carl von Clausewitz's principle that countries could go to war, most nineteenth-century governments accepted that the risks of going to war with another state were high.[2] As a result, most wars conducted between states between 1815 and 1914 were short-lived and limited in their geographic scope. They occasioned more declarations of neutrality (by other states) than declarations of war. In other words, diplomatic restraint and war avoidance were as essential to maintaining the nineteenth-century global order as the ready use of state violence to assert the right to rule over a nation or empire.

On the eve of global war in 1914, then, the world was no stranger to warfare. But it was also no stranger to the idea that inter-state warfare should be prevented. War avoidance and neutrality were common foreign policy strategies in Europe and the Americas after 1815, and in Asia after 1853. Throughout the nineteenth century, many European governments even declared their intention to adopt a long-term policy of neutrality, acknowledging that they would not go to war against another state of their own accord. During the 1890s and early 1900s, some of these countries – including the Netherlands and the Scandinavian states – even considered asking the great powers to guarantee their permanent neutrality as they had previously done for Switzerland, Belgium and Luxembourg. There were, then, three types of neutral states: permanently neutralized states (like Switzerland and Belgium, whose neutrality relied in part on the guarantees of other states), voluntary long-term neutrals (like the United States, China, Liberia and Siam) and occasional neutrals (states who declared their neutrality at the outbreak of a particular war).[3] Significantly, when it came to inter-state warfare, each type of neutral had the same expectations attached to their conduct, some of which were defined by international law, the rest by international custom. On the eve of global war in 1914, then, neutrality was expected to play a prominent role in any inter-state conflict. Furthermore, any European war that developed (which many contemporaries acknowledged as a possibility) was expected to remain localized and geographically contained.

Neutrality thrived in the nineteenth-century international system because it served a number of purposes. By avoiding inter-state warfare, the industrial powers could focus their attention on expanding their industrial economies and empires. For example, the United States used a vast amount of state violence (including genocidal state violence) to extend its formal control over the north American continent in the 1800s. It could do so without seriously worrying about being attacked by another major industrial power. In the 1890s, the United States even managed to acquire overseas territories in southeast Asia (the Philippines), the Pacific (Hawai'i and American Samoa) and the Caribbean (Puerto Rico and Cuba), defeating a weakened Spanish empire as well as mobilizing its own state forces against local and indigenous populations who resisted these developments. Across the same period, Great Britain grew the size of its 'blue water' empire 'on which the sun never set' to administer over 24 per cent of the world's landmass.[4] It utilized a vast amount of state violence against local populations to do so. In both cases, security at home enabled imperial expansionism abroad. Neutrality at home thus also enabled imperial expansionism abroad.

Imperialism and economic expansion also depended on the great power governments' willingness not to compete over access to the world's seas and oceans. Here too the ability to remain neutral when others went to war was essential. After 1815, the British Royal Navy, the world's largest and strongest naval force, protected the seas against piracy threats. All industrializing states, great and small, thrived in the nineteenth century in large part because of their access to these open and free seas. The small neutralized nation of Belgium grew into a major arms exporter, for example, and had one of the world's fastest growing industrial economies. After the Meiji Restoration in the 1860s, Japan too developed into a major industrial power with sizeable regional and global influence, even acquiring its own overseas empire in Taiwan and Korea. Britain was the nineteenth century's biggest winner, but it was not alone. By 1900, Germany and the United States both rivalled Britain in terms of steel production, manufacturing output and advances in chemical output. Their collective wealth and power were, in part, protected by their willingness to localize inter-state wars when they occurred and to avoid them altogether when that was possible. Of course, this collective economic growth also occasioned increased competition, which was manifested in a number of decisive ways, including in diplomatic relations and cultural expressions of national prowess and rivalry.

Despite the rivalries, warfare between the major industrial powers was generally avoided. Even when they did go to war, these powers tended to avoid all-out economic warfare. While it was a belligerent's right to attack ships flying an enemy's flag, to blockade enemy ports and impose other economic barriers to disable their rival's economy, they rarely exercised those rights. For example, during the Crimean War (1853–6, involving Russia, France, Britain, Sardinia and the Ottoman empire), none of the belligerents wished to risk their own access to the open seas and the global economy. They purposely contained the war, focussing on military theatres in the Black Sea, Crimean Peninsula and Baltic. As such, they only imposed a limited blockade on their enemy. Tellingly, both the Austrians and Prussians remained neutral, as did the Americans, and all three utilized their formal neutrality to expand their economic wealth and power by supplying the belligerents with essential goods.[5]

The Crimean War highlights just how essential the unfettered access to the global economy and to the open seas was considered by the world's major powers. They revelled in C.H. Stockton's conception of separating a 'military war' from a condition of a 'commercial peace'.[6] The years 1853 to 1856, then, marked a fundamental shift in how wars were conducted between the Anglo-European states. From the outset of the Crimean conflict, the belligerents ended the practice of privateering, which had been the mainstay of economic warfare in Europe and between the European empires during the early modern period. They sustained the right of neutrals to trade unhindered in non-contraband goods. They also imposed strict rules regarding the legitimate conduct of economic warfare: for example, blockades could only be imposed if they were effective. These ideas were sanctified in international law with the signing of the Declaration of Paris in 1856.[7]

The 1856 Declaration of Paris was the first of several attempts to create a universally recognized international law of war. The 1863 Geneva Convention, signed initially by twelve European governments, established the principle that in time of war, medical units would disperse aid to all who needed it. These Red Cross units effectively functioned as a 'neutral' humanitarian force that operated on (or near) the battlefield. The 1868 St Petersburg Declaration, initially signed by seventeen governments, agreed that some weapons were too horrific for use in 'civilized warfare' (by which they meant wars conducted between recognized states).[8] Fifteen governments met in Brussels in 1874 to define a 'law of war'. Their deliberations would become the basis on which the Hague Conventions of 1899 and 1907 were built. While the Hague conventions represented established wartime practices of most European countries up to that point in time, they were revolutionary in that they projected those expectations outwards to cover the world: China, Japan, the United States, Persia and Siam were all signatories of the 1899 agreements. They also focussed heavily on the rights and obligations of neutral states, entrenching the idea that neutrality was a protected status in time of inter-state war. Forty-four governments were party to the 1907 Hague Conventions, including many of the Latin American states, globalizing the application of international law in the process.

Of course, these international regulations spoke to the ability of the Anglo-European powers to dominate the values regulating the international environment at a political, economic, legal and even sociocultural level. They also spoke to the fact that conceptualizations of 'legitimate' inter-state warfare were commonplace in the lead-up to the First World War, including in the international press. The Hague conventions, for example, offered a key lens for contemporaries to ask questions of a war's legitimacy and to moralize about its conduct.[9] Governments within and outside Europe used these same ideas to mobilize their public diplomacy. For an inter-state war to be considered as legitimate it had to be conducted as a defensive measure only.[10] Increasingly, aggressive warfare between states was considered unnecessary, dangerous and against the precepts of 'civilized' behaviour. Yet, despite such rhetoric, martial virtue played an equally prominent role in Anglo-European political cultures, often defining, racializing and gendering concepts of citizenship and duty to the community, nation and empire.[11]

Most importantly, inter-state warfare was not the most common type of warfare in the nineteenth-century world. The century was filled with people's wars, revolutionary struggles and violent acts of resistance by subjugated communities within these states and empires. The agents of this kind of violence considered warfare an essential means to an essential end. How else was change to come? How else could state power be ceded and replaced? How else could their opposition to such power be registered? This kind of warfare and rebellion aimed at empowerment: it contested the imposition of foreign (colonial) rule and unwelcome governing systems, and aimed at revolutionizing political power from below.

As the historian Antoinette Burton argues in *The Trouble with Empire*, the nineteenth century was beset with wars of rebellion and resistance against imperial authority.[12] These conflicts were a constant reminder that colonized communities did not welcome the foreigners who proclaimed that they ruled their lives. Colonial resistance movements did not only aim to destabilize colonial authority. They were also assertions of agency and sovereignty 'from below'. For the Kurdish tribes who lived in the borderlands between the Ottoman and Persian empires, for example, the ever-changing landscape of great power authority in their territories posed challenges but also offered their leaders opportunities to extend and protect their own regional influence.[13] Another example is that of the desperate battle fought near the town of Adwa which, in 1896, resulted in the Italian forces' defeat and the establishment of Ethiopia as an independent nation-state, a decisive African success story.

In response to internal rebellion, few states and metropoles thought about the rules of war that regulated so-called 'civilized' inter-state warfare. At any rate, a government's policing mechanism fell outside the purview of international law. As a result, most governments felt entirely justified in undertaking almost any military action to repress a local uprising, strike or protest and to suppress the claimed rights to self-determination from among their subjects. They were also adept at policing political activism within and outside their metropoles, appealing to the principles of law, order and stability to justify their actions. They also appealed to their sovereign 'right to rule' to justify their actions against resistant populations. In establishing its control over the Choson peninsula, for example, the Meiji government in Japan repeatedly countered the Korean monarchy's claims to independence by invoking its own right in international law and as a 'civilized' state to acquire and sustain an empire.

Within the numerous empires that stretched across the world by the early 1900s, state violence was an everyday part of life, in terms of both police actions (to repress political unrest, economic strikes and colonial resistance) and the means to acquire new territory, markets and human and material resources. This kind of imperial warfare was seldom considered by its agents in the same way as inter-state military violence. It was generally brutal and rarely restrained. This did not mean, however, that the violence was left unseen or that it did not evoke considered discourses about its legitimacy. For its victims, the violence was all too real and proffered a powerful reason why ongoing military resistance against the empire and its agents was warranted. For its agents – the soldiers of empire – their actions were both legitimated as essential (for the survival of the empire) and celebrated as courageous (not least because they were conducted against supposed 'savage' and 'barbarian' peoples who did not fight fair, unlike the supposed 'civilized' men who undertook the violence).[14]

Somewhat paradoxically, then, Anglo-Europeans in the nineteenth century were *both* ardent proponents of regulating inter-state warfare and limiting its spread in the name of 'civilizing' and humanitarian forces *and* agents of extreme state violence in the name of advancing 'civilization' and imperial glory. Even permanently neutral states, like Belgium, could acquire an empire by means of warfare and rule their imperial subjects with an iron fist. Of course, the paradox only exists if you ignore the racial categorizations that operated in nineteenth-century Anglo-European societies. By 1900, not only were many non-European communities subjugated into one of the Anglo-European empires (including the United States) but they all had to operate in an international diplomatic, economic and cultural system that forced Anglo-European and capitalist values onto the rest.[15] In other words, in the international system that dominated the nineteenth-century world, wars between 'civilized' states and people were considered according to different

ILLUSTRATION 1.1 *This 1898 advertising poster for Barnum & Bailey's circus in the United States included re-enactments of battle scenes from Britain's recent war in the Sudan, which resulted in the defeat of Mahdist communities, the desecration of the Mahdi's tomb and decapitation of his head by Lord Kitchener's troops. In many places across the Anglo-world, the war was both celebrated as a heroic and essential war for the British empire and considered an unnecessary and brutal war of imperial conquest.* **Source:** *'The Barnum & Bailey Greatest Show on Earth', poster, c. 1897, Prints and Photographs Division, Library of Congress, POS - CIRCUS - Bar. & Bai. 1897, no. 7 (C size) [P&P].*

standards than wars conducted by 'white' against 'non-white' people or those fought between or within supposedly 'non-civilized' communities.

From the perspective of many Anglo-Europeans at the time, there was also no paradox. Their version of 'progress' required industrialization and the adoption of standardized principles of governance and order. As such, they defined the rights of communities in terms of the community's relationship to a 'legitimate' or 'civilized' state or empire. They considered that only legitimate states (i.e. countries with a defined international border, recognized governmental structure and system of law and order that protected individual property rights) were allowed to conduct wars to expand their empires and assert sovereignty. If such a state went to war with another legitimate state, the conflict should conform with international expectations, including the international law of war. Any state violence conducted in aid of policing an empire, suppressing a rebellion or acquiring territory where 'non-civilized' peoples lived (i.e. people whom they considered to be living outside a defined state, without set borders, a governmental structure and system of law, or which did not recognize or protect individual property rights) fell largely outside these strictures.[16]

According to these precepts, imposing limits on military violence only worked if all involved understood and worked within the same set of rules. Anyone who fell outside the framing of 'civilization' could not be expected to behave according to the precepts of international law, and thus, need not be treated in a 'civilized' manner. Thus, nineteenth-century industrial imperialism aimed not only at the acquisition of territory, markets and people, but also at imposing these rules, norms and structures on all societies. In effect, the industrializing great powers colonized the world with more than their people, goods and money. They also enforced their ways of governing, thinking, believing and behaving on the world in order to aid global economic and political interaction on their terms.

Still, it must be said that at no time was the use of state violence universally condoned or accepted among these same Anglo-Europeans. While there were certainly numerous Anglo-Europeans who accepted the need to use military violence to advance an empire, to repress a rebellion, to overthrow colonial resistance or even to quash an 'alien' people or culture, many others disagreed and critiqued these violent acts. Context, as the historian Andrew Fitzmaurice so ably explains, is everything.[17] Consider, for example, the British war of conquest in the Sudan in 1888 and 1889. Lord Kitchener's army's successes in the region were celebrated in Britain and throughout its settler colonies (see Illustration 1.1). Yet some of the excesses of Kitchener's violence were also criticized.[18] The *Mataura Ensign* newspaper in New Zealand, for example, described the destruction of the Mahdi's tomb and decapitation of his body as ghoulish and unnecessary, while in England the *Anglo-Saxon Review* lambasted these same events:

> It will be a bad day for Britain when a piece of needless brutality can pass unquestioned because the men who are responsible for it have been brilliantly successful on the battlefield.

The perspective included in the *Review* argued: 'we' British must set the right example of 'superior civilisation, superior humanity, superior gentleness and consideration' because humanity expects more of civilized states than a 'barbarous orgy of revenge'.[19]

Such critiques of imperial violence took place within a wider global discourse about the potential of extending international norms, heightening international integration and bettering all humanity within the existing international system. At the turn of the century, internationalist idealism thrived in many places. With the media revolution of the 1890s, such opinions became more commonplace and globalized in part because news about acts of state violence spread more easily and in part because there was greater recognition of how the world and its people were interconnected.[20] Many of these media reflections focussed on the regulation of the international law of war. Even before the first Hague peace conference was held in 1899, newspapers around the world considered its potential to improve international affairs. There was widespread recognition that wars were destructive and, even if they could not be avoided, should be ameliorated and restricted. These Hague principles and agreements certainly played a prominent role in the public sphere between 1899 and 1914. In reporting on The Hague conferences, but also on wars, conflicts and uprisings, global newspapers repeatedly reflected on the concept of legitimacy: was a war or instance of state violence conducted according to the rules? And, if not, what might that say about the agents of the violence? Were they 'civilized'? If they transgressed, how did that complicate global expectations and the international situation?

The Russo-Japanese War (1904–5) offers a useful example of these competing visions of war, not least because it was an intensely documented media event.[21] In the global press, the war was overwhelmingly recognized as an inter-state war, pitting the Meiji empire against its Romanov counterpart. As such, newspaper reports focused mostly on the military conduct of and the diplomacy surrounding the war. In conducting their military campaigns, the Japanese government was extremely careful to uphold the international law of war.[22] Japan needed to be seen as operating within the constricts of 'legitimate' warfare to confirm its status as 'civilized' and as an equal in the international system. As a result, international lawyers accompanied Japan's armies in the field and Russian prisoners of war were offered all due care as specified by the 1899 Hague Conventions.[23] In the international press, the war was also assessed in terms of the requirements of 'legitimate' warfare and the prescriptions of international law. This was particularly important because of Russia's attempts to interfere in Japan's trade with the neutral great powers. A considerable body of academic work appeared on the international law of war and neutrality in relation to the conflict, much of which also received commentary in the global press.[24]

In keeping with the inter-state war depiction, many editorials also considered the Russo-Japanese War as a heroic struggle of competing industrial empires, a war in which the Japanese 'tiger' defeated the Russian 'bear'.[25] In Japan, the war offered a means to advance nationalism and the idealization of soldiers as archetypal citizens.[26] The costs of warfare were also amply illustrated. Russia's military defeat inspired anti-Tsarist revolutions across the Romanov lands, highlighting the unpredictable domestic impact of warfare on the volatile subjects of this sprawling empire.[27] The socialist revolutionary Rosa Luxemburg described these anti-Romanov protests as reflective of the interconnected nature of global warfare. The destiny of Europe, she suggested in 1904:

> isn't decided between the four walls of the European concert, but outside it, in the gigantic maelstrom of world and colonial politics. ... This war

brings the gaze of the international proletariat back to the great political and economic connectedness of the world.[28]

For Koreans and the inhabitants of Manchuria, of course, the Russo-Japanese War was one of conquest, confirming Japan's rising imperial power and *de facto* control of the Choson kingdom. These people, most of whom were non-combatants, were nevertheless the war's primary victims: the battlefronts passed across their homes and lands, their cities were bombarded. Surprisingly, the civilians in the Russo-Japanese War remain the least studied by historians.[29] They are also the least visible in the contemporary newspaper record. After 1905, any hopes that the Korean people might have had to be freed from Japan's imperial yoke disappeared.[30] The war confirmed Japan's international right to empire. Manchurians too now looked with unsteady eyes to the competing claims of the Qing, Romanov and Meiji emperors to their lands. For other southeast Asian peoples, the rise of an aggressive Japan was also a frightening prospect, complicating the imperial power stakes at play in their own communities.[31] Filipino intellectuals, for example, looked to alternate visions for their own future, seeking independence from the United States and advocating for the long-term neutrality of the Philippines to heighten their security.[32]

Meanwhile, neutral Anglo-European observers racialized the conflict and questioned the martial virtues and (waning) abilities of the 'white' world. For if a 'yellow' people could win this war, then what might that say about the supposed superiority of European civilization?[33] Among most non-Europeans, however, Japan's victory was considered a fundamental military success, which they might one day emulate. As such the war offered inspiration for their own anti-imperial struggles.[34] As the Gujarati newspaper the *Jam-e-Jamshed* described the war: 'the twentieth century could not have breathed a more ... encouraging message of hope into the ears of the downtrodden nations of the East'.[35] Yet depictions of the conflict around the globe also focussed on the frightening reality of industrial warfare. Thus, when the American president, Theodore Roosevelt, successfully mediated a peace treaty at the war's end he also came to be represented as a heroic figure of international peace, the limitation of war and the promotion of liberal internationalism more generally.

Quite in contrast to the Russo-Japanese War, the global press presented the maelstrom of violence that typified the Balkan Wars in 1912 and 1913 as a 'people's war'. The neutral press fixated on the national stakes involved in the conflict, pitting the various Balkan communities (both ethnically and religiously defined) against the Ottoman empire first and then against each other. War reports fixated on its human cost: its 'outrages', massacres, pillaging and the great number of refugees.[36] In the Balkan Wars, international law seemed not to apply because people, rather than states, were the driving force behind the war.[37] Few Anglo-European observers reacted with anything other than abhorrence at the conduct of the war, although some 'Othered' it as a form of military violence that was only possible on the margins of Europe among 'semi-civilized' people.[38]

Yet in the public diplomacy conducted around the war, the belligerent Balkan governments utilized international legal norms to condemn their enemies and promote their own cause. Such claims found ready voice in the international press.[39] For its part, the Carnegie Endowment for International Peace, an internationalist organization set up in 1910 to facilitate peaceful relations in the world, commissioned an official enquiry into the conflict by sending observers from neutral countries (most of whom were international lawyers) to the region and interviewing locals. The Carnegie report, published in 1913, both documented the conflict's extreme violence and registered its purpose of ensuring that 'public opinion' be duly informed about what happened. The report eyed the improvement of international law so that wars like this one would become increasingly rare.[40] Of course, for the Balkan peoples who were at war, the war was not an 'idea' or 'observation'. Its violence was a lived reality.

It is one thing, then, to describe a conflict as witnessed from afar, mediated through a neutral newspaper article, photograph, artwork, poem or endowment report. It is quite another to assess its value in the moment. After July 1914, warfare became an increasingly universal reality (albeit a distinctly different reality depending on who you were and where you lived). Nevertheless, between 1914 and 1918, more and more parts of the world were formally *at war*. Even if they remained formally neutral and removed from a military front, the socio-economic consequences of conducting this multifaceted global war had a decisive impact on most societies. If anything, the 1914–18 conflict globalized and normalized warfare and extreme violence for its agents, victims and observers alike. It also removed many of the distinctions that contemporaries in the nineteenth century made between inter-state warfare and other forms of state and non-state military violence.

Of course, when contemporaries considered the possibility of a future war in the Balkan region during the July crisis in 1914, they did so entirely in keeping with their expectations of inter-state warfare at the time. Very few expected the assassination of the Austro-Hungarian Archduke Franz Ferdinand and his wife, Sophie, Duchess of Hohenberg, to lead to global war. As an example, on 1 July 1914, the Dutch-language *Sumatra Post* editorialized that general opinion acknowledged this murder as a 'political crime' but one that 'will have no influence on the development of Austro-Hungarian politics'.[41] The historian Michael Neiberg shows just how surprised Europeans were by Austria-Hungary's declaration of war on Serbia on 28 July.[42] At that stage, most contemporaries did not even expect a large-scale inter-state war to develop, although a Balkan war was always a possibility.[43] A number of Latin American and Japanese newspapers meanwhile talked of a potential European war breaking out along the lines of what had happened between France and Germany in 1870–1.[44] In that conflict, the rest of Europe remained formally neutral. At any rate, most commentators in 1914 recognized that Balkan crises were common and that, in the end, the recent Balkan Wars had been successfully mediated by the neutral great powers without them all becoming embroiled. In July 1914, then, the tenets of the European-backed international system seemed to still be in place. They also analysed the outbreak of war between Austria-Hungary and Serbia as an inter-state conflict and expected that it would (and, at the very least, should) be conducted according to established principles of international law.

The responsibility for the war's expansion from a Balkan conflict to a world war definitely lay with the European imperial governments. The 1914–18 war was the product of decisions made at the highest levels of government, by heads of state, ministers and cabinets. This is not to say that Europe's crowds did not come out in patriotic support of the wars declared by their governments. They certainly did, although not as enthusiastically or universally as historians used to claim.[45] But the First World War did not begin as a people's war. The impetus for the declarations of war was embedded in the decisions made by the continent's governing elites. The First World War clearly began as an inter-state conflict determined by the vagaries of European diplomacy and government decision-making processes.[46]

As a result, and as they read about unfolding events in July 1914, newspaper readers around the world expected the same diplomatic principles and restraints that had shaped previous international crises to apply. Thomas Munro shows how active the calls to arbitrate or mediate the crises were using the mechanisms of The Hague's Permanent Court of Arbitration.[47] Munro reminds us that many of the people watching the July crisis unfold were not passive receivers of information, they were also active agents in attempting to alter the course of government decision-making and promote particular foreign policies.

Europe's governments were certainly aware of the power of the people and the dangers of rebellion and revolution orchestrated 'from below' both within metropoles and across their empires. As a result, they framed their public diplomacy around the outbreak of the war in defensive terms, which was as true for neutral governments as those who had just become belligerents. It was also on defensive grounds that the public's patriotism came into play in late July and early August as the European states went to war.[48] The German parliament's *Burgfrieden* (literally 'fortress of peace', political truce) saw even the anti-military Social Democrats (SPD) declare their support for the nation under attack from Russia.[49] The Russian *Duma* declared a similar truce with the otherwise unpopular Tsar.[50] In the neutral Netherlands, a *Godsvrede* (literally 'God's peace', political truce) saw its parliamentary parties work in unison to implement effective strategies to guard the country against possible invasion and protect it from the economic impact of an uncertain war situation.[51] Declarations of a 'state of emergency'

ILLUSTRATION 1.2 *This depiction of Germany at war was published in the* Münchner Kriegsblätter *[Munich War News] in August 1914. It highlights not only the military strength of the German nation in arms (the knight and the well-disciplined troops) but also the relative weakness of its enemies: the Russian bear with its mouth wide open in agony, the toothless British lion flanked by a Japanese monkey and a frightened Gallic rooster (France). The depiction reminded its readers that Germany was conducting a defensive war and underscored the expectation that it would come out victorious.*

Source: *Bruno Goldschmitt, artist, for* Münchner Kriegsblätter *Munich, Hans von Weber, 1914, Library of Congress, LC-USZ62-21811.*

proved a very useful mechanism for governments to obtain widespread buy-in to their belligerency and neutrality.

Of course, the benefit of hindsight allows us to see that the First World War did not remain a war of states. As the conflict rapidly globalized and radicalized it grew in size and scale. In response, the war acquired different faces depending on who was affected and involved. At times it was a war of empires, at other times, a war fought within empires or between peoples and communities. At other moments, it was a war of revolutions, anti-colonial resistance, religious fervour, self-determination and irredentism. In some places it took the form of civil war. A study of the transformations effected by the war years can tell us a great deal about how a conflict that began as an inter-state war fought in Europe turned into a war of the world. Such a study can also tell us much about how contemporaries internalized, considered, debated and acted upon the changes and challenges occasioned by the war as it evolved. The following chapters bring out the importance of those transgressions and transformations.

Essential to this book and to our definition of total war is the acknowledgement that not only states, but also ordinary people, were agents of the global war. Whether as belligerent or non-belligerent actors, they helped to shape the war's various parameters. As a result, this book focuses on both states and societies. It looks both to government authority at a state level and to the individuals and communities that comprised that state or empire. Our second major distinction is between belligerents and neutrals. It is important to recognize that neutrality was a formal condition assigned to a state that remained non-belligerent during a war fought by others. In every war fought during the previous century, there had always been more neutrals than belligerents. As a result, by 1914, it was expected that at the outbreak of a war uninvolved governments would declare the intention of their country (or empire) to remain neutral. Neutrality was the fall-back position of most states. As we will see, however, neutrality did not remain a stable foreign policy choice through the course of the 1914–18 conflict. One of the key transformations of these war years was a universal shift away from neutrality.

But in 1914, it was generally acknowledged that a country could remain neutral as long as its government maintained a good relationship with the belligerents. That is to say, neutrality was sustainable as long as the country was not invaded (when it automatically became a belligerent) and as long as any violation of the legal and political requirements of neutral states in time of war was policed by the neutral government and was validated by the belligerents. According to these legal rights and duties, neutrality maintenance was a complicated and involved business. Regardless of how far away a military front was, neutral governments had to be seen to mobilize troops and naval ships to patrol territorial borders. They had to design domestic laws to prevent neutral subjects from signing up to serve in a belligerent armed force or to keep them from smuggling contraband to a belligerent. Above all, neutrality maintenance involved constant vigilance and diplomatic negotiation with belligerents, for any violation could lead to a charge of 'unneutral behaviour' and a corresponding declaration of war on that neutral.

Successful neutrality maintenance was also a matter of domestic politics. While in terms of international law, a private subject of a neutral state could not endanger that country's formal position of neutrality, in practice how neutral communities behaved in relationship to a war mattered both to the political stability of the neutral country and to their government's relationship with the belligerents. Neutral subjects internalized these responsibilities in varying ways. They often mobilized their identity as neutrals to proffer humanitarian support in the war or to engage in 'good offices' or mediation attempts. They usually advocated for the international good of their own neutrality in keeping the war from expanding. None of these positions prevented individuals from neutral countries from sharing their opinions and perspectives on the war, including in their news media. The Carnegie Endowment report on the Balkan Wars, described above, is an apt example. Its report on the 'rights' and 'wrongs' of the war was made from the self-proclaimed position of a neutral organization manned by international lawyers from neutral countries, who professed they could adjudicate the war because of their 'impartial' standpoint and their mutual respect for the universal values of peace and justice embedded in international law. From all these perspectives, neutrals considered themselves the peace-keepers of the world.

Through the course of the First World War, this peace-making role came under such intense strain that by late 1917, many contemporaries argued that neutrality's peace-keeping function had not only come to an end but that an entirely new world order was needed. But what that new world order might look like and how it might impact one's own life were openly contested. For in unravelling the many foundations of the nineteenth-century world order, neutrality included, the 1914–18 war years inspired a wide array of alternative political narratives.

2

Germany's invasion of Belgium and the expectations of 'civilized' war

After Austria-Hungary went to war with Serbia on 28 July 1914, most observers feared that the conflict might escalate and expand across the European continent. Yet many of them also hoped that the situation could and would be localized like so many European inter-state wars of the past. As a result, governments within and outside Europe dutifully declared their formal neutrality. They mobilized their armed forces and manned their borders – as was required by international law – to defend against a potential invasion and against any violations of territorial neutrality. Although they were wary of Russia and Germany's mobilizations, they also anticipated that wiser heads would rule and that this Balkan conflict might remain geostrategically contained. These expectations of restraint and containment altered drastically on 2 August 1914, after the German government issued an ultimatum to neighbouring Belgium requesting free passage for its armies on their way to attacking France.[1] The following day, the Belgian Foreign Minister refused Germany's demand. That night (3–4 August 1914), the German armed forces enacted their Schlieffen Plan, simultaneously invading neutral Belgium, Luxembourg and northern France in an attempt to encircle the French capital, Paris.[2] These German invasions transformed the character of the European war in fundamental ways and forced observers to acknowledge that this war was evolving into a rather frightening new reality.

Germany's act of aggression against Belgium shocked. Neutrality was a relatively sacred concept in the international state system in large part because it kept inter-state warfare geographically constrained and, with it, neutrals' security intact. Belgium's neutrality was particularly important to sustaining the European balance of power system.[3] The country's neutrality was also guaranteed by all the European great powers. By invading neutral

Belgium, Germany not only dismissed the validity of the system's stabilizing features, it also violated the principles that underwrote the Anglo-European international order.[4] When reports subsequently circulated of German soldiers engaging in indiscriminate reprisal killings of Belgian and French civilians, global outrage followed.[5] As many observers saw it, the Germans had assaulted the principles of 'civilized' warfare in two fundamental ways: firstly, by ignoring Belgium's and Luxembourg's rights as permanent neutrals and, secondly, by flagrantly breaching the laws of war that regulated the conduct of inter-state warfare and occupation.

Across the neutral world, Germany's actions were condemned as barbaric and its behaviour considered unworthy of a 'civilized' state. In Argentina, an entire magazine dedicated itself to explaining *los horrores* (the horrors) of the war in Belgium with references like 'the shame of the German army'.[6] Yet to the subjects of Germany's colonial empire, the violence enacted by the German soldiers in Belgium and France was less surprising.[7] To many other non-European communities subjected to the rule of an Anglo-European empire, the violence was also unremarkable. They had been exposed to all manner of atrocities in the name of 'civilization' for generations. Germany's 'transgressions' in invading Belgium and northern France thus seemed to bring the excesses of imperial violence back 'home' to the metropole. They seemed to turn Belgium into a colony of Germany.

In Chapter 1, we highlighted some of the paradoxes of the nineteenth-century international system, which created a world where warfare between supposedly 'civilized' states was restricted and avoided where possible. At the same time, this world of 'civilized restraint' also enabled all manner of state violence against subject communities to take place. When Germany invaded Belgium, Luxembourg and France in August 1914, then, it did more than expand an inter-state war to a new military theatre in Europe. In transgressing the accepted norms and laws of inter-state warfare, it blurred the lines between acceptable and unacceptable forms of state violence. It made inter-state warfare look like the unregulated forms of violence used in 'people's wars', like those that raged across the Balkan region in 1912 and 1913. It also made Germany look like an imperial power subjugating a colonial people into submission, much like it had done in Africa and elsewhere.

According to these nineteenth-century standards, Germany's invasion of Belgium, Luxembourg and France could not be considered a legitimate act of inter-state warfare. As a result, the invasion signalled that whatever the ensuing conflict would turn into, and whomever it would involve, it would not be a war of restraint. As such, the invasion of Belgium in 1914 represented the first major transformation of the First World War, one that altered pre-existing conceptions of warfare and state violence in important ways.

As we will see in the next chapter, without this German act of war, Britain may not have become a belligerent. Yet when the British government declared war on Germany on 4 August 1914, the German Chancellor Bethmann-

Hollweg exclaimed that he could not understand why. After all, the Treaty of London of 1839 that guaranteed Belgium's neutrality was merely a 'scrap of paper'. In response, the British Ambassador to Berlin, Edward Goschen, explained that Britain was honour-bound to defend Belgium and uphold the sanctity of its international agreements or else lose the good faith and credit it enjoyed in the world.[8] As the historian Isabel Hull shows, when Goschen used the word 'honour' here he referred to 'an amalgam of legal, moral and security considerations', but above all, he did so to assure the world that the British government would uphold the systemic principles that defined the established international system.[9] Many in Germany, Bethmann-Hollweg included, summarized Britain's position as naked self-interest and nothing to do with honour or morality. Yet even in this exchange, the two governments vied for the upper hand in defining the international values at stake in this war.

Germany's breach of its neighbouring states' neutrality, the subsequent murder of civilians in Belgium and northern France and the destruction of cultural heritage in these same regions posed powerful questions about the nature of this new European war. The rest of this chapter reflects on the sense of rupture occasioned by these acts of violence both locally and globally. For in an ever-expanding world of war after 4 August 1914, Germany's acts of aggressive violence took up a special place, both in the experience of its victims and within global public opinion. It certainly took up a considerable amount of attention in Allied propaganda, where the German enemy was consistently conceptualized as a barbaric brute unable to uphold the standards of 'civilization' that were supposedly embedded in the rest of the Anglo-European world.

Allied commentators often invoked the metaphor of rape, including its sexualized, gendered and racial connotations. In these framings, 'poor little Belgium' was typecast as either an innocent child or a brutalized woman. Germany was represented as a barbarian, no better than any supposedly 'uncivilized' non-European. The trope also turned the violence committed against civilians, including women and children, into an explanation as to why they were at war with the Germans. In so doing, they could easily portray themselves as defenders of 'civilization', of 'hearth and home' and of the weak everywhere. The trope mobilized the gendered and racialized inequities in operation in the pre-1914 international order to underscore the righteousness of the Allied war cause.[10] Furthermore, by asserting the just nature of their war against this 'barbaric' enemy, the Allies also mobilized a potent narrative to justify their own transgressions of international law as the war progressed.

For neutral countries, which included much of the world in early August 1914, the 'rape of Belgium' metaphor was also effective. It certainly seemed to require a response. Embracing their roles as the 'peacemakers' and 'humanitarians' of the international system, neutral populations acted accordingly. As 'objective observers', they looked to occupy what they

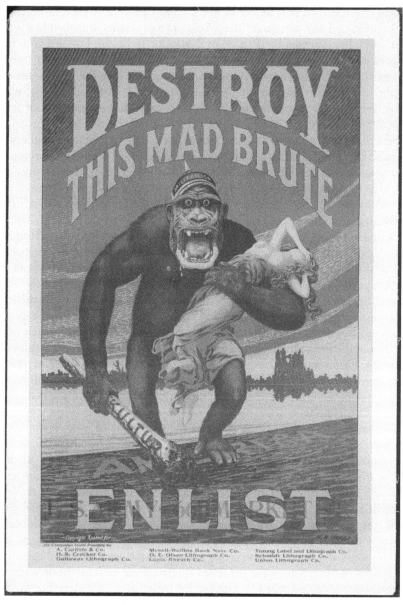

ILLUSTRATION 2.1 *This popular recruitment poster, designed by Harry R. Hopps in 1918, aimed to persuade Americans that the United States' declaration of war on Germany in 1917 was entirely justified since Germany was an 'uncivilized' beast. Hopps included the iconic ruins of the Cloth Hall at Ypres in the background of the poster to make sure there was no room for misunderstanding that the United States was going to war because Germans had violated neutral Belgium in 1914.*
Source: *Harry Hopps, 'Destroy This Mad Brute' poster, 1917, Library of Congress Digital Collection, LC-DIG-ds-03216.*

considered the moral high ground in the war. They asserted their right to investigate any wartime atrocity – much like the Carnegie Endowment had done in the Balkan Wars of 1912 and 1913 – and looked for opportunities to alleviate the suffering of the war's many victims, which in 1914 included sending Red Cross and ambulance units to the war fronts and marshalling charitable aid for Belgian refugees.[11] In so doing, they mobilized as neutrals to affect the course of the war and to determine which side had the moral imperative to win. In general, Germany was demonized in the neutral press for its military actions in western Europe. As a result, Germany found it very hard to reclaim the 'hearts and minds' of neutrals, not least because few neutral communities considered that the country was conducting a legitimate inter-state war along the principles of the Hague conventions and international law. To succeed in the war, then, many Germans pinned their hopes on a quick and decisive victory.

Another way to read the transgressive nature of Germany's invasion is to remember that all states were formally neutral until their government declared war or their borders were invaded. While they waited, they mobilized their armed forces and guarded their borders. If they bordered a powerful belligerent country like Germany, they waited under enormous emotional stress. The Dutch newspaper *De Telegraaf*, for example, reported on the Netherlands' mobilization orders on 31 July 1914 with the comment, 'humanity, and especially its female component, watched [the mobilized soldiers], leave as if their path led them straight to the battlefield.'[12] In France, the news of mobilization on 1 August was met with markedly more enthusiasm, in part because of the possibility that France might finally defeat its German foes.[13] Yet here too, many of the newly mobilized troops waited for something to happen. As one soldier recalled in his diary:

> Slow hours .... Everything before us looks vague and empty .... No one is hurried. All feverishness is gone. I don't think about the war anymore. I feel again that wretched sadness of empty hours in the barracks. All these men who don't know each other, sitting there together, no one knows why anymore, with their bundles wrapped in a coloured kerchief. When the quartermaster comes to talk to us about the war, I say to myself: Hey! It's true![14]

Another, finding himself in a part of France he had never been before, noted: 'we were given some beautiful apples. We gaze at the sea, which a lot of the men have never seen.'[15] All of these mobilized men anticipated an unknown and frightening wartime future. Back home, their families also grappled with this possibility. Anxiety ruled supreme.

Germany's invasion on the night of 3–4 August broke this timorous calm. It also registered as an emotive flash point. From this moment on, the war in Europe had become so much more than a Balkan crisis. It now involved millions of Europeans and destabilized the perceived security of all of Europe's remaining neutral countries. But what confronted the world above all else was the news of Germany's military actions against civilians in Belgium and northern France. In their ground breaking study *German Atrocities: A History of Denial* (2002), John Horne and Alan Kramer meticulously reconstruct the violence perpetrated by the invading soldiers.[16] About 5,500 civilians in Belgium and another 1,000 in northern France were murdered in acts of military reprisal through the course of August and September 1914. These actions spoke not only of the military violence of a pre-modern European world, they also invoked images of the ongoing colonial violence conducted by Europeans against non-Europeans, including by the Belgians themselves in Belgian-controlled Congo.[17]

Horne and Kramer outline the character and development of the killings in Belgium and France and contextualize them according to the expectations of the German soldiers who committed the acts. These Germans anticipated meeting a hostile and treacherous population, one that would resist their occupation by any means be it by shooting at them from within their family home, poisoning water supplies or mutilating their wounded comrades. They expected a host of *franc-tireurs* (free shooters) like those that had plagued their predecessors during the Franco-Prussian War (1870–1).[18] They also expected Belgians to resist the occupation like the subject communities in their empire. Despite the fact that there were clear laws of war that applied to the occupation of an enemy state, which were communicated to all involved, many German soldiers were filled with fear and rage as they advanced through Belgium and northern France.[19] In their fury, they turned to the local population to exact revenge for illegal deeds that almost certainly did not occur. There were no Belgian girls who gouged out the eyes of German wounded. No wells were poisoned by locals and it would have been a rare act of defiance if a farmer shot at an invading soldier. Yet in response to the illegality of these imagined acts of civilian aggression, the Germans committed equally illegal acts of military violence.

These soldiers' desire for exacting revenge was also fuelled by an expectation that they should be able to defeat the Belgians quickly and easily. To avoid a two-front war developing with Russia in the east, Germany needed a speedy victory in western Europe. If France fell quickly, then Germany could concentrate fully on Russia. The 'beast in the East' was Germany's greatest foe, after all. But because the German advance in Belgium and France was slower than expected, it was easier to blame the locals than the logistical nightmare of marching and fighting without a break along an ever-widening arc towards Paris. Germany's Schlieffen Plan was logistically flawed.[20]

Instead, the Belgian and French populations bore the brunt of Germany's collective military frustrations. As Kaiser Wilhelm II angrily wrote in his private notes on 9 August 1914:

the population of Belgium [...] behaved in a diabolical, not to say bestial, manner, not one iota better than the [Russian] Cossacks. They tormented the wounded, beat them to death, killed doctors and medical orderlies, fired secretly [...] on men harmlessly standing in the street – in fact by prearranged signal, under leadership [...] The King of the Belgians has to be notified at once that since his people have placed themselves outside all observance of European customs – from the frontier on, in all the villages, not only in Liège – they will be treated accordingly.[21]

His words reflect what was written in many German newspapers and ego-documents of the time. While there were some Germans who did not believe that Belgian and French civilians attacked their troops, they also considered it understandable that they might want to defend their homes.[22] For the German soldiers involved, it was all too easy to see the civilians as the enemy, even if the reprisal killings were much harder to rationalize. As one of them recalled:

We were given order to kill all civilians shooting at us, but in reality the men of my regiment and I myself fired at all civilians we found in the houses from which we suspected there had been shots fired; in that way we killed women and even children. We did not do it light heartedly, but we had received orders from our superior officers to act this way, and not one single soldier in the active army would know to disobey an order from the senior command. My company did not kill more than about thirty civilians in the conditions I have just described.[23]

Yet some of these soldiers were no strangers to exacting extreme violence in the name of Germany. As Mary Fulbrook shows in her book *Dissonant Lives*, violence travelled from empire back to metropole in surprising ways. She cites the example of a captain serving in the Colonial Army in German South-West Africa (present-day Namibia) who, on returning to Germany before the outbreak of the First World War, readily wielded the same whip he had used on Africans on his wife, children and servants. According to a neighbour who recalled the incident in later life, the man 'often told me how good things were in Africa, because one could beat up the blacks ... then in 1915 he was sent to Belgium'.[24]

As such, it is unsurprising to find some German military leaders condemning all Belgians as 'uncivilized' and 'barbarian' and as a 'lesser race'. After all, Germany had a duty to 'civilize' and thus could assert their 'right to rule' as needed. Hans Weseler, the Commander of the German Third Reserve Corps serving near the town of Leuven/Louvain in August 1914, explained this 'right' in a letter to his wife as follows: 'I do not like these [Belgian] people ... they give one the impression of being a race which has been kept down.'[25] Beseler saw the Belgians as a kind of savage, immature people who, if 'treated with understanding' would one day 'come to trust us [the Germans]'.[26] In Beseler's view, Belgium required a colonial-style occupation with a German civilizing mission operating at its heart. Another German general, this one retired, responded to the stories of Belgian *franc-tireurs* with the comment that such behaviour was common to 'the hordes of inferior races, and which will serve to strike this [Belgian] people from the ranks of the civilized nations'. Consequently, 'the Belgians rank with the Herero well below the level of the Hottentots!'[27] According to the general, Germany had a right to crush the rebellion on colonial and racial grounds.

Few people outside Germany saw the invasion in this way, and there is some evidence to suggest that a number of Germans did not either. For many of them, the images from the invasion of Belgium – of ravaged towns and communities, of bombed libraries and cathedrals, of refugees in uncountable numbers – were the first hellscapes of the First World War they encountered in their newspapers and illustrated magazines. As the British soldier-poet Rupert Brooke described it, the fall of Antwerp mid-August 1914 was like 'a Dantesque Hell, terrible' followed by an even 'a truer Hell. Hundreds of thousands of refugees, their goods on barrows and hand carts and perambulators and waggons, moving with infinite slowness into the night'.[28] The Argentine lawyer, Juan P. Ramos, used similar language when he described the war in August 1914 as barbarism run amok:

> People are killing each other, on all the seas and in all the lands; millions of soldiers are simply out to kill or be killed; it's raining fire and steel; huge battle cruisers are sinking; cities are burning and fields are being destroyed; everywhere there is murder, immolation, plunder, violence; the only law calls for destruction and death; mankind has stepped aside for the lecherous and savage gorilla.[29]

Perhaps unsurprisingly, it was Germany's invasion of Belgium that contemporaries returned to as familiar iconography to explain the war as it evolved.[30] It was also this invasion that determined the rights and wrongs of the whole war in many neutrals' eyes. They did so regardless of the fact that equally awful acts of military violence existed in the war between the Serbs and Austro-Hungarians and would soon be occurring in military theatres across eastern Europe, the Middle East and Africa.[31]

When it came to making sense of this new war caused by Germany, many neutrals turned to familiar tropes and looked for testimonial accounts. Before 1914, such reports were furnished by newspaper correspondents or self-proclaimed neutral 'experts' collecting evidence of atrocity and excess. The 1896 Sassun report, for example, narrated the Ottoman empire's extermination of Armenians.[32] The 1901 Hobhouse report investigated British atrocities against Afrikaners in the Second Anglo-Boer War, while the Carnegie Endowment became famous for its 1913 Balkan War accounts.[33] When the British-led Bryce report appeared in 1915, fulsomely describing Germany's atrocities in Belgium, its contents thus made for familiar reading.[34]

Alongside a relentless stream of newspaper horror stories 'straight from the mouths' of Belgian refugees, Germany could not escape the bad press.

In combination, the 1915 Bryce Report and these atrocity stories had an enormous impact on how neutral populations considered the war and how Allied propaganda portrayed Germany's actions. It fuelled widespread anti-German sentiment. Already in late August 1914, Swiss newspapers wrote lengthy reports lauding the Belgian government's official protestations to the German government for the breaches of international law, neutrality and humanity committed during the occupation.[35] In the United States, the Bryce report appeared around the time a German U-boat sunk the *Lusitania* passenger liner and made a distinct impact on Americans' readiness to consider the war in Europe as an American concern.[36] The Dutch sent their own journalists to the war fronts and into occupied territory to obtain their own 'reliable' news, reporting on many of the massacres soon after they occurred.[37] As the war lengthened, neutral reporters extended their gaze, reporting on the excessive use of violence in other theatres of war as well, including in Serbia and in the Ottoman empire.[38] They also reported on the use of illegal military weaponry, like dum-dum bullets.[39] The German authorities responded swiftly and fully to these assertions of wrong-doing. They misdirected information, published their own 'neutral' newspapers, disseminated doubt and asserted that the Belgian atrocity stories were inventions and all part of a clever disinformation campaign orchestrated out of France and Britain.[40] In the aftermath of the war, this media effort was remarkably effective. In 1914 and for many of the war years, these German disinformation campaigns largely failed to impress.[41]

Nevertheless, even in the war's early months, neutral observers were particularly adamant that they needed to see the evidence of transgression for themselves. They were particularly wary of the possibility of exaggerations creeping into the reports written by the belligerents and prided themselves on their supposed objectivity, which they described as a 'genuinely neutral stance'.[42] As an example, the Amsterdam professor of international law A.A.H. Struycken insisted Germany was innocent of any 'wrong-doing' until proven guilty. That required a thorough and fair investigation, conducted by an impartial neutral interlocuter.[43] Only by upholding the standards of international law, so Struycken argued, could the power of neutrality and a stable post-war international order be effectively restored.[44] From this perspective, neutrals ought to remain the arbiters of peace and justice.[45] The British jurist, John Macdonell, echoed the sentiment:

> True neutrality has not meant *silent* neutrality; silent in the presence of offences against laws and usages, part of the common stock of civilisation. Nor has it meant silenced neutrality; neutral Powers, dumb spectators, because [they are] afraid to speak of momentous controversies .... International law has its main origins in impulses proceeding from the consciences of men. But its only effective sanction ... is the public opinion,

the collective moral influence, of the world, the open disapprobation of those who are impartial.[46]

As the war progressed, however, such expectations as Struycken and Macdonell still possessed about the role of neutrals in 1914 and early 1915 increasingly faltered as the violence committed by belligerents on all sides expanded and as their propaganda machines went into overdrive.[47] While Germany's conduct was rarely considered virtuous or praiseworthy, the moral high ground asserted by the Allies in 1914 also quickly disappeared. Neutrals too were increasingly held accountable for the material support they extended to the belligerents: were they little more than war profiteers?

Yet throughout the war, the idea of the 'rape' of Belgium underwrote how most neutrals and Germany's enemies considered the Central Powers' war cause. Even though most of the victims in Belgium and France were men, the representation of these events was purposely gendered to prioritize the women. This is not to say there was no rape in Belgium and northern France. Every war front experienced that barbarity. But it is hard to know the true scale of gendered violence in part because the victims of sexual assault rarely told their stories.[48] When it came to the invasion of Belgium, however, the power of the rape metaphor lay in the fact that it raised the levels of outrage that could be exhibited by the predominantly male reporters who narrated the crimes, and did so in the most lurid tones. As a result, the stories provided a 'narrative truth' (as Horne and Kramer describe it) to explain the rights and wrongs of the war as it evolved.[49] The 'truth' was hard to escape and ensured that voyeuristic tales of sexual assault committed by an army of 'Attilla the Huns' against hapless and helpless victims were repeatedly mobilized in Allied propaganda to heighten the sense of Germany's transgressions against 'civilization'.[50] As the historian Nicola Gullace shows, these depictions provided 'propagandists with a vivid and evocative set of images that could be used to explain the arcane language of international law to a democratic public increasingly empowered to support or reject its enforcement'.[51] It turned the clear breach of the rule of international law by Germany into a real-life horror story, where the privileges supposedly enjoyed by European women and children in the safe space of their homes were brutally cast aside by an 'uncivilized' beastly force.

In this way, the rape metaphor also reasserted the traditional patriarchal order of war. Men fought for women, both to conquer them and to protect them from conquest.[52] Even in neutral China, commentators framed the war as a reflection of European civilization in general. Western states were militant in nature, as the journalist Chen Duxiu explained, and militancy implied men conquering women.[53] Such gendered representations also impacted women's ongoing roles within occupied societies. As Susan Grayzel points out, at a certain level, women were considered a national liability because of their vulnerability to rape and 'infection with the bacteria of sin' forced on them by enemy soldiers.[54] This influenced how women living in the occupied territories of France and Belgium were seen during and especially after the war since a degree of distrust always circulated around them about possible (consensual or forced) sexual relations with the occupier.

The gendered and racialized nature of the commentary around the rape metaphor was particularly important because it typecast wartime behaviour in terms of the supposed ethno-racial characteristics of a nation or community. The German version categorized Belgians much as it did Poles and Slavs as 'uncivilized' and 'un-European'.[55] Germany's enemies did the same with their depictions of Germany's reprisal killings and rape stories: the German Huns were inhuman beasts, no better than any non-white and 'uncivilized' people. In both cases, such representations helped to essentialize the nature of the war and who was fighting it. The war was no longer an ordinary inter-state conflict, but a war pitting cultures, 'civilizations' and, thus, essential values against each other, a war of eschatological proportions.[56]

Typecasting the enemy as the 'barbarian' also offered a handy rationale to justify one's own breaches of the law of war. If the enemy was not 'civilized', it did not need to be dealt to with restraint. In the process, these depictions essentialized the ethnic and cultural identities of the various belligerents and made race a powerful lens through which the conduct of the war was considered. For Catholic communities in neutral Latin America, for example, the German Teuton race not only threatened Belgium (a small neutral country, 'like them') but also risked the long-term survival of European civilization itself. Accordingly, the Columbian writer Santiago Perez Triana argued in 1915 that no Spanish American could be 'pro-German'.[57]

The responses to the German invasion of Belgium deserve close attention. For Dutch soldiers mobilized along the neutral Netherlands-Belgian border, the horror of the German-Belgian war was all too real. Not only could they hear and feel the thunder of artillery shells hitting nearby towns, they could see the German armies pass by the frontier. Along with several journalists, medics and a number of curious adventurists, some of them breached the security of their own neutral zone to bring wounded soldiers back with them and offer shelter to Belgian refugees. They also wondered fearfully about the future of the world and the safety of their own homes.[58] In response, the Dutch government declared a 'state of siege' in the country's border regions, placing border municipalities under military control and surveillance. They enacted laws to limit the movement of people and goods, brought in curfews for the population and identified strangers as potential foreign spies.[59]

For Belgians, the reality of warfare was even more horrifying. Alongside the dangers of the military occupation, Belgium's non-Belgian-born residents also had to consider their immediate futures. How should Belgians treat a German neighbour, married to a British man, living in a Flemish town with Belgian-born sons? The diary of Constance Graeffe offers incredible insights into the impact the German invasion had on cosmopolitan communities across the country.[60] After 4 August 1914, a person's national and racial identity largely determined how they were treated by others, including by their neighbours and the occupation authorities. Race and nationality would continue to have an enormous impact on the evolving violence of the war within civilian and military spaces within and outside Europe. In Chapter 5 we explore this civilian face of war in greater detail.

For Belgians, news and rumours about the executions and the destruction of villages also sparked tremendous upheaval. Reliable news was, of course, scarce. When Liège fell in mid-August and as the German troops marched towards the major cities of Brussels and Antwerp, burning the historical city and famous library of Louvain on the way, an exodus of refugees made its way southwards into France and northwards into the Netherlands. By October, almost a million Belgians had fled across the northern border, increasing the population of the Netherlands by a sixth. Another 500,000 Belgians arrived in France and from there many reached Britain.[61]

This desperate face of humanity inspired an extraordinary humanitarian relief effort in their host communities.[62] And as the neutral world read this news, they responded with extraordinary acts of charity aimed at alleviating the suffering of this 'unjust' war waged against these 'poor Belgians'.[63] Even though the First World War would displace tens of millions of people in Europe, the Middle East and Africa (including more than six million subjects of the Russian empire), these Belgian refugees transfixed the charitable responses of much of the neutral world until the armistice of 11 November 1918.[64]

The news stories from Belgium in August 1914 confronted readers in every sense. They provided a powerful rationale for Britain going to war. When Italy joined the war on the side of the Allies in 1915, Italians too were urged to rally behind the war cause by posters emblazoned with the warning: 'Italians! The horrors of Belgium and France are being repeated in invaded Veneto!'[65] Similar references were made in the United States when it declared war on Germany in 1917 (see Illustration 2.1).

Even among non-European communities across the British empire, Belgium's fate provided a reason to support the war against Germany. An anonymous poet in *The Times* (London) published his 'Thoughts of an Indian Soldier' in September 1914 with the lines:

The foes are not sahibs
They break the word they plight
On babes their blades are whetted
Dead women know their might.[66]

In New Zealand, members of the Ngati Porou *iwi* (tribe) assembled on 3 October 1914 to declare their collective 'appreciation of the gallant efforts of the Belgians to repel the invader'.[67] They honoured a large Belgian flag, which they hoisted underneath the British ensign. One *rangatira* (chief) even explained how the paternalistic 'duty of care' extended by the British government over New Zealand now also extended over the Belgian people.

In recognition, at least as the English-language *Poverty Bay Herald* recounted the event, 'The Maoris [*sic.*] were met to honour the flag of the Belgians, a people who had raised one of the hurdles over which the enemy would have to jump before New Zealand could be reached ... The meeting ended with solid cheering for the British and the Belgians, and cordial salutes for the allied flags.'[68] In this way, the horrors encountered by Belgian families crossed imaginative thresholds around the world and offered an identifiable and familiar cause to fight for. In the case of Ngati Porou, it offered a clear route to support the British empire in a just war against a clearly identifiable moral and imperial enemy.[69]

It is highly significant then that as the war expanded globally after 4 July 1914, the trope of 'civilization' continued to dominate many local and imperial justifications for the war. Non-European communities also utilized it, at times to justify their support of their own metropole's war against the Germans and at other times as a critique of their empire's own wartime activities. For Kuki communities living on the contested frontiers of the British empire in north-eastern India, for example, news of the war in Europe filtered through even to the 'most sleepy hill villages' who were as 'thirsty of information about the war' as anyone else.[70] Their understanding of the 'strange weapons of destruction' and the actions of the German 'archrival' ensured that few were willing to be recruited into British labour corps for service in Europe when officials called for volunteers. In their words, they 'preferred to die in their own country'.[71] The Kuki's militant resistance to the British empire in 1917 illustrates one way in which local resistance to empire became fully integrated into a world of total war.

For its part, the German government readily critiqued Britain and France for breaching the laws of war by mobilizing non-white ('uncivilized') soldiers against them, firstly in Africa and the Middle East then in Europe, suggesting that they (as opposed to the Germans) were in violation of the standards of 'civilized' warfare. On 2 September 1914, Bethmann-Hollweg even attacked the British for employing non-white soldiers and damaging the racial integrity of Europe.[72] In response, the British invoked Germany's genocidal activities against the Nama and Herero peoples in South-West Africa (present-day Namibia) in 1904–5 to further underline Germany's lack of restraint and inherent 'barbarism'.

When the British forces stationed in South Africa defeated their German equivalents in German South-West Africa in 1915, the new imperial authorities decided to collect evidence of Germany's brutal repression of the Herero and Nama uprising in 1904. The revolt came in response to clear breaches by German colonists of the Damaraland Concession of 1892, which guaranteed the Nama and Herero communities rights to land and resources. In response, the colonial authorities decimated these communities in what can only be called a genocidal campaign that resulted in a 45 to 50 per cent death toll.[73] By invoking the outrage of the invasion of Belgium and linking it to outrages committed by Germans against the Herero and Nama, the British hoped to strongly underline how truly 'uncivilized' the German state actually was.

What came to be known as the 1918 Blue Book *Report on the Natives of South-West Africa and Their Treatment by Germany* remains an important eye-witness account of the 1904–5 genocide. Like the 1915 White Book on Belgium, the 1918 Blue Book offered a gruelling and often voyeuristic read for contemporaries. In keeping with the long tradition of 'impartial' or 'neutral' accounts noted above, it marshalled the testimonies of witnesses (Herero, Nama and local colonists) to make its case. The theme of 'civilization' appeared regularly throughout, including in claims from the indigenous Africans that they were more 'civilized' than the Germans. In the words of Chief Daniel Kariko:

> We decided that we should wage war in a humane manner and would kill only the German men who were soldiers, or who would become soldiers. We met at secret councils and there our chiefs decided that we should spare the lives of all German women and children. The missionaries, too, were to be spared, and they, their wives and families and possessions were to be protected by our people from all harm. We also decided to protect all British and Dutch farmers and settlers and their wives and children and property as they had always been good to us. Only German males were regarded as our enemies, and then not young boys who could not fight these also we spared: We gave the Germans and all others notice that we had declared war.[74]

This testimony spoke to a set of norms that were familiar to the text's target audience: that the rules of war required the protection of civilians, of women and children. *Ergo*, Germans were even less civilized than these indigenous Africans.[75]

It is worth noting that in the aftermath of the war, both the 1918 Blue Book and the 1915 White Book were dismissed as products of malignant British propaganda against Germany. Obviating the content of the books helped to improve Anglo-German relations in the 1920s and offered South African and British authorities a 'clean slate' to reassert their imperial authority in the Namibian region. It certainly reasserted a sense of the superiority of 'white' civilization writ large. In so doing, the very real suffering endured by the Herero and Nama in 1904–5 as well as by the Belgians in 1914 was largely silenced.[76] Yet during the war, both of these cases of state violence helped to underwrite a global discourse around the values at stake in what many considered a war of 'civilization'. In so many ways, then, the German invasion of Belgium, Luxembourg and France in August 1914 set the tone for an unprecedented new scale of war which, as the next chapter shows, would soon encompass much of the world.

3

Short-war ambitions: The global importance of Britain's declaration of war

While the German invasion of Belgium, Luxembourg and France was perceived as conceptually transgressive around the belligerent and neutral world, it was Britain's subsequent declaration of war on 4 August 1914 that globalized the conflict. Britain's declaration ensured that few communities could avoid the question: 'what now?' Their governments had to make vital decisions about their country's future as either a neutral or belligerent in a global war in which the security of the seas and the stability of the international economy were no longer *prima facie* protected or safe. As news of Britain's war declaration spread on 5 August 1914 and economic uncertainty surged, many also recognized that the key precepts of the nineteenth-century international system – open seas, limited warfare and diplomatic restraint – were imploding. The war was transforming into a global reality that left few communities unaffected.

Britain's entry into the war registered as a decisive shift at all levels of experience. On 7 August, for example, the Colombian newspaper *La Linterna* described the expansion of warfare as a 'horrendous catastrophe … that can only end with the definitive destruction of Europe, or perhaps the total ruin of the old western civilization.' By 20 August it was clear that the war could not be contained within Europe. *La Linterna* registered this shift and its potential impact as follows: 'we are on the eve of a terrible economic crisis that can only have the most fatal results'.[1] What might happen next, however, remained unclear: the fog of war emitted a haze of unpredictability. What did happen next was a violent reshaping of the global economy and the world of war.

Over the course of the next few months, as a military stalemate developed between the European belligerents, what was a short-war ambition turned into a long-war reality. While most contemporaries clung on to the hope

ILLUSTRATION 3.1 *The fear of the outbreak of war's economic impact on the Latin American republic of Argentina is clear from this stark magazine cover published on 5 September 1914. The Buenos Aires'* Caras y Caratas *editors chose the symbolic representation of the 'sword of damocles' (in this case, scissors that might 'cut' the economy) to remind its readers of the war's potentially devastating impact on Argentina. Such fears were replicated around the neutral world.*
Source: Caras y Caratas *5 September 1914, Buenos Aires, front page.*

that the war would come to a speedy conclusion, the fact that the world's foremost economic and naval power was now at war effectively ensured that the war 'would not be over by Christmas'. This chapter shows how Britain's shift to belligerency opened up a gamut of new challenges for states and communities around the world. It explains how the war globalized after 4 August 1914, drawing in ever more belligerents.

The British government faced a stark choice when Germany went to war with France and Russia: either join the war and help its *Entente* partners or remain neutral and hope that the war in Europe did not alter the geostrategic environment too radically. As many in the British Liberal Party understood, British neutrality would in all likelihood keep the war contained in Europe and thus keep the seas open for commerce (a vital British interest). It would enable an agreement to be reached to keep the French and German colonies from fighting each other as well. A European war without Britain might be containable. It might even be highly profitable. But, as the British Conservatives argued, a war in Europe in which Britain stayed neutral might also lead to a German victory. In the end, the British cabinet chose war on 4 August 1914 to avoid the possibility of a German hegemon appearing in Europe. Before the German invasion of Belgium, Luxembourg and France, a considerable number of ministers threatened to tender their resignations if Britain went to war to defend France. After the invasion on the night of 3–4 August, only two held to that threat. The others were now convinced that a continental war involving Germany was too great a menace to British interests.[2] From this perspective, Britain's belligerency was imperative and focused entirely on containing German power, although it certainly helped that the German invasion also transgressed some powerful public norms about war.

The rather ill-conceived desire for a short war that could quickly remove the German invaders out of France and Belgium was paramount for these politicians. In their public rhetoric, they certainly expressed their faith that the war 'would be over by Christmas'. Of course, the possibility that the conflict might evolve into a long and protracted affair was a risk they willingly took, much as the Austro Hungarian, German and Russian leaderships had also done in the preceding days. Still, while these men might have imagined the prospect of an all-out war between Europe's industrial powers, at heart, they also expected that the war would not radicalize in that way.[3] None of the governments that went to war in July and early August 1914 were eager to engage in a drawn-out conflagration. None of them had planned for such a scenario. No strategic plans even existed for warfare between the imperial rivals in Africa, for example.[4] Instead they pinned their short-war ambitions to a small number of decisive military victories in Europe. Ideally, the continental war would last a matter of weeks, at most a few months.[5]

For Britons, the war declaration presented as a major break with the past. For almost a century, Britain dominated the international system as the world's super power. Its repeated use of neutrality and its overwhelming naval strength sustained the peace of the seas, helped to grow a globally interconnected capitalist economy and facilitated the expansion of an enormous global empire. By and large, Britons were proud of these successes. They also understood that the *Pax Britannica* protected the wealth and power of their global banking system and London's money markets.[6] Many of London's bankers and economists pushed for the empire's ongoing neutrality in July and early August 1914 and, in so doing, joined a vocal pro-neutrality faction.[7] When the country declared war on 4 August, however, support for king and empire became the norm among all but the most ardent British pacifists. The invasion of Belgium helped to sell this new norm.

Britain's century of neutrality between 1815 and 1914 had enabled its empire to bourgeon. By 1900, the British crown ruled more than 446 million subjects.[8] On the night of 4 August 1914, all 446 million plus officially went to war. So too did the Royal Navy. And because the British empire went to war, so did the outposts of the French and German empires, drawing in several million more imperial subjects formally into the war. As of 4 August 1914, the world's seas and oceans became potential warzones too. If Germany's invasion of neutral Belgium concerned neutrals on a conceptual level, Britain's declaration of war sent the global economy into a tail spin, taking almost everyone along with it. After 4 August 1914, the entire world economy was at war.

Altogether then, Britain's entry into the war presented the world with a profoundly transformative reality. At one level, they were all confronted with the impact of the global economic crisis occasioned by Britain's decision. How to manage that crisis was their most immediate concern. At another level, they were also confronted with the prospect that new military fronts might open up in Africa and the Asia-Pacific as enemy colonies mobilized their imperial forces against each other. In these ways, by merely going to war, Britain helped to ensure that this war could not remain a short-lived event. Yet in the heady early days and weeks of the war, most contemporaries couched their expectations of what would happen next in terms of what they hoped would happen, namely that the war would be quickly won by one or other side. In this way, while their warmongering language was also couched in terms of defending empires and 'civilization', a short-war ambition underwrote most of their desires and hopes for the future.

How essential the impact of Britain's war declaration was as a globally transformative moment is ably illustrated by Kathryn Meyer's engaging history of the Chinese treaty port of Shanghai.[9] In 1914, Shanghai was a 'city of strangers', a key international port of trade and commerce that thrived in the nineteenth-century age of open seas and open commerce.[10] Both Britain and the United States had acquired official concessions from China to run parts of the port, while the city's administration was split between various local, imperial Chinese and foreign interests. Wealthy merchant families largely ran Shanghai, but the transnational Chamber of

Commerce that represented the various mercantile, industrial and banking interests in the city also wielded a considerable amount of power. With Britain's declaration of war this transnational commercial zone could no longer sustain its networks of interdependence.

The war hit locals and foreigners alike hard and fast. Firstly, British and German ships left the port, escaping to the safer havens of Weihaiwei (a British concession) and Tsingtao (a German concession). All other ships delayed their departure. Most of them were unsure of global shipping conditions or unable to acquire affordable maritime insurance. They feared seizure by a belligerent and were uncertain of the security of their destinations and of the economic stability of any markets for their wares. Almost no new ships arrived in port for weeks. Unemployment skyrocketed. Because there were no ships, labourers were not needed to unload them. The local silk and tea industries came to a standstill as there were no foreign buyers for these luxury items. Stock piled up in the port. Inflation hit on imported goods but also on staples like rice. Money became scarce, gold and silver prices shot up and gold shops closed. International business came to a standstill. The Shanghai stock market shut down and never reopened. Shanghai's telegraph stations refused to transmit coded messages to protect China's official neutrality declared on 6 August. The transnational Chamber of Commerce, including its neutral Chinese, Japanese and American and belligerent British, French and German representatives, met to discuss suitable and cooperative solutions on 8 August. Their negotiations failed and the Chamber dissolved.[11]

Everyone in Shanghai hoped for a short war. They recognized a short-term economic crisis as manageable; a long-term one was not. Only in early 1915, as the short-war illusion dissipated, did the formally neutral port of Shanghai entrench its commercial activities along belligerent lines. By late 1915, the British and Americans set up their own nation-specific Chambers of Commerce. Germans in Shanghai could no longer bank with British firms or purchase insurance from them. Joint stock companies wound up their business.[12] Over the ensuing war years, the Japanese and American presence in Shanghai increased and China asserted more sovereign and economic power over the future of the port, in part ennobled by a 'new and patriotic language of trade'. Like many other non-European and neutral societies, China gained economically from supplying the war needs of the European belligerents and from the removal of foreign competitors in its own regional economy. All of these opportunities only became apparent, however, once the long-war reality set in.[13]

Shanghai's story was replicated all around the world.[14] In Europe, stock market jitters first appeared with the Austro-Hungarian ultimatum to Serbia on 23 July and entrenched when it declared war on 28 July. By 1 August, most European stock markets were closed. So was Wall Street. Tokyo followed suit. Panic ensued. As the middle classes around the world recognized the financial dangers of a global war, they attempted to empty their bank accounts. Gold, silver and copper disappeared from circulation as everyone hoarded what were acknowledged as more valuable species of exchange. Governments closed their treasuries and banks shut their doors, fearing depletion of their reserves.[15] Emergency paper money was issued to cover basic transactions, often for the smallest denominations. The aim was to avoid economic collapse and disaffection among populations. Prices soared while markets and shops emptied of wares. There was no clarity on when new supplies would arrive. Nervousness and anxiety permeated the globe. For example, in Peru's isolated Canete valley, a three- or four-day horseback journey from Lima, the prefect called an emergency meeting of local merchants on 10 August aimed at avoiding food shortages and rioting. Meanwhile, in the Peruvian cities, banks and factories closed, unemployment spread and food prices mounted.[16]

Britain's war declaration and the general war situation in Europe in August 1914 had a schismatic impact on global trade and, thus, on local economic and social realities. As ports lay idle, crops around the world rotted away. The agricultural economies in Latin America, Asia and Africa had trouble recovering from the loss of a stable European market. The impact was particularly heavy for luxury crops, like coffee, tea, silk and even 'exotic' feathers.[17] These export industries did not recover during the war as the warring states prioritized shipping of essential goods. But even Chile's nitrate crops, which sustained the country's economy and were an essential war material, could not reach manufacturing plants in Europe in August 1914. This caused immense economic suffering for Chileans.[18] The Japanese government, for its part, felt compelled to subsidize the local silk industry for the loss of its profits.[19] Cotton farmers in the southern United States would recoup their 1914 losses once trade with Britain, France and the European neutrals could reasonably resume but in August 1914 they were only fearful of a complete collapse of their industry.[20]

Shanghai's cotton weavers sourced new cotton supplies from the Chinese mainland in 1915, illustrating how enterprising individuals could and did profit from the changing economic landscape of war.[21] In August 1914, as African cash crops accumulated on docks, locals outed their frustrations by rioting and looting. As an example, social unrest permeated British-controlled Nigeria once it became clear that palm oil and palm kernels could no longer be traded with their main pre-war markets in Germany.[22] Colonial authorities across the continent were duly concerned. But given that imports of European manufactured goods also ground to a halt– a more permanent development – long-term inflationary pressures were guaranteed. Although they could not know this at the time, this war for resources would only radicalize after 1914, accentuating the strains on workers and their families alike. In referencing these economic impacts, Marxists felt justified in asserting that the global war was a tragedy for the world's working classes, who were exploited as soldiers and labourers to sustain a capitalist world at war.[23]

In the long term, the ability of a local or regional economy to recover from the initial economic shock occasioned on 4–5 August 1914 depended in large part on its ongoing role in the war, its proximity to 'safe' trade routes and distance from military theatres on land and sea. It also depended on whether its society remained neutral or became a belligerent. As a 'long-war reality' dawned in December 1914 (as the next chapter shows), the expansion of the belligerents' economic warfare tactics ensured that all these economies and communities were subsumed as economic agents in the wider world of war. Very few escaped the impact of global industrial warfare.

But in August 1914, global anxiety was fed in part by the realization that the free-trade and open-seas principles of the past had ended. For one, enemy belligerents could no longer trade with each other, a particularly disruptive realization given that Germany was Britain's second biggest export market and London's banks financed much of Germany's mercantile trade.[24] In turn, Germany blockaded Russia's Baltic ports, hampering Russia's access to the open seas and its economic security.[25] For the neutral world, Britain's entry into the war also ended any certainty about the ongoing legitimacy and security of their rights as neutrals to open and free trade. What measures would the belligerents impose on neutral trade with the enemy? Would they adopt the terms of the 1909 Declaration of London, which Britain had refused to ratify in 1911, but which offered broad guarantees for neutral trade? What kind of contraband declarations would the belligerents impose? How would they conduct their military campaigns against each other's shipping? Were German ports in Europe and around the German colonies still open to neutral ships? How would such shipping be protected or insurable? What would happen when neutral ships were sunk by military action? Would the conduct of maritime warfare risk neutrality and turn neutrals into belligerents?

These questions were urgent in a way that they had not been in the wars of the previous century. At no time between 1815 and 1914 were there so many great power belligerents or so many powerful navies at war with each other. While the rights and expectations of neutrals were more clearly defined by international law in 1914 than ever before, the changing ratio of neutrals-to-belligerents expanded the uncertainty. For only the United States, the Ottoman empire and Japan were left as neutral great powers on 5 August. Of the three, only the United States would remain a neutral great power by the end of the year. In this light, Germany's invasion of neutral Belgium signalled further uncertainty for the security of the world's many smaller and weaker neutral states and their imperial outposts.

The British government had not planned effectively for the possibility of a general European war, let alone a global economic war. From 4 August on, it improvised a range of economic policies focused on reassuring its own people, banks, insurance companies and merchants that their economic futures were secure.[26] Thus, even before its declaration of war (at 11 pm on 4 August), the British government established a State Insurance office to prevent a collapse of global shipping (or rather of global shipping that advantaged British interests). The office opened its doors the following day. Effectively, such policies were the British government's way of announcing that the seas remained 'open for business' for all bar its enemies. The government also (rather controversially) agreed to abide by the Declaration of London in line with its allies France and Russia, thereby fully embracing a short-war plan and reassuring the world's neutrals that their long-term economic security was safe.

Still, the London banks also refused to issue any international credit, called in international loans and rethought their peacetime insurance policies. The impact was felt around the world. Many ships stayed in port, and the recall of loans and investments made an immediate impression on the struggling investment economies in Africa, the Middle East and Latin America.[27] As Britain also declared all-out warfare on German and Austro-Hungarian trade, blockading Germany's ports from afar and seizing all merchant vessels flying a German or Austro-Hungarian flag, the German merchant marine disappeared from the world's oceans within days. Most of it would eventually be reflagged by enterprising neutral companies.[28]

The German leadership, for its part, had planned more effectively for a war with Britain, even if it had not expected the British to go to war. While Germany's armies invaded neutral Belgium, it avoided an invasion of its other western neutral neighbour, the Netherlands, in order to maximize its access to the substantial Dutch network of global trade. The Netherlands and the other border neutrals in Scandinavia and Switzerland would offer Germany an economic 'windpipe' through which it could breathe, as General von Moltke planned when he revised the Schlieffen Plan in 1909.[29] Throughout the war, these same border neutrals were considered the bane of the Allied blockade. But on 4–5 August 1914, these neutrals were as economically and psychologically distressed as the rest of the world.

For Germans and Austro-Hungarians, the British-French actions of early August 1914 made the necessity of a short war all too pressing. That sense of urgency was heightened when British troops disconnected the German telegraph cable laid across the Atlantic Ocean on 4 August and disassembled German telegraph stations in Samoa, New Guinea, and German East and West Africa over the coming weeks, severing the communication networks between the German metropole and its imperial outposts.[30] The Central Powers, then, pinned their hopes on the successful implementation of the Schlieffen Plan in western Europe, the defeat of Serbia by Austria-Hungary and a slow mobilization of Russian forces in the east. All three plans proved unrealized by December, but in the opening weeks of war their potential fulfilment underwrote German and Austro-Hungarian ambitions.

The cutting of telegraph cables, however, illustrates another fundamental transformative impact of Britain's war declaration. Where until 4 August 1914, the world's waterways were highways of relatively open communication, trade and exchange aided by the expectation that ships and cables should be able to cross those waters unencumbered, after 4 August the security of these same communication routes ended. Not only did the ownership of the cables determine which ones continued to function, it also determined what kind of information could circulate on them. To protect the territorial integrity of neutral states, for example, telegraph stations in neutral territories were instructed to refuse enciphered messages as they might contain military sensitive information that favoured one belligerent over another. Coded business transactions that passed across neutral and belligerent networks thus became beleaguered. The German-controlled cables no longer worked. Trade and investment relationships around the world faltered in turn, while clandestine use of neutral telegraphic networks became a major issue for neutral and belligerent governments alike.[31]

Mercantile and passenger shipping companies also had to consider the dangers of maritime warfare. As the British, French, Russian and German navies were now at war, the seas around Europe and the belligerent colonies became militarized. How to protect passengers and cargo, and thus profits, preoccupied business leaders in belligerent and neutral countries alike. It was not only a question of who could trade with whom and what could be carried on board neutral and belligerent ships but also which shipping routes and ports were safe from attack, blockade and interference. Access into and out of Europe's port cities was now precarious, which had the dual effect of making trade with Britain and Europe more lucrative (as prices would inevitably rise there) and less predictable. After August 1914, then, great profits could be garnered but almost always only at great risk. The economic, social and political reverberations of these consequences impacted the whole world, not least when the great power belligerents stepped up their economic warfare measures after December 1914 and coopted neutrals in the process.

But in August 1914, the economic situation was already dire. It heightened further as the British and French navies blockaded access to the North Sea and Channel and patrolled the Mediterranean, and as the German navy mined the entrance of the Baltic Sea and kept the Russian navy in its northern ports. The battle of Heligoland Bight fought on 28 August between the British and German navies highlighted the dangers of navigating Europe's seas. That all the world's oceans had become highways of warfare became all too evident when the Royal Navy bombed German telegraph stations in Dar-es-Salaam and Tanga in August, and as German raiders sunk enemy merchant ships in the Pacific Ocean, Mediterranean and Caribbean Seas, around the African continent (including on Lake Tanganyika) and along the Atlantic coast of Latin America.[32] It was made even more obvious to neutral newspaper readers when on 22 September, two German cruisers bombed the Tahitian port of Papeete, devastating the town and killing two residents.[33]

Beyond the seas, Europe's colonial empires also went to war on 5 August. This too was a radical development. Most nineteenth-century wars between

ILLUSTRATION 3.2 *On 22 September 1914, the German armoured cruisers* SMS Scharnhorst *and* Gneisenau *bombed the Pacific port-town of Papeete in French-controlled Tahiti, sinking the French gunboat Zélée and freighter* Walkure, *damaging the town's fortifications and defences and killing two residents. The local authorities had already destroyed the town's stockpile of coal to prevent its capture by the German ships.*
Source: Le Miroir, *6 December 1914, Wikipedia.org.*

the European states purposely avoided spill-over into their colonial empires. Wars in Europe were almost always kept separate from colonial warfare (another feature of the Anglo-European 'limited war' ethos). If Britain had stayed neutral in Germany and Austria-Hungary's war with Russia, Belgium and France in 1914, the neutrality of the British empire would in all likelihood have prevented conflict between the German, Belgian and French imperial outposts. The principles of the 1885 Treaty of Berlin would probably have applied. Certainly, a neutral Britain could have made a very strong case that a war in Europe did not need to extend into the extra-European world.

But as a belligerent, the British empire was too formidable not to take war to its much weaker German imperial rival. The opportunity to eradicate and acquire the German empire presented an enticing opportunity for the British and French governments, upon which they quickly capitalized.[34] New Zealand soldiers were asked to invade the islands of German Samoa, which they successfully completed on 29 August, without loss of life. An Australian force acquired German New Guinea on 11 September.[35] In Africa, German Togoland fell on 26 August to a combined French-British force. Cameroon's German ports were occupied in September, while German South-West Africa was invaded by South Africans that same month too. It submitted to British control in the middle of 1915.[36]

The African continent remained at war until 1918, costing millions of people their lives and livelihoods, particularly in south-east Africa.

The military campaigns pitting the largely African army of the German Lieutenant-Colonel Paul von Lettow-Vorbeck against British- and (later) Portuguese-led forces decimated local communities in a prolonged war of attrition. Central Africa too sustained long-term military campaigns between Belgian and German forces, with decisive impact on locals. Most of the communities affected by these military actions experienced them as extensions of European imperialism: their lives continued to be interrupted by Europeans in highly violent ways. Yet, as we will see in Chapter 6, these conflicts also brought about opportunities for local agency and resistance.

The net result of Britain's war declaration was that hundreds of millions of people across the world came to experience warfare in very direct and immediate ways. In the space it took the earth to make one full turn on its axis, warfare had become a global reality. The mobilization of armies and navies unsettled the normal state of affairs in neutral and belligerent communities alike. P.H. Ritter described the impact of the Netherlands' mobilization declaration on one Dutch town:

> Such a deadly silence hung around the packed-together crowd that one could hear the birds chirping in the gardens behind the houses. When it was announced that fifteen military intakes of conscripts would be called up, a breath of dismay, like a sudden wind surge, spread through the crowd. One woman fell unconscious. Other women started to cry silently, and buzzing and stumbling the crowd parted into the small streets where their dull footsteps echoed from the walls of the houses, which absorbed an unrest never known before.[37]

Ritter's description bears and eerie resemblance to a diary entry of a Shi'ite cleric in the southern Lebanese village of Nabatiyya on 3 August when the (still neutral) Ottoman empire declared its general mobilization:

> The people were deeply troubled and agitated .... They gathered in small groups in public spaces, astonished and bewildered, as if confronting the Day of Judgement. Some wanted to flee – but where could they go? Others wanted to escape, but there was no way out.[38]

Meanwhile in eastern Africa, as Michelle Moyd shows, the war arrived first 'as a rumour'. She narrates how:

> Mzee Ali ... recalled how he first heard in late 1914 of the 'great and terrible war' ... : From the talk around the campfires we knew this was to be no ordinary war. ... We knew from the gravity of the discussions that this war would come to our land and that only then would we fully comprehend its nature.[39]

In Europe, Africa and the Middle East, more than 18 million men took up arms in late July and early August 1914. Millions more volunteered for military service over the coming months; others were forcibly conscripted. Aside from the emotional shock mobilization engendered in these families and communities, let alone the cataclysm of violence many of them would soon experience, the removal of so many men from the civilian workforce had a decisive impact. It also militarized familial and communal settings. Uniforms and military declarations dominated civilian life in many communities after August 1914.

The white British Dominions were particularly enthusiastic in mobilizing for the war. While Ireland and South Africa posed some issues, not least when a group of opportunistic Afrikaners under leadership of Niklaas 'Siener' van Rensberg attempted to take over the government (a rebellion that was quickly repressed by the local authorities), even here the call for a war against 'barbaric' Germany was well supported.[40] Among non-white subjects of the British and French empires, the mobilization for war was generally received with more circumspection but also with recognition that the war offered opportunities to advance a range of political ambitions, be they in support of or against the Anglo-European imperial authorities.

Some Maori, for example, saw a possibility in loyally serving King and empire to gain greater political recognition as full citizens of Aotearoa New Zealand.[41] Some Australian Aborigines, Polynesian, Caribbean, Vietnamese, Cambodian, Algerian and Canada's First Nation communities mobilized in support of their empire's war effort for similar reasons: the promise of greater political representation, racial equality and recognition within the empire and local polity.[42] In India too, numerous elites argued in favour of war to advance their status as loyal imperial subjects worthy of greater self-governance and possible Dominion-status.[43] The opening months of war thus reflected the equivalence of *Burgfrieden* and expressions of national honour in a number of colonial outposts. Support for an embattled empire would (so these supporters thought) only lead to political advantages within the empire once the war finished. Their loyalty to empire seemed well founded, particularly when they were endorsed by supportive appeals from the imperial authorities themselves. That motivation remained for many months, sometimes years. Much of it would not survive the whole war.[44]

Equally alert to the geostrategic opportunities presented by the outbreak of global war were other indigenous and colonized communities who looked to advance their pre-existing anti-imperial agendas. Many south-east Asians had a nuanced understanding of the global implications and geostrategic parameters of the war. Whether they were formally neutral (as was the case for China, Siam and the Dutch East Indies) or formed part of a belligerent empire (as was the case for Singapore, Malaysia and French Indo-China), the global war influenced how these communities considered and reconfigured their political and economic interests after 4 August. As the historian Heather Streets-Salter highlights, many anti-French and anti-British revolutionaries in south-east Asia successfully lobbied for German government support to fund and resource their resistance activities against their common enemy. They often did so from neutral territories. These activities helped to destabilize the British and French wartime empires in due measure.[45]

For the United States, the expansion of the war was also of grave concern. The country declared its neutrality on 4 August, as it had in all foreign wars since 1796. There was some hope that the European war might benefit the American economy.[46] The opening of the Panama Canal on 15 August 1914 further heightened the opportunism for the neutral Americans to take over a large portion of European trade in the Atlantic and Pacific regions as well as sustain the war economies of the belligerents in Europe. The Latin American states also declared their neutrality: why partake in a war of empires that offered no clear advantages? The neutrality of the two American continents (barring Canada of course) established a key geostrategic neutral zone, sustaining the regional economy in ways that particularly favoured the United States and also offered the belligerent British and French essential advantages.

Many of Europe's smaller states also adopted neutrality, as did Spain. Even Italy declared its neutrality in early August. The Italian government's decision not to join its allies Germany and Austria-Hungary in their war was based on a foreign policy of 'sacred egoism', as the Italian foreign minister announced.[47] In August 1914, Italy had nothing as yet to gain from the conflict and much to lose. The Italian government was particularly wary that if it went to war it would embolden the anti-imperial opposition against Italian rule in Abyssinia (Ethiopia).[48] Italy's neutrality in 1914 held off an Ethiopian independence movement's bid for power, albeit only until 1916. When Italy's government entered the war against the Central Powers in May 1915, it did so with other imperial aims in mind, particularly acquiring a number of Austro-Hungarian territories.[49] Yet Italy's gamble did not pay off. By the war's end not only was Italy facing social, economic and political disarray, a civil war in Abyssinia brought an end to the Italian administration there and initiated Haile Selassie's regency.

Many communities in Africa and the Middle East also understood how the war altered their futures. As early as August 1914, Tutsi tribes in German-controlled Rwanda raided their Hutu neighbours in the Belgian-held Congo, utilizing the imperial governments' belligerency as part of their rationale.[50] This local war escalated so that by 1916 a Belgian-led *Force Majeure* from the Congo, peopled largely by local soldiers, invaded German Rwanda and Burundi and successfully seized Tabora in September. The Belgian government formally extended a protectorate over Rwanda on 6 April 1917.[51] For many African and Middle Eastern communities, the war of the world thus became part and parcel of their local and imperial rivalries. Similarly, after the Ottoman entry into the war, several Kurdish communities mobilized in support of the empire, helping to occupy Russian-controlled

Azerbaijan and raiding and razing local Nestorian Christian communities, who supported their co-religionist Russians and attacked the Muslim Kurds in turn.[52]

For the Persian (Iranian) government, however, the outbreak of war was disastrous. Aiming to protect Persia's sovereign independence, it declared formal neutrality. But since a belligerent Russia occupied the northern reaches of Persia and a belligerent Britain administered the southern region, remaining non-belligerent proved impossible. Both powers eyed up Persia's oil reserves. Meanwhile, for the Swedish police troops already serving in Persia as neutral peacekeepers (they were there to train police officers, aid with tax collection and combat brigandage), the dangers were deemed too great. After declaring Sweden's neutrality in the war, its government recalled the entire force back to Sweden.[53] Persia became a key warfront. Representatives of the great power belligerents repeatedly negotiated with local communities, including Kurds, Assyrians, Armenians, Azerbaijani and Muslim groups, for their support in an attempt to destabilize their enemies' interests.[54] These deals not only prevented the Persian government from sustaining effective rule, but also had long-term legacies for the stability and political cohesion of the region after 1918.[55] Persia, then, was the third neutral state (after Belgium and Luxembourg) to fall victim to the great powers' war. It was not the last.

Still, in 1914, neutrality was a respected and expected foreign policy choice for states. The great power belligerents well understood the importance of keeping particular countries neutral. They were also cognizant of the obligations and requirements of neutrality. But with Britain's entry, the war involved more great power belligerents than any previous conflict fought since 1815. Who was going to advance and protect neutral rights in a war dominated by great power belligerents? President Woodrow Wilson's United States seemed willing to take up this mantle. Japan's future as a neutral, however, was less obvious.

Britain's war declaration presented the Japanese government with a tantalizing prospect. With much of Europe at war, virtually all of Japan's imperial rivals in the Asia-Pacific region (aside from the United States) were pre-occupied. Given that Japan could legitimately call upon its formal alliance with Britain to go to war with Germany, it faced the possibility of expanding its Asia-Pacific empire without much opposition.[56] Japan declared war on Germany on 27 August 1914. It attacked and occupied the German-Chinese treaty port of Tsingtao, which fell on 7 November, and acquired the Marshall, Mariana and Caroline Islands and the Jaluitt Atoll by the end of the year.[57] The Japanese Navy further patrolled the Pacific and Indian Oceans, hounding what was left of the German navy out of these seas, convoying British and French troop ships and securing these waters for the safe passage of merchant vessels.[58] The regional Asia-Pacific economy grew during the war in large part because of Japan's protective role. While the Atlantic Ocean, the Mediterranean, Baltic and Black Seas would become increasingly treacherous to navigate, the Pacific and Indian Oceans remained relatively safe zones for shipping. That Japan was the ultimate beneficiary of these developments was almost inevitable. The longer Europe's war lasted, the greater Japan's economic gains.

In China, the shift to global warfare on 4–5 August 1914 registered as *weiji* (great crisis, literally 'danger opportunity').[59] The loss of European imperial agency in the region meant that only the American government was left to protect the 'open door' policy that had dominated Chinese foreign and economic relations throughout the previous two decades. Japan's invasion of Tsingtao frightened the Chinese. Their fears were fully realized when Japan capitalized on its position of power by issuing a set of twenty-one demands expanding Japanese control over Tsingtao, Manchuria and Chinese economic affairs for the foreseeable future. The twenty-one demands signed by China in March 1915 are considered one of China's ignoble moments. For the United States too, Japanese belligerency and expansionism during the war heightened the rivalry between these two major Pacific powers. Meanwhile, the notion that Japan might threaten other Asia-Pacific communities permeated the region. Still, as the historian Xu Guoqi shows, the changing landscape of imperial order in the Asia-Pacific region was also regarded as an opportunity for the Chinese to reassert themselves into the international diplomatic order.[60]

If Japan's war declaration was unimaginable without Britain's entry into the war, so too was that of the Ottoman empire. Until Britain joined the war, the Young Turk government could imagine itself as a neutral power, situated on the periphery of a European continental war. With Britain's entry in the war, the geostrategic threats to the empire mushroomed, as did the possibility that the victors (on either side) would not hesitate to dismember the empire at the conflict's conclusion. Since Russia presented the greatest threat, a war fought on the side of the Allies was unthinkable. A war on the side of the Central Powers offered a wealth of opportunities, not least the possibility to expand and Turkify the empire.[61] From early August 1914, then, the Ottoman government negotiated an alliance with the Central Powers, promising military aid against Russia at the earliest opportunity. It took until late October to fulfil this secret promise.[62] On attacking the Russian fleet in the Black Sea on 29 October, the vast Ottoman empire with its immensely diverse population went to war. It opened up new military fronts in the Caucasus, Mesopotamia and Persia, made the Suez Canal less safe and cut Russia off from the Mediterranean Sea.[63]

Even if opportunism drove its decision to enter the war, the Ottoman government publicly presented the war as a defensive enterprise.[64] Much like Christianity was mobilized as a rationale for war and in the defence of 'civilization' in Europe, the Ottoman sultan declared *jihad* (holy war) on all Christians in early November.[65] *Jihad* had numerous faces aimed both at mobilizing Muslim subjects of the Ottoman sultan in a 'just' and 'necessary' war and at inspiring Muslim subjects of enemy empires to incite anti-imperial rebellion from below.[66] *Jihad* confronted all the Christian powers, including the neutral Netherlands whose East Indian colonies counted millions of Muslims.[67] With good reason, the British and French colonial authorities worried about the potential impact of *jihad* on a colonial rebellion among their Islamic subjects. Across Africa, south and south-east Asia, Muslims were inspired by the *jihad* to reassess their relationships to the local imperial authority and the wider world at war.[68]

There is much historiographical debate about the success of the 1914 *jihad* declaration.[69] At one level, *jihad* legitimated certain wartime actions, not least the systematic targeting of Christian populations within the Ottoman realm. Christian-Muslim relations in the Middle East, which were shaky at the best of times, drastically declined after August 1914.[70] There is also evidence to suggest that for some Muslims, the call to battle helped to solidify their support for the Ottoman war effort. But *jihad* also validated a massive Turkification enterprise throughout the empire. On the grounds that only loyal subjects to the empire could be trusted and to pre-empt the creation of 'fifth-column' guerilla forces, the Ottoman government ordered the massive displacement of 'suspect' civilians, including millions of Christians.[71] Through the course of 1915, these Christians would be systematically eliminated by the Ottoman government in a distinctly genocidal campaign. Identifying the 'enemy within' was a common strategy utilized in all belligerent societies, however, and one that reflected widespread colonial imperial practices before the war too.

In the opening months of war, the giddy heights of the short-war ambition were reached. These are best reflected in the extravagant plans of military leaders on all sides. In hindsight, British expectations for the defeat of Germany and its own rising global power, Germany's hopes for an enlarged central European empire, and France's expectations for the restitution of Alsace-Lorraine and other territorial acquisitions seem fantastical, callous reflections of how out-of-touch these leaders were with the desperate suffering of their subjects and soldiers. Still, these military men were not the only ones looking to maximize the opportunities a successful short war might provide. Japanese hopes for a sizeable Asian empire and recognition of their great power status and the Chinese government's wish to reinsert itself on the international arena were equally prominent ambitions in the opening months of war. So too were Vietnamese hopes for independence and many indigenous communities' desires to achieve political recognition for their wartime military service, Indian and Irish hopes for Home Rule, and even some suffragettes to achieve the vote for women. The expectation that wartime service and support could lead to post-war gain were all too common in the 1914 war months.

These 1914 ambitions lingered as a reference point as the war progressed. But in December 1914, everyone first had to endure the recognition that the war would not be over before 'the leaves fall off the trees' as Kaiser Wilhelm II had promised the German population in August.[72] Their collective

ILLUSTRATION 3.3 *This photograph, taken on the Greek island of Lemnos in 1915, shows soldiers from the various Allied armies preparing to invade the Gallipoli peninsula. The invasion, waged from 25 April 1915, involved troops from around the French and British empires, including from India, New Zealand, Australia, Ireland, Malta, Egypt, Senegal, Algeria, Tunisia and Newfoundland.*
Source: *Photograph, Lemnos, 1915, Bain News Service, Library of Congress, LC-DIG-ggbain-20400.*

short-war ambitions were overtaken by a long-war reality. That realization proffered terrifying prospects, not least because the first five months of war had already cost millions of people their lives and livelihoods, including a casualty count of a third of the Russian army (around 1.8 million men), half of the Belgian army, 90 per cent of the Ottoman Third Army and 1.25 million Austro-Hungarian troops.[73] From 1915 on, the lack of a decisive victory by any of the great power belligerents would lead the world on a path to total war.[74]

4

Long-war realities: Economic warfare and the evolution of total war in 1915

The opening months of war in 1914 were immensely destructive for the European belligerents. By the time winter descended, not only had they endured phenomenally high casualty counts, their military stockpiles were also largely exhausted. By November, the British Expeditionary Force in northern France and Belgium had run out of sandbags. In the middle of November, the German army facing them across the western front only had enough artillery shells to last them four more days of concerted attacks.[1] By this stage, generals in every belligerent army complained about serious armaments shortages, alongside the scarcity of much else, including blankets, uniforms, fuels, fodder, medical supplies and horses.[2] For the belligerents involved, restocking their armies in the field with essentials had become a priority. But the logistics involved were staggering, requiring wholesale increases in manufacturing capacity which in turn necessitated the building of factories and machinery, the acquisition of skilled labour, raw materials and fuels, the expansion of transportation capacity and enough money to pay for it all. Given that in August 1914, none of the belligerent metropoles were self-sufficient even in terms of food supply, prioritizing access to the foods, fuels and raw materials had become essential to the viability of the belligerents' war campaigns.[3]

That all the major belligerent powers experienced serious military shortages in these early months underlines how deeply embedded their desire – and perhaps even their expectation – for a quick victory had been at the war's outset.[4] It also underscores how deeply they had underestimated their enemies' ability to defend. As the western front entrenched after the Battle of the Marne and as victory eluded the armies on Europe's extensive eastern and Caucasian fronts through November, the likelihood of a 'long war' dawned as an inescapable reality.[5] That realization presented the belligerent governments with unenviable options. None of them were willing to sue for peace. But they also recognized that to have a realistic chance at victory, radical changes needed to be made to their wartime policies, especially in terms of logistics and military supply. The prospect of a long war required careful consideration of these enduring economic and material needs. If their material advantages could be maximized and those of their enemies minimized, then the possibility of a quick victory remained.

The 'long-war reality' that set in during the European winter of 1914 thus did not end the belligerent governments' hopes for a speedy victory.[6] Rather, it repositioned their planning around how to achieve victory by recognizing the central importance of mobilizing all available human, industrial, financial and material resources for the war.[7] Where before 1914 most European states expended around 4 per cent of their GDP on their armed forces, the shift to total war ensured that their entire economic output was repurposed to serve the needs of the war.[8] After November 1914, the global economy was also weaponized to serve the needs of the belligerent powers. Inevitably, neutrals and the 'limited' economic warfare practices of the past became targets of the shift.[9] This chapter explains how the shift to a long-war reality transformed the conduct of the economic war. It does so by describing the impact of these developments on neutral and belligerent communities alike, including the Netherlands, Colombia, the United States, Liberia, Shanghai, Port Said, India, Japan, the Ottoman empire and Russia.

By traversing the world of economic warfare in 1915, the chapter illustrates how deeply interconnected the global economy remained during the war and how singularly important the shift to economic warfare was to communities everywhere. It also shows how banks, shipping companies, manufacturers, suppliers of raw materials and insurers aided and abetted the belligerents' insatiable need for money and military supplies. It highlights how the premise of neutrality – the right to stay out of another country's war – was affected by the shift to economic warfare and how the actions of neutral governments, people and institutions influenced wider perceptions of what 'the war' was about. Chapter 5 follows on by describing how no civilian community anywhere was *prima facie* safe from the destructive violence of the war from 1915. At any rate, by the end of the year many of them understood, as the German newspaper the *Kölnische Zeitung* explained it on 3 October 1915, that this was a 'war of holding out', a war of survival.[10]

If in August 1914, people laboured under the illusion that the war might present a short-lived interruption of pre-war economic practices and that 'business as usual' would soon resume, after November 1914 that illusion had surely burst. From this point on, the belligerent governments prioritized the material and industrial needs of victory. At home, they reconfigured domestic laws and bureaucratic practices, requisitioned and rationed resources, imposed new taxes and mobilized civilians into essential 'war work'. Peacetime industries converted into arsenals. Raw materials, food and fuel stuffs were consigned to prioritize military production and supply. In metropoles and imperial outposts alike, 'the war' increasingly governed the contours of everyday life.

Military planners in all the major belligerent capitals reconsidered their strategic plans after November 1914, with an eye to securing key resources and disrupting their enemies' supply routes. The Indian Expeditionary Force attacked and occupied the Mesopotamian city of Basra on 11 November, for example, to protect British access to the Anglo-Persian Oil Company's installations at Abadan.[11] In February 1915, an Ottoman force of 22,000 troops assaulted the British-controlled Suez canal hoping to dissever this key international highway of trade and troop movements.[12] In April, a combined force of British, French and imperial troops invaded the Ottoman empire's Gallipoli peninsula seeking to reinstate Russian shipping access through the Dardanelles Straits and to disrupt the land-bridge by which the German, Austro-Hungarian and Ottoman empires supplied and supported each other by road and rail. As the historian Hew Strachan explains it, in 1915 'the attack on the Dardanelles provided the epicentre for the hopes and fears of all the belligerents'.[13] When the Gallipoli invasion failed, the Allies looked to support the Serbian war effort by driving a wedge into the region from out of the (formerly neutral) Greek port of Thessaloniki. The Salonika front tied up tens of thousands of troops and placed the region under long-term military occupation.

Across the 1914–15 winter months, the belligerent powers also expanded their economic warfare practices, targeting first their enemies and then the neutrals who supplied them.[14] The expansion of these economic policies might have looked like a tit-for-tat series of reprisal measures, each step escalating its reach so as best to interrupt the enemy's war effort.[15] In reality, the belligerent authorities on both sides carefully considered the short- and long-term liabilities of their economic policy decisions: the French and British governments argued about them incessantly, while their legal advisers clearly explained how the measures violated existing international laws.[16] Balancing the needs of victory in the immediate term against the dangers of alienating a neutral government (who might join the war against them) and the fear of setting new legal precedents that might disrupt their own interests as neutrals in a future war remained an utmost consideration.[17] But where in August 1914 the belligerents accepted the principles of the Declaration of London and the rights of neutrals to trade, the shift to a 'long-war reality' ensured that belligerency increasingly overruled neutrality.[18] Throughout the previous century, the reverse had been true.[19]

When Germany mined parts of the North Sea in August 1914, it sought to prevent the British Royal Navy from directly blockading its ports. In October 1914, the Royal Navy mined the mouth of the English Channel hoping to keep neutral cargo from reaching Germany through the ports of Amsterdam, Copenhagen and Hamburg. At this point, however, both navies also provided neutrals with maps to navigate around their mines.[20] A British

Order of Council on 29 October, subsequently, expanded the war on neutral trade by declaring all foodstuffs destined for the enemy as contraband and thus liable for capture. The declaration also made neutral ship captains responsible for 'proving' that their cargo would not reach Germany, Austria-Hungary or the Ottoman empire. The legal protections offered to neutral traders to freely cross the open seas had effectively ended.[21] Four days later, the British naval vessel HMS *Audacious* sank on a newly laid German minefield off the northern coast of Ireland. In retaliation, the British government declared the entire North Sea a 'military area' and warned all unauthorized ships to keep away. Effectively, the British used the rationale of 'military endangerment' to allow it to monitor, intercept and board all neutral ships found in the zone.[22]

The North Sea became even more treacherous when on 4 February 1915, the German government announced its own warzone around the British Isles and declared all ships caught in the zone at risk of being sunk without warning by its fleet of submersible U-boats.[23] The French and British felt compelled to adopt a more coordinated 'offensive economic warfare' strategy in response, one that targeted the trade of Germany's contiguous neutrals especially.[24] Collectively, these actions ensured that no neutral cargo intercepted by a belligerent navy anywhere in the world was *prima facie* safe from capture after March 1915. Furthermore, no neutral ship intercepted in and around the European continent was safe from being sunk on sight.

Historians often explain the shift to 'total war' during the First World War as the product of the belligerent governments' willingness to prioritize victory at any cost. Their definition of total war stresses three interdependent components: firstly, the mobilization of all elements of state and society in aid of a country's war effort; secondly, the conscription and coercion of all available human and material resources to support a belligerent's war effort; and, thirdly, the strategic targeting of an enemy's economic, material and human resources.[25] In other words, the shift to total war made everyone in a belligerent society responsible for the successful conduct of the war. In a society at 'total war', as Illustration 4.1 emphasizes, the female labourer working in a factory making artillery shells was often considered as important to the success of a country's war effort as the male soldier on a battlefield. The corollary was, of course, that the labourer working in an enemy factory was deemed as legitimate a target of military violence as any enemy troops. But so was a neutral shipping company supplying an enemy with goods or a neutral bank underwriting an enemy war loan.

The shift to total war ensured not only that the belligerents willingly wielded blockade and hunger as weapons against enemy civilians but also against neutral populations. The shift to total war thus presented neutral states, neutral commerce and neutral populations with a new set of wartime expectations and realities as well. Their economic security, their sovereign independence and their non-belligerency were all at risk of succumbing to the shifting sands of total war. While neutrals had subsidized the financial

ILLUSTRATION 4.1 *This propaganda poster, first published in 1916 by the German War Office, reminded its audience of the essential role German women played in sustaining the military war effort. Entitled 'German Women Work in the Home Army', the poster depicted a female factory labourer passing a grenade, that she has presumably built, to a male soldier. Positioning her at the centre of the poster and assigning her equal size and space to the male soldier communicated the essence of the concept of total war: civilians and soldiers alike were needed to win this war. She had his back. Without her, the war could not be won.*
Source: *Gottfried Kirchbach, 'Deutsche Frauen arbeitet im Heimatheer!' Poster, 1916, Deutsches Historisches Museum, 2013/3085.*

and material needs of belligerents for centuries, their right to do so was always contested. The maintenance of neutrality always involved a balancing act between belligerent and neutral interpretations of international law and diplomatic agreement. Throughout the nineteenth century, however, neutral rights had stabilized. Until 1914, the right of neutrals to trade freely with each other and in limited capacity with belligerents was well-established. Great Britain's position as the nineteenth-century's economic and imperial superpower, for one, was predicated on its ability to remain non-belligerent when its industrial rivals were at war. But in the context of the shift to total economic warfare in early 1915, a neutral country's right to profit from the war or to supply a belligerent came under increasing scrutiny and attack. Moreover, as the historian Pierre Renouvin explains, if it was 'on the backs of neutrals that the economic warfare was pursued' then neutrals' economic agency was increasingly considered a weapon in the war. As a result, to conduct a successful total war required the curtailment of neutral rights.[26]

The economic war for and against neutrality played out in a surprising number of ways. The capture of the Dutch merchant vessel, the *Zaanstroom*, by a German U-boat in 1915 offers a compelling example. The *Zaanstroom*'s captain recounted the incident in a compendium of Dutch-language stories entitled *The Dutch Merchant Marine in Wartime*, which was published in the Netherlands in 1930. According to the account, the *Zaanstroom* left its neutral Dutch port on 17 March bound for England. It soon entered the English Channel looking to evade a known minefield but was intercepted by the *U28* instead. In keeping with long-established search-and-visit practices at sea, the U-boat crew set a small team on board to determine the nature of the *Zaanstroom*'s cargo. Alongside a number of guns and other (unspecified) military contraband, the team found several Belgian men, all of whom claimed refugee status. By international law, a belligerent could seize a neutral merchant ship if it suspected it of carrying contraband. Furthermore, the Hague Conventions of 1907 specified that any enemy soldiers found on board a neutral ship were liable for capture as prisoners of war, as long as the neutral vessel had not rescued them during a naval battle. As a result, and all very properly, the *U28* crew raised a German flag on the *Zaanstroom* and accompanied the ship to the German-occupied Belgian port of Zeebrugge. In Zeebrugge, the Belgian men were imprisoned. The Dutch crew was offered safe passage back to the Netherlands, by way of an armoured train with boarded windows (so they could not spy on German military installations). The ship was requisitioned. A Hamburg prize court subsequently declared that no compensation was due to the Dutch ship owner for the vessel or its cargo since the *Zaanstroom* carried enemy soldiers and contraband. In the end, the ship lay idle in Zeebrugge alongside dozens of other requisitioned vessels until the Germans abandoned the city in October 1918 and sunk them all.[27]

The fate of the *Zaanstroom* tells us many things about the expansion of economic warfare in 1915. Firstly, it highlights just how precarious global shipping had become. In an environment where the capture or sinking of neutral ships (and their cargo) became all too likely, no ship was safe. Thus, its passengers and crew were not safe either. Between 1914 and 1918, thousands of ships were sunk off the coasts of Europe, Africa and the Middle East and across the Atlantic Ocean. As a random example, Tanzania's territorial waters in the Indian Ocean today host no less than thirteen First World War wrecks.[28] Thousands more ships were requisitioned by the belligerents. Such losses were not as prevalent in the Asia-Pacific region however, largely because the German and Austro-Hungarian navies did not operate there as consistently. As we will see, the boon this safety offered the regional Asia-Pacific economy was substantial.

The *Zaanstroom* incident thus also highlights how the capture and destruction of neutral vessels simultaneously made shipping more precarious and more valuable. As the historian Samuël Kruizinga describes it, the crews of neutral ships suffered mental health breakdowns as readily as neutral shipping companies enjoyed massive profits from sending their ships out to sea. At least until April 1917 – when the United States entered the war and changed the global economic landscape yet again – neutral and *Entente* shipping companies like the one that owned the *Zaanstroom* made phenomenal profits.[29] So did their insurers and the farmers and manufacturers who successively supplied the wartime needs of the belligerents. The economic impact of the First World War was one of extremes. A select range of states, businesses and companies, individuals and communities became very wealthy during the war and particularly so in the 1914–16 years. But most did not.[30]

Balancing the cost-benefit ratio of neutral trade played a key role in all the belligerent governments' economic warfare strategies. It also ensured that neutral governments were in constant diplomatic negotiation with the belligerents, balancing their own security and economic needs with the diplomatic requests and demands of the warring states. As a result, neutral governments felt compelled to micro-manage the economic behaviour of their citizens and subjects, with an eye to mobilizing, requisitioning and rationing essential resources when necessary to protect the neutral nation as it navigated through the war. As a result, 'the war' governed the contours of everyday life in neutral states and empires.[31]

The *Zaanstroom* incident also shows up just how much rules and protocols continued to matter in the waging of economic warfare. Even though the *U28* might have sunk the *Zaanstroom,* the German war effort had more to gain from boarding and capturing its cargo than sinking the vessel immediately. If we are to believe the captain's account, the *U28* intercepted the *Zaanstroom* 'by the book'. The German crew kept strictly to the legal requirements of international naval practices. The 1930 Dutch compendium is chock-full of similar boarding and requisitioning stories. Keeping to 'the rules' mattered for Germany's ongoing relationship with the Netherlands, a border neutral its government wished to court and mobilize as an essential supplier of its economic war needs. It also enabled the Germans to claim that they were not 'uncivilized' and that their war was conducted as international law dictated, an essential weapon in their ongoing propaganda campaign to win the 'hearts and minds' of neutrals.[32]

From the belligerents' perspective, managing neutral trade and finance made all the difference in the success of their economic warfare strategies. The Allied blockade of Germany, Austria-Hungary and the Ottoman empire, for example, could only be effectively maintained if these enemies did not receive undue aid from a border neutral. In managing these neutrals' access to global trade, however, they inevitably contracted their economic well-being. As a result, while some European neutrals made immense profits from the war – not least by smuggling goods into belligerent territory or offering private bank loans – most of them despaired in the face of shortages, rationing, inflation and a burgeoning black-market economy.[33]

For more distant neutrals, like the Latin American countries, the shift to a 'long war' had equally decisive economic and social consequences. The already weak Colombian economy, for example, suffered acutely from the long-term loss of access to the European import and export market. Through the course of 1915, foreign credit disappeared, coffee and banana prices fell further and the loss of customs duties from European imports crippled the state budget. The ensuing deficit saw José Vincente Concha's government reduce expenses by shutting down government ministries, defunding schools and public work schemes and deferring pensions. According to the historian Jane Rausch, even the leprosy asylum in Agua de Dios 'disgorged its hapless inmates' onto the streets for lack of funds to pay staff. Colombians' dissatisfaction with these developments had numerous political repercussions which heightened the already violent rivalries that existed between the Republican and Liberal camps in society.[34]

Colombia's pre-war economic relationships with Europe did not improve during the war. Increasingly, the only hope for economic recovery lay with the highly unpopular United States.[35] Given the United States' role in the seizure of the isthmus of Panama in 1903 and the subsequent opening of the Panama Canal in 1914, Colombians were extremely wary of American imperialism. That wariness heightened when the United States Congress repeatedly refused to ratify the Thomson-Urrutia treaty that was signed in April 1914, offering an apology to the Colombian people for the Panama situation and providing their government with US$25 million in compensation.[36]

That both the United States and Colombia participated in the Inter-American High Commission that met in Washington DC in May 1915 to discuss 'closer and more satisfactory financial relations among the American republics' is, therefore, highly relevant.[37] That event, a pre-cursor to the Pan-American Union, brought representatives of Latin America's independent states and the United States government together to negotiate a common approach to banking, transportation and commerce in the context of the global war.[38] After May 1915, Colombia became increasingly economically dependent on the United States. Whereas Colombian exports to and imports from Europe had almost halved since 1913, the United States' share of Colombian exports increased by a quarter and its import share expanded by nearly two-thirds by the end of 1915.[39] Furthermore, investments by American-owned companies in Colombian oil, platinum mines and banana crops heightened the United States' informal interests in the country. Between 1915 and 1918, Colombia 'moved steadily into the United States commercial orbit', as did many of its immediate neighbours.[40]

For the United States, the 1915 Inter-American High Commission meeting signalled greater regional security and heightened its own economic advantages as the world's sole remaining neutral great power.

Its economic growth through the course of the war was built in part on its ability to replace European investors, shipping and exports across the south American continent.[41] Even more decisively, it utilized the European powers' preoccupation with the war to expand its formal empire across the Caribbean too. The United States invaded the island of Haiti in July 1915, with an eye to protecting the mouth of the Panama Canal.[42] The Dominican Republic and Cuba followed in 1916 and 1917 respectively.[43] As the United States expanded its imperial power in the context of the lengthening global war, it reinforced the notion that the entire central and south American region had become a neutral bulwark in the war.

Across the region, Latin Americans viewed the United States' 'commercial conquest' of their economies as troubling. Their newspapers lamented that their people were being treated as 'war booty' of the powerful northern neutral. Their governments were placed under considerable political pressure from the people to counter the expansionism.[44] Still, the reorientation towards the United States also helped to stabilize what were increasingly unstable economic entities.

This regional American geostrategic neutral zone also offered decisive advantages to the belligerents who could most easily access them.[45] The United States' direct support of the Allied war effort between 1915 and April 1917 (when it formally joined the war as a belligerent) was enormous.[46] In oil supplies alone, the United States dominated. Where in 1914, the British army had operated 827 cars and 15 motorbikes and owned a few dozen aeroplanes, by late 1918 it utilized 56,000 tanks, 58,000 motor vehicles and 55,000 aircraft in its daily military operations.[47] All of these machines required oil to run. The United States supplied the majority of Britain's wartime oil needs, although the Basra oil fields increased their output from 1,600 barrels per day in 1914 to 18,000 in 1917.[48]

Well beyond oil, though, the British government maximized its purchasing power in the United States by commissioning the J.P. Morgan company to be its financial representative. As a private enterprise, J.P. Morgan could raise bank loans in the United States for the British state as well as acquire a wide array of essential goods, which it then shipped on to Britain. After May 1915, the newly established British Ministry of Munitions employed a further 1,600 private individuals to buy up even more American products. Collectively, these efforts ensured that by early 1917, the British government spent a phenomenal US$83 million (approximately US$1.6 billion in today's terms) per week procuring American resources.[49] Without the United States, the Allied war effort would have faltered.

It is really no surprise then that Germany aimed to undermine American shipping access to Britain and sought to maximize its own access to (neutral) Romania's oil fields as well as to the oil resources under (belligerent) Ottoman control.[50] Increasingly, its economic warfare practices aimed not only to intercept ships and acquire cargo, but also to sink as much of the neutral merchant marine destined for Britain and France as possible. In turn, the

British-French blockade of Central Powers increasingly targeted Germany's border neutrals. Neutral governments and trading companies invented a range of innovative trade agreements with the belligerents to accommodate these changes. As an example, the Dutch government set up the Netherlands Oversea Trust Company (NOT), a private shareholding entity consisting of banks, shipping companies and commercial enterprises. The NOT acted as an official 'back-channel' to the Dutch government and entered into commercial agreements with the British government that covered all Dutch overseas trade. In turn, the NOT guaranteed that all consigned goods carried by Dutch ships would be consumed domestically and, thus, not re-exported to Germany. While the NOT agreements tied Dutch wartime trade to British oversight, it also opened up the possibility for the wholesale export of Dutch-origin products to Germany.[51] Despite heightened NOT controls and British interference, Dutch-German trade flourished well into 1916.[52] Smuggling along the Dutch-German and Dutch-Belgian borders was also rife, as it was on Switzerland's and Denmark's land borders too, where similar consignment policies were implemented.[53]

One of the most drastic signs of the radicalization of British economic warfare practices in 1915 was its government's decision to blacklist all German companies and enterprises regardless of whether they operated in a neutral country. Even hiring German-born workers could result in a blacklisting of a neutral company and, thus, an end to its ability to operate effectively within the global economy. Blacklisting bankrupted thousands of German-owned enterprises globally, causing widespread unemployment and heightening social tensions in a number of neutral countries. In Latin America, alongside numerous public protests against blacklisting, the suspension of British coal supplies to several German-owned electricity companies even resulted in blackouts in the cities of Valparaíso (Chile), Vina del Mar (Chile) and Buenos Aires (Argentina).[54] According to the historian Philip Dehne, the Allied powers' full-frontal attack on German commercial and financial interests was a powerful weapon of war.[55] It also had a fundamental impact on neutral communities.

The African neutral state of Liberia offers an excellent example. Surrounded by the belligerent outposts of Sierra Leone (Britain) and French West Africa (present-day Ivory Coast and Guinea), Liberia was a particularly vulnerable neutral state. Before the war, 80 per cent of its government revenue came from customs duties, a substantial amount of which came from German import trade.[56] Almost two-thirds of Liberia's external trade in 1913 was with Germany. German investors owned Liberia's key electricity and telegraph companies as well as the steamboat service that navigated the Kavalli River.[57] The outbreak of the First World War devastated the Liberian economy. Not only was neutral Liberia not a priority supply port for the French or British, who preferred Sierra Leone and the Ivory Coast, but Germany's shipping trade with Liberia also halted.

In a recent book, the historian Jyotirmoy Pal Chaudhuri describes how the impact of the war, the cessation of German shipping and the blacklisting of German companies by the British in 1915 resulted in a 'complete disaster'. The numbers of ships calling into Liberian ports fell from 1,322 in 1913 (more than half of which were German) to a mere 245 in 1917 (two-thirds of which were British).[58] In response to the declining size of its coffers, the Liberian government (much like the Colombian government) attempted to cut costs by drastic means. Its freeze on paying out wages and the introduction of stamp duties on gin, tobacco and other luxuries failed to recoup anywhere near the lost revenue. Instead, it turned to a controversial Hut Tax imposed on every building structure in the country, the collection of which only resulted in widespread social upheaval, political strife and police violence. Meanwhile, Liberian produce and products piled up in warehouses and ports, unable to find ships and export markets.

The cosmopolitan entrepot cities of the world, like Shanghai and Bombay, also made drastic readjustments in 1915 to accommodate the new global realities of economic warfare. Shanghai's Chamber of Commerce wound up and the various commercial enterprises in the city were regulated along belligerent lines. Others, like the Deutsche-Asiatische Bank were forcibly shut down.[59] The growing animosity between rival resident communities made the management of social cohesion in Shanghai especially difficult.[60] This was particularly so between Shanghai's Chinese and Japanese populations. After Japan's invasion of Tsingtao and the issuing of the twenty-one demands in early 1915, Shanghai Chinese protested by boycotting Japanese goods and stores. Animosity increased on Shanghai's streets. In response, the Japanese Residents' Association formed armed self-defence units and 'vigilance committees' that looked to shield the city's 30,000 Japanese residents and their children from such attacks.[61]

Port Said, at the mouth of the Suez Canal, faced equally challenging realities. At the outset of the war, the Egyptian government had declared its intention to keep the canal open for all warship traffic (as it was obliged to do according to the terms of the 1888 Constantinople Convention). Very quickly, the impact of global economic warfare resulted in the British interfering with these Egyptian directives and canal trade. In September, British troops landed in the canal zone, looking to defend it against attack and in December, Britain expanded its authority over the khedive with the appointment of Sir Henry McMahon as High Commissioner.[62] The impact of Egypt's incorporation into the world of war was particularly acute in Port Said. Not only did tensions between various ethnicities (particularly those from enemy communities) repeatedly spill over, so did the demographic composition of the city's residents change, especially once the city's authorities denied access to the port to crew who held enemy passports (even if they came in on a neutral vessel). During 1916, German U-boats repeatedly shelled Port Said, heightening residents' insecurities and ensuring an increased military presence in the city and across the canal zone. In recounting these developments, the historian Valeska Huber stresses that while the cosmopolitan composition of Port Said altered during the war, the heightened presence of troops from all over the French and British empires (including from Madagascar and India) leant an ongoing cosmopolitan and military nature to its socio-economic landscape.[63] The war entrenched Port Said's and the Suez canal's place within the British empire.

Meanwhile, Indians also quailed at the impact of the early months of the war on their economic interests. In the twelve months before May 1914, only 37.6 per cent of Indian exports were sold within the British empire. The rest ended up elsewhere, often in Germany or Russia. With the outbreak of war in August 1914, not only did India lose their second largest source of imported goods (Germany), but with Ottoman entry into the war in October, it also lost access to the Black Sea economy.[64] The bombing of the port city of Madras (Chennai) on 22 September 1914 by the German light cruiser *SMS Emden* further signalled to the entire British empire that it was as much at war as Britain itself. With the shift to long-war economic planning, the British government assessed the potential of mobilizing India's vast human and material resources. It was reluctant to ask too much of India, fearing protests and anti-imperial rebellion. Still, by the end of the war, the south Asian sub-continent had supplied 172,815 animals and 3,691,836 tonnes of supplies to the Allies, alongside more than 1.4 million troops.[65] In 1917 and 1918, India offered two vast 'gifts' of 100 million pounds to the British government, paid for by 'war loan' subscriptions made by the Indian population.[66] India thus played a key role in sustaining the British war effort.

Between 1915 and 1918, India's balance of trade also shifted: it exported more than it imported and its financial wealth expanded, not least because it became a stable investment economy. India's industrialization (much like that of Japan) expanded in turn. The Tata Iron and Steel Works grew, as did the number of hydro-electric projects, bringing electricity to cities like Bombay.[67] By redirecting some of its export trade to the Asia-Pacific region, including to the Russian port of Vladivostok and Japan, India was able to come out of the war economically rejuvenated, even if its population suffered from the same inflationary pressures as the rest of the world.[68] These economic developments had a significant impact on south Asian perspectives of their role in the empire and heightened the politics of nationalism and demands of self-rule and self-determination.

How ably well-functioning and industrial economies could supply the belligerent needs of the European great powers is well illustrated by the example of Japan. While Japan mounted military campaigns against German-held territories in the Asia-Pacific, in general the Japanese government did not sustain a heavily militarized nation-at-arms between 1914 and 1918. Rather, the war years offered only incentives to grow Japan's industries, finances and economy.[69] The economic power of the Japanese state grew as its banks offered more than 1 billion yen's worth of loans and shipped a multitude of goods, products and crops to its European allies.[70] Japanese cities witnessed a 17 per cent growth as their industries boomed. But its slums also grew alongside.[71] The loss of European ships out of the Asia-Pacific region offered further opportunities. By 1917, Japanese companies controlled 55 per cent of the Pacific Ocean's mercantile trade, much of which had been dominated by Britain before 1914.[72] By 1918, its foreign trade share had increased by 300 per cent, its gold reserves ballooned and Japanese investments in the Malaysian and Borneo plantation economies heightened.[73]

Yet the war did not leave all Japanese people better off. Inflation, declining wages and the scarcity of rice crops seriously affected the daily lives of most Japanese. Discourses about 'wantonly wasteful' war profiteers resulted in the imposition of an Anti-Profiteering Law in 1916 and the government imposed rationing, price checks and restrictions on the sale of essential goods as well.[74] Many Japanese protested the undue interference in their economy by the British, not least when German-Japanese firms were blacklisted and a ban on luxury imports was imposed in Britain in 1916.[75] The gap between rich and poor grew drastically during the war years, drawing more middle-class men and women into the wage economy in the hope of making ends meet. The socio-economic impact of the war left Japan facing significant political challenges, including a spate of 'rice riots' and workers' strikes involving tens of thousands of people in 1917 and 1918.[76]

For the Ottoman empire, the economic consequences of the shift to long-term economic warfare were truly drastic. The British and French navies blockaded the Ottoman empire in the Mediterranean and Red seas and around the Arabian gulf from the moment the Ottoman government declared war in October 1914. They also intercepted camel traders entering the empire from across Arabia.[77] The Ottoman empire's own closure of the Dardanelles further exacerbated the supply problems, as did its requisitioning policies and heightened taxation.[78] The impact was fundamental for all residents of the empire. Starvation affected communities across present-day Syria, Lebanon and Palestine in 1915. The combination of blockade, a locust plague and the Ottoman empire's inability to centralize the movement of resources effectively brought these regions close to social collapse that year.[79] In 1916, the entire empire (and much of Persia too) faced starvation as a drought exacerbated the already meagre local supplies.

Given that the Ottomans were also dependent on foreign coal supplies and that the Allied blockade prevented the export of local cash crops, locals kept themselves alive by burning trees. The ecological consequences were phenomenal and resulted in widespread deforestation and the cutting down of old-growth olive groves and fruit orchards.[80] Hyper-inflation ensued and criminality expanded in the wake of these developments as did reports of cannibalism and the spread of serious diseases like bubonic plague, typhoid and typhus.[81] Social crisis was inevitable. It is no surprise then to find that for Middle Eastern communities, the First World War registers as a 'war of civilians', a war, as the historian Najwa al-Qattan describes, of 'near annihilation' that created a 'world of beggars and beasts, animals and cannibals'. A war that caused a rupture in time.[82] Already in 1915, the Ottoman empire's subjects understood the meaning of total war in the most fundamental of terms.

The Russian Romanov empire struggled in similar ways. The example of India highlights how essential the impact of the German blockade of the Baltic ports and the Ottoman closure of Dardanelles Straits was to the viability of Russian wartime economy.[83] As any good history of the Russian revolutions of 1917 explains, the origins of Russian unrest and social instability in 1917 lie in the inability of the Russian state to coordinate its resources effectively to ensure an adequate standard of living for the Russian people.[84] The questions at play were not only about the ability of the Russian government to effectively mobilize the domestic economy and industry for total war. Russia's troubles were also a product of the economic warfare strategies conducted by its enemies. Whereas in 1913, the Russian balance of trade sat at a healthy 146.1 million roubles, by the end of 1914 it faced an import-export deficiency of 141.9 million roubles. By the end of 1915 the Romanov government's deficit sat at 8.8 billion roubles, a staggering 75.8 per cent of its overall outlay that year.[85] Increasingly, the government relied on its French and British allies to rescue it from financial disaster, although it never managed to break through these essential supply issues.

Altogether the disruptive changes brought on by the shift to total economic warfare in early 1915 were global in nature and impact. They caused enormous alterations in trade patterns impacting on living standards and human suffering. The shift ensured that food security became a weapon of war, a weapon wielded against belligerent and neutral communities alike. As the next chapter highlights, the limits of this 'total war' did not end with the economy, they expanded to military violence as well. But as this chapter highlights, very few people in the world were left unaffected by the war's economic effects.

Unsurprisingly, it was also in response to these everyday impacts of the economic war that people around the world recast their understanding of what 'the war' was about. The language of 'just war' – what was allowed, permissible or expected in terms of the belligerent and neutral behaviour in time of war – altered as the war progressed. Those perspectives involved neutrals as much as belligerents. The 'war profiteer' was a hated trope in neutral and belligerent communities alike. As such, the experience of economic warfare in 1915 helped to 'de-bound' the norms and expectations of the war globally.[86] In many neutral countries, heated and at times polemical political debates evolved about the value of remaining neutral and of which belligerent side to support. These debates were informed by local knowledge and prejudices as much as they were a reflection on the military and economic progress of the wider world at war. The relative value of a country's ongoing neutrality played a powerful hand in these debates.[87] For neutrals like the United States in 1915, for example, the idea that the war had unleashed a 'will to profit' at almost any cost evolved. While President Woodrow Wilson continued to assert America's right to 'innocent trade', this conceptualization became increasingly untenable.[88] As Chapter 6 highlights, neutral communities responded to such claims by asserting alternative neutral virtues, like humanitarianism. Unsurprisingly, then, it was in neutral countries that the inherent value of the war was often most contested.[89] But as the next chapter also shows, after 1915, there was nary a community that did not consider their future without some reference to 'the war'.

5

The 'barbarian' next door: Total war at home and abroad in 1915

As the Sixth Division of the Indian Expeditionary Force D (IEF-D) fought its way on behalf of the British empire through Ottoman-ruled Mesopotamia in 1915, it occupied the towns of Basra, Qurna, Nasiriyah and Kut al-Amara. Amidst the violence, one of the division's Indian officers, Captain Kalyan Kumar Mukherji, wrote a letter to his family asking an important question: what had the enemy done to deserve this destructive fate?[1] Privately, he may also have wondered what he might have done to deserve a similarly destructive fate. For by the time the IEF-D retreated from the Battle of Ctesiphon back to Kut al-Amara on 3 December, it had endured tremendous casualties.[2] Soon, they were besieged in the town by the Ottoman Sixth Army. Cut off from logistical support and without adequate rations, the 3,350 residents and 11,600 combatants in Kut suffered from severe malnutrition.[3] Many died. The Hindu, Sikh and Gurkha troops were particularly affected as they could not eat the only available protein: horse and mule flesh.[4]

Disaffection set in among the rank-and-file, helped along by some judicious Ottoman leaflets, written in Urdu and Hindi that urged the soldiers to defect. All up, seventy-two of them took up the offer. The few who were caught escaping were summarily executed by their officers.[5] In an attempt to prevent news of the calamitous siege spreading through India and the rest of the British empire, the military leadership in Kut denied the Indian troops the right to write home.[6] As an officer, Mukherji was exempt from the ban. He wrote to his mother in April 1915:

> After three months with very little to eat the troops are starving. The mortality rate in the hospital has soared. In the last 15 days many have died for lack of food. Of what use is medicine now? There's nothing to eat. People are coming to the hospital because starvation has made them weak. With nothing to give them, how can we help? Apart from that, there are no medicines left either.[7]

When all the food ran out on 29 April 1916, the town surrendered.[8] It was a jubilant day for the Ottoman empire. As one veteran recorded in his diary: 'the English have never faced such a defeat anywhere'.[9] For the emaciated survivors of Kut, however, only more horror followed. The Jewish and Arab civilian residents were held responsible for aiding the British occupiers and were hanged from gallows to die.[10] The British and Indian occupying soldiers were taken as prisoners of war, most of them forced on a 160-kilometre march across the desert to Baghdad. Thousands of them perished, either due to starvation, dehydration, sunstroke or when they fell behind and were left to the mercy of local raiders. Many of the survivors, Mukherji included, subsequently died working on the Anatolia to Baghdad railway or in one of the Ottoman empire's neglected prisoner-of-war camps.[11]

In 1928, Mukherji's grandmother published a memoir, in which she included copies of her grandson's war letters.[12] One of those letters, written before the siege of Kut in October 1915, reflected on the violent and seemingly endless nature of the world war:

> Unless something surprising happens suddenly – I don't see why a war of this kind should not go on for 20 years. So long as Germany can keep itself supplied with provisions and weaponry I don't think this [the British] side will be able to advance. Nor does it seem possible for Germany to advance any further into France. ... In this one year of war a *crore* of people (English, German, Russian, French, Indian, African together) have been killed or wounded. Another *crore* of families are heart-broken because of 'Selfish nationalism: a most inhuman sentiment'. In other words this war is proof that this brutal and selfish love of country – that this awful, malign, sentiment is an obstacle for all humankind.[13]

Meanwhile, the British commander at Kut, Major-General Charles Townshend, mobilized his sense of ethnic superiority and loyalty to empire to reposition blame for the Kut disaster away from himself. He placed it squarely at the feet of the Sixth Division's Indian 'sepoys'. 'How easy the defence of Kut would have been,' he wrote, 'had my division been an all British one instead of a composite one.'[14]

The siege of Kut al-Amara offers an all too telling example of the human costs of the shift to total war in 1915. The military stalemate or state of 'mutual siege'[15] that evolved in 1915 ensured that the belligerent powers not only expanded their economic warfare's parameters (as discussed in the previous chapter), but also escalated their use of military violence against soldiers and civilians alike. The warring governments' willingness to mobilize their military power to win 'at almost any cost' ensured that few communities were effectively safe from harm. Total war required total commitment to a belligerent cause: every advantage needed to be exploited, no leeway could be allowed. Ultimately, the questions of 'who to trust?' and 'what to do with those you distrust?' dominated the military, economic

ILLUSTRATION 5.1 *This photograph of a group of Indian survivors of the siege of Kut al-Amara (1915–1916) was taken during an exchange of prisoners between the Ottoman and British empires in 1916. The soldiers not only suffered from severe malnutrition during the four-month siege but also from maltreatment by the Ottoman authorities once they were taken prisoner.*
Source: *Wikipedia.com.*

and cultural mobilization of societies at war. Increasingly, they dominated neutral societies too.

As explained in Chapter 4, the move to a long-war reality in 1915 helped to radicalize the actions of the belligerent powers *vis-à-vis* their enemies and neutrals. That chapter highlights some of the human costs of the shift to total economic warfare. This chapter focuses on the totalization of the military conduct of the war through 1915. It concentrates on the uses made of state violence to facilitate military, strategic and economic advantages in the war and to enforce compliance on subject, occupied and neutral populations. Above all, it asks how the concepts of 'loyalty', 'identity' and 'responsibility to the state' were mobilized within communities to justify and warrant the escalation of violence against those who 'could not be trusted' and against those who were not 'on one's side'.

The expansion of the total war ethos and the need for victory at almost any cost had numerous consequences. At a state level it ensured that belligerent governments mobilized the human and material resources at their command to augment their chances of military success. This made the civilian working for the war economy as valuable (and by extension expendable) as the front-line soldier. It also made anyone aiding the enemy's war efforts – be they an actual enemy, a neutral, or a suspicious 'Other' living in one's own community – a justifiable target for surveillance, incarceration and even eradication. The 'barbarian' living next door was as dangerous as the one trying to kill you from afar. The results of the shift to the 'total war' mindset, then, were decisive.

Some of the most enduring images of the First World War's many hellscapes are of the industrialized trench lines that appeared on Europe's western front through the course of 1915. The belligerent powers did everything they could think of to break the impasse on this front. Through 1915, their industrial production geared up. New weapons were invented; their calibres expanded. The number of aeroplanes, machine guns, artillery pieces, bullets and explosive shells proliferated. So, too, did the number of soldiers manning the front. Their attacks across 'no man's land' were repeatedly repelled. Craters great and small pockmarked the trench lines that snaked for thousands of kilometres across southern Belgium and northern France, filled with mangled barbed wire, military debris and half-buried fragments of dead horses and human bodies. Along the more mobile fronts in eastern and southern Europe as well as in the Caucasus and Middle East, villages and towns disappeared under the waxing and waning onslaught of repeated military attacks.

As the war entrenched, both sets of belligerents experimented with new weaponry, willingly violating the international laws of war. Their scientists, including those working in universities across Britain, France and Germany, experimented with chemical weapons, militarizing their academic institutions in the process.[16] The French trialled tear gas bullets on the battlefield in August 1914 (to little effect), while the British worked on sulphur dioxide weaponry. The Germans inserted tear gas and other chemicals into artillery shells, which they fired across the western front in October 1914 and used against the Russians on the Vistula in January 1915 (again with little effect).[17] On 22 April 1915, however, Germany successfully released chlorine gas from carefully placed cylinders on the Gheluvelt peninsula near Ypres (in Belgium). As the gas distended across 'no man's land' and the Allied trenches, it caused panic, then havoc among the troops stationed there. This silent 'unseen' weapon that attacked the internal organs was feared by soldiers and condemned by neutral and belligerent communities alike, only in part because it was proscribed by The Hague Conventions.[18] As the German writer serving as part of the Saxon Hussar regiment at Gheluvelt, Rudolf Binding, noted while retrieving his fallen enemies' guns: 'The effects of the successful gas attack were horrible. I am not pleased with the idea of poisoning men. Of course, the entire world will rage about it first and then imitate us. All the dead lie on their backs, with clenched fists, the whole field is yellow.'[19] From this point on, and despite the fact that gas warfare was far from effective in ensuring a strategic breakthrough, chemical agents were produced by every belligerent (and many neutrals too) and featured as a weapon on almost every military front.[20]

What the use of chemical agents in 1915 highlights, above all, was the belligerents' desperation to win. Not only did they accept almost any degree of suffering endured by their soldiers, but they were also willing to risk the lives of enemy and neutral civilians. Bombs dropped from aeroplanes and dirigibles extended the range of the violence, including against factories, towns, railway lines and depots.[21] These bombs made total war a military reality for the many Europeans who otherwise lived far away from a military front. Even the European neutrals were not safe when stray bombers accidentally released their loads on neutral territory. The indiscriminate mining of seas and waterways – sinking fishing vessels, passenger ships and neutral commerce – further extended the violence. The expansion of the Allied economic blockade in 1915 to include all foodstuffs, which risked malnutrition and starvation among enemy and neutral civilians, further expanded and intensified the conflict. The retaliatory use of U-boats by Germany to target any ship sailing to or from Britain and France from February 1915 on made the war fought against civilians in Europe all-encompassing. It certainly did not stay contained in Europe.

Across 1915, the unprecedented expansion of military violence ensured that the war became, what the historian John Horne so evocatively describes as, a 'world in itself'.[22] Soldier artists and poets reflected on the personal hell that was their war, often invoking the industrial and impersonal nature of the violence they faced: the artillery that blew limbs right off or bodies to smithereens, the shrapnel that shattered skin and ruined organs, the gas masks that disfigured faces, the barbed wire that trapped them in 'no man's land', the 'chiwaya' sound of machine guns popping like popcorn in a tin (as the Chichewa soldiers from south-east Africa recalled from their western front experiences).[23]

But, as the historian Stéphane Audoin-Rouzeau reminds us, none of this violence was actually impersonal. Soldiers were the war's first victims but also its primary agents. Their weapons were both friends (protecting them from potential harm) and turned them into killers.[24] Unsurprisingly, a soldier's war experience was profoundly transformative. The trauma reshaped personalities, inspired reflections about the war and why they were fighting (much like Mukherji's letters cited above) and incited questions of loyalty to their comrades-in-arms and the authorities who caused them to fight.

Given that soldiers came from all over the world, their war experiences reverberated globally too. The *In Flanders' Field Museum* in Ypres lists more than fifty nationalities of veterans who served and died in the region between 1914 and 1918.[25] The cosmopolitan nature of the western front, which by the end of 1915 included soldiers and military labourers from China and all parts of the French and British empires in Africa, Asia, the Pacific and Caribbean, astounded some of them. One South African soldier serving with the South African Native Labour Corps in France was surprised 'to see the different kinds of human races from all parts of the world'.[26] Other African troops acknowledged that they lost their fear of 'killing a white man' on the western front.[27] Many were only too alert to the ongoing racial hierarchies at play in this war of the world, which was being fought for the power and prestige of Europeans.[28]

Neutrals too bore witness to military violence, often at a distance through refugee accounts or voyeuristically through newspaper articles, photographs and moving pictures.[29] Occasionally, they witnessed it first hand, as medics at a war front, as passengers or crew on a ship navigating the militarized seas, or even when stray bombs dropped on neutral soil or a loose sea mine exploded on a neutral beach. They asked equally searching questions of their own loyalties, identities and responsibilities in the war.

If 'soldiers are made to get themselves killed', as Napoleon so famously quipped, then belligerent states needed persuasive reasons to promote, enforce and, at times, coerce their citizens and subjects to undertake this vital role. In all cases, soldiers needed to be convinced that the cause for which they were offering up their (and their families') lives was worth the sacrifice. The question of loyalty to a war cause was always riven with tensions. Why would a young man from a west African town leave everything familiar behind to fight in a war on behalf of a colonial government who did not recognize his rights as a citizen of France? Why would Kalyan Mukherji join the Indian Expeditionary Force to fight for an empire that repeatedly rejected his country's requests for self-determination? Why would the families of any new soldier allow them to serve in a war that might get them killed?

The answers to these questions lay in a complex web of loyalties and obligations, in which personal convictions and concepts of duty played vital roles. As we saw in Chapters 2 and 3, some soldiers were convinced that the war was fought for the survival of civilization itself. For others the violence committed by the enemy fixated a hatred or a desire for revenge.[30] Yet others went to war for the adventure, a chance to see the world or to 'test one's manhood' as one Nyasaland volunteer noted years later.[31] For many, the opportunism of 'proving' one's loyalty to the nation or empire by showing up to fight, regardless of the costs, was all-important. Others went to war because they had no choice. Loyalty, in this sense, could also aim at political and economic gains. As we noted in Chapter 2, this could include ambitions for gaining greater equality be it for a colonized community or a marginalized group. Most women in belligerent societies did not have the right to vote, for example. Some of them hoped that by fully supporting the war they might gain greater recognition of their right to participate as equals in political society alongside men.[32]

The belligerent governments certainly mobilized the promise of post-war gains to persuade volunteers to join up and to assuage the fears of conscripted troops. Recruitment posters in India, published in an array of local languages, enticed volunteers with the promise of free clothes and a good wage alongside an opportunity to fulfil a duty to King and empire, to 'demonstrate bravery' and 'do one's family proud'.[33] Across the British Dominions and in Ireland too, similarly styled posters asked 'Your chums are fighting? Why aren't you?'[34] Meanwhile Bantu recruits for the South African Native Labour Contingent were asked by their local newspaper to 'play our part' in this 'world war' because 'without you, your white comrades cannot do anything, they cannot fight and provide labour at the same time'. Thus, 'please, everyone who loves his country and respects the British Government, join this war without hesitation. Forward! Forward!'[35]

As will become clear in the next chapter, maintaining these loyalties became increasingly difficult as the war lengthened into 1916 and beyond. Loyalties could shift, and they were much more likely to do so in the face of terrible odds or consequences. As a western-front veteran from Nyasaland recalled: 'The government told the chief that there was war; the chief informed his people. He asked us young people to help the [British] government fight the Germans. I lost confidence in the chief; he was a betrayer. He would make us die in the war.'[36] For an Indian soldier, the 'moral contract' he thought he had signed with the British empire was nullified when he was not sent home after suffering a terrible wound and enduring an extensive stay in a British hospital. His loyalty, as Santanu Das explains, was not honoured by the government who had called on his gallant services in the first place.[37] Instead he was made to go back to fight a war of horrors. Another Punjabi soldier serving on the western front also begged his family in 1915: 'For God's sake, don't come, don't come, don't come to this war in Europe … tell my brother Muhammud Yakub for God's sake not to enlist.'[38] His words are almost identical to those of a Vietnamese soldier who wrote home urging his friends to resist recruitment: 'My friend! It is better that you do not come here. I would advise you to come here in peacetime. But it is wartime. Stay there.'[39]

What all these developments also had in common was that the shift to total war resulted in an ever-increasing emphasis on identity. National and imperial identities sat at the heart of most belligerent discourses: their war was fought in defence of the nation, the empire, the people and the foundations of 'civilization' against the existential threats presented by enemy nations, empires and people. To that end, military service supposedly existed as a unifying force, bringing the nation and empire together against a common enemy.[40] The result of such 'unifying' conceptualizations was that anyone who was not a clearly identifiable member of the nation or empire, or did not abide by the requirements to serve the nation or empire, could be targeted as a potential threat.

As John Horne explains, these enemies lived not only far away, but also in one's own community, in one's street, and could possibly be counted among one's friends and colleagues. The shift to total war, thus, also resulted in a shift to identifying 'treasonable element[s] who potentially threatened the national or imperial effort with betrayal'.[41] Fear and suspicion about these alien 'Others' heightened popular anxieties. States, communities and individuals alike played up pre-existing prejudices to root out these 'enemies within'. Nationality, ethnicity, religious or pacifist beliefs, even gender, age and class, all played their part in informing on suspicious 'Others', whose loyalty to the war cause was not immediately obvious and, at the very least, ought to be policed.

Acting on these suspicions often resulted in more violence. In almost every belligerent society, enemy subjects were incarcerated in internment camps. Foreign shops and businesses were eschewed, while spy mania captured the public's imagination. Most states introduced border security measures, extended passport-control systems and supervised the movement of people and goods across their territory. The state played an increasingly invasive role in the lives of individuals, monitoring communities for signs of wavering loyalty and pushing them to sacrifice even more in service of the war. But so too did ordinary people. The shift to questioning the loyalties and identities of one's neighbours also extended to neutral countries, whose governments and populace increasingly feared that an unseen 'enemy within' was working for one or other belligerent and would force them to join the war.[42]

Altogether, throughout 1915 the idea that countries and communities had a 'right to use violence' to police their societies against the threat of the 'enemy within' became normalized. The socio-political dynamics of the war thus also framed new conceptions of 'loyalty' and 'belonging', purposely excluding those that did not fit. None of this happened, however, without also inspiring a massive amount of public questioning. A case study of the global response to the sinking of the British luxury liner, the *RMS Lusitania*, on 7 May 1915 brings out the interplay of these dynamics of violence, loyalty and identity all too well.

When the commander of the *U20* U-boat decided to torpedo the *Lusitania* on intercepting the large Cunard liner off the coast of southern Ireland, he understood many things.[43] He knew that the ship was sailing under instruction of the British Admiralty and had enough weapons on board to be converted into an armoured cruiser, ready for war service.[44] He knew it was travelling within Germany's declared warzone while visiting two enemy harbours (Liverpool and Cherbourg). He also understood that the *Lusitania* was a luxury cruise ship, with nine passenger decks, transporting hundreds of civilians from Britain via France to New York. There is no question that the commander felt within his rights to torpedo the ship, sinking it and leaving its hapless passengers and crew to drown or be picked up by nearby vessels. This was war, after all. The neutral Americans on-board had, at least, been warned by the German government, who had placed advertisements in a number of New York newspapers not to travel through Germany's declared war zone at the risk of losing their lives.

Lusitania's sinking cost 1,198 passengers and crew their lives. Their bodies beached on the Irish coast, to be buried in local cemeteries. While it was not the first (or, for that matter, last) passenger ship to be sunk as part of Germany's U-boat campaigns in 1915, it was the largest and caused the greatest number of civilian deaths as well as the greatest number of deaths among citizens of neutral countries (including 128 Americans). What almost no one could have foreseen was the storm of protest and outrage that ensued in response to the sinking, nor the acts of violence that it provoked against Germans, Austrians and other enemy 'aliens' around the Allied world.

The *Lusitania* inspired emotive responses among all who encountered the news of its sinking. If they were pro-German, they were enraged by the need for Germany to use such horrifying and retaliatory tactics in the first place. After all, the German warzone was established to fight back against the British and French-imposed 'hunger blockade' which, as the German Foreign Office's formal response to the *Lusitania* attack argued, constituted a barbaric 'plan of starving the civilian population of Germany'.[45] '*Gott mit uns!*' (God with us!) and '*Gott strafe Engeland!*' (God punish England!) became rallying cries for revenge across Germanophone communities.[46] These popular German representations celebrated the *Lusitania*'s sinking as an essential act in a righteous war against a barbaric enemy.[47] German academics published treatises that carefully explained the legalities of Germany's actions and emphasized the breaches of the law made by their enemies.[48]

Outside these German communities, the more common response was outrage directed at Germany for breaching the standards of civilized warfare, yet again. For centuries, the law of war at sea required warships to warn targets that they would be sunk, so that the people on board could safely exit them. It also required that nearby vessels (including the warship itself) would pick up any survivors. Neither of these things happened in 1915. Given the concurrence of the *Lusitania* incident with Germany's release of gas warfare at Ypres and the publication of the Bryce report, any value that pro-German propaganda may have had in neutral and enemy communities before May 1915 collapsed.[49] Americans were particularly outraged. They also feared that due to Germany's actions, the United States might be forced to become a belligerent, ending their long-term isolationist foreign policy.[50]

Importantly, this neutral outrage mattered to the German government. It could not afford to risk the United States' entry into the war, nor that of its closest neutral neighbours. It relied too heavily on the economic resources that could still be obtained from the Scandinavians, Swiss and Dutch, and feared what opening another military front so close to its borders might do to its chances of victory. As a result, in September 1915, it officially halted its indiscriminate U-boat campaigns. This did not mean that neutral ships or passenger liners were not sunk by German warships after 1915. Several dozen were, and Germany resumed its wholesale U-boat attacks in 1917. But when these sinkings involved a neutral vessel, the German government often extended some kind of compensation or formal apology, as they had done with the *Zaanstroom*.[51] But the public relations damage could not be undone. As Frank Trommler so persuasively argues, the *Lusitania* became a 'free floating signifier of aggression' that Germany could not escape.[52] Much like the 'rape of Belgium' motif, the *Lusitania* fed anti-German propaganda and popular actions throughout the war.

The *Lusitania* also inspired a range of popular reprisal actions against German communities. Throughout May 1915, in Britain, France and Russia, locals targeted (alleged) German families and businesses with violence. The riots in London were some of the worst recorded in British history, resulting in the mobilization of 30,000 special constables and the wounding of 257 people, the looting of shops and widespread damage to German and Austrian community spaces.[53] These 'amazing scenes of wreckage', as a New Zealand newspaper described them,[54] were also repeated in Moscow, where locals combined anti-Semitism and anti-Germanism to attack 'alien' residents with German-sounding names regardless of whether they had lived in their community for generations or whether they were actually German.[55] Despite the fact that both London and Moscow had thrived as cosmopolitan spaces prior to the war and contained tens of thousands of Germanophone residents, after May 1915 their identity as 'Germans' made them particularly unsafe.

The *Lusitania* sinking thus offered an emotionally charged outlet for the pent-up fears and frustrations that the war exacted in many belligerent communities. It provided a justifiable rationale to identify, isolate and (in the case of Russia above) even to murder these alien 'Others'.[56] Such acts of 'civic cleansing', as Nicoletta Gullace describes them, offered the powerless a measure of control over 'the war' by identifying even more vulnerable individuals they could attack. Inevitably, these acts of identification, isolation and eradication reimagined entire communities.[57]

In the ethnic melting-pot port city of Liverpool, for example, the *Lusitania* inspired a group of slum-dwelling Irish port workers, whose families had lost so many of their 'best' men to the western front, to the Royal Navy and to the merchant marine, to take action. Once the list of *Lusitania*'s drowned passengers and crew (many of whom were locals) were released, their communal grief broke. As the then fourteen-year-old Pat O'Mara recalled in his memoirs, the local fish-and-chip shop owner, Mrs Seymour, led the mob to attack anyone and anything remotely German. Previously well-respected and admired members of the community, who were now identified as having some (however tenuous) link to Germany, had their shop windows knocked in and looted. Mr Yaag, the butcher whose sons were serving in the British army in France, had no inkling that he might be considered 'suspicious'. When the mob came to his shop, he appeared at the

ILLUSTRATION 5.2 *This powerful and emotive recruitment poster, designed by the American artist Fred Spear in response to the sinking of the* RMS Lusitania *in 1915, reminded its (mainly British) audience about Germany's perfidy in sinking the passenger liner, killing innocents. It hoped to inspire belligerent populations to volunteer their service to fight the 'barbaric' Germans who allowed such acts to happen.*
Source: *Fred Spear, artist, 'Enlist', recruitment poster, 1915, Sackett and Wilhelms Corporation, in Library of Congress, POS - US.S656, no. 1, LC-DIG-ppmsca-50552.*

door full of smiles, but he nevertheless had his belly 'kicked in'.[58] As Gullace describes: 'The bonds of friendship and even kinship rarely mitigated the attacks on Germans. O'Mara even sacked the house of his own uncle and thought little of "having fun" at the expense of his former friends.'[59]

Across Britain and its Dominions in Canada, New Zealand, Australia and South Africa, similar riots broke out. They were particularly heated in multi-ethnic South Africa, where the war had repeatedly strained the competing loyalties of South Africa's various communities. In Pietermaritzburg, a town of 8,000 Europeans (Anglophone, European and Afrikaner), 8,000 indigenous Africans and 7,000 Indians, the heated language of the *Lusitania* news led to an outward showing of support for the British empire by the Anglophone community. Over the course of two nights, this mob, singing patriotic songs accompanied by bugle and drum, attacked German shops, burnt property and damaged public spaces.[60] Johannesburg also experienced such riots, as did Cape Town and Durban. Here too, the chance to assert control over public space by invoking loyalty to the wider imperial war cause played a key role. For, as the Johannesburg *Star* explained: 'it was not the hooligan who was at work [during the *Lusitania* riots of 12 May]. It was the well-dressed man, ... who was determined to wipe something off his slate.'[61]

The *Lusitania* incident highlights how the emotions of war preyed on the interchange between state and society. Governments certainly mobilized this popular anti-enemy fervour through their own propaganda and laws, in part to keep the loyalty of their population fully focused on 'winning the war'. After May 1915, the Allied governments also heightened their actions against enemy 'aliens' residing in their countries. In Australia, parliamentarians called for the seizure of German businesses and private property.[62] In New Zealand's capital city of Wellington, the local German-language professor at Victoria College was asked to 'abstain from communicating with other Germans' in order to keep his academic appointment.[63] Ultimately, German and Austrian residents, regardless of whether they were naturalized or born locally, were picked up and imprisoned in camps. Across the British empire, from Gibraltar to Sri Lanka to the Samoan islands, tens of thousands of enemy 'aliens' were corralled into camps, quarantined from the rest of society.[64] The rest of the belligerent world followed suit, setting up prison camps to intern their enemy 'Others'.[65] Even neutrals used imprisonment as a way of controlling foreign residents who might complicate or endanger their neutrality.[66] Between 1914 and 1918, the neutral Netherlands had camps for Belgian refugees, for foreign soldiers who had violated neutrality by entering Dutch territory, for former prisoners of war who had escaped their camps in Germany, and even for impoverished Dutch migrants who returned from Belgium and Germany but could not afford the cost of living 'back home'.[67]

These acts of incarceration ensured that the First World War, as the historian Panikos Panayi argues, became a 'turning point in the persecution of minorities'.[68] The impact on internees was predictably powerful.[69] As Richard Noschke, a German-born clerk who lived in London's East Ham, explained to his children:

> I often wonder how was it possible that the English people after me being a Resident in that Country for 25 years with an English wife, a grown up Family, the best of Character, 20 years in one situation, could turn on me so bitter … I had made many friends … but I am sorry to say, that nearly all … have turned against me, even my own direct family relations never even sent me as much as a postcard all the time I was interned.[70]

Yet even in neutral countries, these popular inclinations to strident nationalism, racism and xenophobia pitted migrant communities (from enemy countries) against each other.[71] Across the world, these empathies estranged family members and rejigged loyalties. They also offered a ready feeding ground for more extreme acts of violence.[72]

In territories newly occupied by an invading army, the interplay between violence and loyalty was particularly volatile. The Germans who invaded Belgium, Luxembourg and France in August 1914 were by no means alone in treating the local population with extreme violence. Even though The Hague Conventions outlined basic humanitarian responsibilities for occupying armies, conquest bred its own logic, as Sophie de Schaepdrijver notes.[73] Inevitably, the needs of the war outweighed any responsibility that the occupying forces may have felt to uphold the international laws of war. The occupier's law prevailed, militarily and administratively. As a result, any resident in occupation who could be considered a danger to the war effort – such as a spy, propagandist or even a person of the 'wrong' religion or ethnicity – could be suppressed, incarcerated or removed. 'Needless mouths' had to be made productive to support the war effort, which included forcing enemy civilians to work in essential industries and moving them into prison-like work camps.[74] Occupation also opened up spaces for colonization and imperial expansion, be it in Europe or the Middle East, Japanese-occupied Tsingtao or the New Zealand-occupied Samoan islands.

Across 1915 and beyond, occupied territories became, in the words of Annette Becker, a testing ground for population displacement and repression: 'To some extent these zones became the laboratories of an atypical front whose "artillery" and "gas" took the form of exodus, deportation, forced labor or the concentration camp.'[75] The transgressions that occurred on the military fronts, thus, had their counterparts in the transgressions that occurred against these 'suspicious' civilian populations. In occupied territories that experienced invasions and counter invasions in quick succession (including for the residents of Kut al-Amara described at the start of this chapter), the dangers were particularly acute. How one differentiated an enemy from a friend altered with each oscillation of power and authority. How to prove one's reliability to the new authorities could mean the difference between life and death, deportation or a chance to share in the spoils of war.[76] Civilians in occupation were rarely passive victims. They played vital roles in the dynamics of power, control and governance of occupied regions. Some of them saw new opportunities when an invading army arrived because they had suffered so much under the previous regime. Others collaborated to save their own lives, to profiteer or to advance their own political influence. A few resisted the occupation authorities, risking everything in the name of loyalty to a bigger cause, or because alternate routes were closed to them, for example, when they were classified as enemy 'aliens' or as traitors by the state or their neighbours.

As an example, consider the war experiences of the people who lived in the expansive Galician borderlands of the Austro-Hungarian empire, where the Russian armies first attacked Austria-Hungary in the autumn of 1914. Well before the Russian invasion, the Austro-Hungarian authorities were fearful of the anti-imperial loyalties of Galicia's population, including its Poles, Ukrainians and Ruthenians. As 'little Russians', the 3.2 million Ruthenians of Galicia were particularly worrisome, not least as Tsar Nicholas II had ambitions to reacquire Galicia as part of the Russian empire.[77] As a result, some 600,000 Ruthenians were forcibly moved out of Galicia's border regions by the Austro-Hungarian authorities and housed in improvised refugee camps further west. If they refused to move, they faced instant retribution and were treated as potential enemy collaborators. Paranoia spurred the violence. Already in 1914, the corpses of Ruthenian villagers littered roadsides, 'bobbing in the wind' hanging from trees, in scenes that would be replayed in occupied Serbia in 1915.[78] As the Austrian Chief of the General Staff, Franz Conrad von Hötzendorf, explained: 'we fight on our own territory as in a hostile land.'[79] Of the Ruthenians who made it to the camps, more than a third perished of malnutrition or disease.[80]

Once the Russian forces captured Galicia in 1914, they too used extreme force to cleanse the region of its 'unreliable' civilian residents. In first instance, they targeted the region's 872,000 Jews and 90,000 German-Austrians.[81] Pogroms, robberies, sexual assaults, murder and the wholesale destruction of property were common place activities conducted by the Russian forces in Galicia through the course of 1914 and 1915.[82] They also promoted local Ruthenians to the status of full Russians, in the hope of Russifying the region quickly.[83] Yet because of their desperate and violent efforts, the Russian occupiers increasingly alienated the locals. Hundreds of thousands fled into Austria-Hungary, escaping the Russian occupation. These refugees needed places to stay and food to sustain them. Through 1915, Galicia's refugees as well as those escaping the empire's Italian territories (after Italy joined the war in April) were perceived as 'unnecessary co-eaters' by the communities in which they reluctantly re-housed.[84] Annoyance, fear and anxiety upset social cohesion and loyalties even in these unoccupied regions.

Significantly, Galicia was recaptured twice more before the end of the war. In May 1915, a combined German and Austrian force drove the Russians out, re-occupying the territory. In response, hundreds of thousands of Ruthenians fled to Russia. In 1916, under the leadership of General Brusilov, the Russian occupiers returned, reclaiming large parts of Galicia as their own. Each invasion, hugely violent and costly in terms of military casualties, also caused immense civilian suffering. For as Alexander Watson explains, 'the warring Habsburg and Romanov Empires' racialized fantasies of treason and brutal reprisals interlocking and spiraling' ultimately uprooted, killed and deported millions of supposedly 'disloyal' residents and turned Galicia into a bloodbath.[85]

Across the borderlands between Russia and its enemies, similar acts of 'civic cleansing' and 'denationalization'[86] occurred. These included the deportation by the Russians of hundreds of thousands of 'hostile' locals from the Baltics and Poland, many of whom ended up in exile in Siberia.[87] Each side framed the religious and ethnic ties of the various communities as a reason to displace, incarcerate or kill them off.[88] Russian pogroms against Jews and Muslims in the Caucasus were common.[89] The Russians also mobilized Armenian and Georgian volunteers into regiments to attack Kurdish tribal forces. These Kurds, in turn, mobilized themselves in support of the Ottoman empire's declaration of *jihad* against their Christian opponents and in the hope of obtaining greater regional autonomy.[90]

Through the course of 1915, the Turkish rulers of the Ottoman empire authorized the 'cleansing' of its Greek Orthodox and Armenian Christian communities. The claim that these Christians were loyal to the enemy because of their religion and their history of anti-imperial politics presented an emotive rationale to declare them an internal security threat. Policing that risk empowered the agents of the Ottoman state to forcibly relocate 1.1 million Greeks out of the empire's Balkan borderlands in 1914 and to murder more than 1.5 million Armenians through the course of 1915.[91] The Armenian genocide involved mass executions, death marches, concentration camps and starvation tactics. Many of the young Armenian women – estimates range up to 200,000 in total – were not killed but kidnapped, married off to Muslim men, enslaved and sexually assaulted. As one of these women recalled of her enslavement at the age of twelve by a Kurdish family:

> The Vali's wife loved me like a mother, and he loved me like a lover ... and I love nobody. What did they leave me to love when they killed the last of my family?[92]

In combination with the famine that wrecked much of the Middle East in 1915, these acts of personal violence cleft the social fabric of the Ottoman empire.[93]

These stories of wartime suffering also illustrate how a 'home front' was rarely a 'safe' place or an 'escape' from the war. Death, disease and violence occurred on all the war's fronts, at home and abroad. Soldiers worried about the families they left behind as much as any family worried about those who had 'gone to war'. In this world of total war, then, belligerent civilians were far from passive agents or bystanders. As Leila Fawaz explains in her history of Ottoman society coping with the daily struggles of wartime survival: 'while those in more modest social circles avoided drawing the attention of officials, relying for survival on their own wit, resourcefulness, and networks of family and friends, others played the system and sought out ways to profit from the war.'[94] That sentence could also have been written about occupied Belgium, northern France, Serbia, Romania, Galicia or Poland during the war or about any number of belligerent societies in Europe, Asia and Africa.[95]

Significantly, neutral communities did not escape the war's spiral of violence nor the questioning of the loyalties that it entailed. A neutral country was not necessarily a 'safe' space, even if it was usually safer than a belligerent space. Chapter 6 describes some of the ways in which neutral communities and governments mobilized their neutrality to 'do good' in the war and to mediate or alleviate its violence. Yet more often than not, there was very little neutrals could do but bear witness to the war's violence and to write their reports. Yet in reporting, they also undertook a vital role: they made the war's extremes more publicly visible. As David Monger argues, the neutral diplomats stationed in the Ottoman empire helped to make sure that news of the Armenian genocide was shared with the world.[96] And in sharing the news, these neutrals ensured that questions of whether such violence was warranted permeated the global media as well.

The belligerents were also highly alert to the power of the neutral press. Capturing the 'hearts and minds' of the neutrals was considered vitally important. After all, today's neutral could be tomorrow's enemy. As a result, while public diplomacy was important before 1914, the First World War elevated its stakes exponentially.[97] To this end, the British government set up a secret War Propaganda Bureau in 1914 to influence neutral media.[98] The Germans too quickly realized that offering neutral journalists access to the warfront helped to mitigate some of the anti-German war news.[99] It took the French much longer to mobilize neutral reporters in the same way, but soon even Belgium's government-in-exile operated an active press campaign in neutral countries.

That so much energy was expended on the 'war of words' in neutral spaces highlights just how significant the belligerent governments believed the support of neutrals to be. It also recognized how essential the global public sphere was to determining acceptable 'norms' of warfare. As a result, much of the propaganda that aimed at shaping the loyalty of neutrals was similar to the messages that belligerent governments projected to their own populations. In both cases, presenting a convincing case for the necessity of a certain wartime action, especially when it transgressed existing norms or breached an international law, was paramount.

All the great power belligerents engaged in extensive propaganda campaigns aimed at persuading neutral and subject populations that their side was fighting a 'just war' against an ideological enemy and that, unlike their enemies, their own war activities were lawful. Such messages were promoted in a multitude of ways. They published books, pamphlets and documents 'proving' the enemy's responsibility for the war. They payed journalists to publish belligerent-friendly reports. The British were particularly adept at circulating glossy illustrated war magazines. Of these, the Spanish-language *America Latina* and Portuguese *O Espelho* circulated across Latin America on fortnightly basis. Around 75,000 copies of *Al Hakikat* were regularly disseminated across the Middle East in Arabic, Persian, Hindustani and Turkish. *Cheng Pao*, a Mandarin-language periodical promoting the Allied war effort, had a regular distribution of 108,000. Even more impressive was the distribution of 750,000 copies of the monthly *War Pictorial* in English, French, Dutch, Spanish, Portuguese, Italian, Russian, Greek, Danish, Swedish, German, alongside *Senji Gaho* (Japanese), *Warta Yang Tulus* (Malay), *Satya Vani* (Bengali, Hindi, Gujarati and Tamil) and *Jang Akhbar*, which was published in Hindi, Urdu and Gurumkhi.[100]

Some of this neutral targeting was very specific. The French government, for example, funded a newspaper in Spain entitled *Iberia*, which was run by a pro-Catalan independence group and aimed both at Catalan self-rule and at advancing a pro-*Entente* neutrality policy for Spain.[101] For its part, the Ottoman government used its special services to promote *jihad* and incite Muslim communities across the world to rise up against the British and French empires.[102] In response, the British targeted Muslim communities with anti-German messages that also aimed at discrediting the Ottoman empire. They even tried to persuade Chinese Muslims that the Germans were anti-Islamic in intent.[103]

The neutral United States presented a particularly important and captive audience for these belligerent propaganda ministrations. The American media landscape was inundated with opinions, perspectives and calls for and against wartime action.[104] Even the *Encyclopedia Britannica* – the British empire's foremost authority on knowledge – advertised its *Britannica Book of the War* in American newspapers on the grounds that 'you want to know the merits of the Great War, of course'.[105] Hollywood produced a range of full-length cinematic documentaries, often funded directly by the belligerent governments, looking to persuade American and other neutral audiences of wartime events and their significance.[106]

As we have seen, Germany had a distinct disadvantage in these media wars. But, as both belligerent sides expanded their warmongering, targeted civilians and repeatedly breached the laws of war, their representations of the enemy's inherent barbarism, left many wondering whether the descent into total war had caused morality itself to collapse globally.[107] The journalist Juan José de Soiza Reilly, who was stationed in Europe to report on the progress of the war for an Argentine newspaper, mobilized increasingly more anti-war reflections in his reports. At times, he critiqued the 'silent war of famine' that Britain enforced on Germany. At others, he despaired at the 'true war, the one I see, the one I hear, the one I smell', 'the common war, the vulgar, dirty, stinking war of human beings who eat one another, like cannibals', a war which had its own dynamism of destruction.[108]

While many neutrals grew weary of the war through 1915, many belligerent communities grew wary of neutrals. In Britain, German-speaking Swiss nationals were often interned as enemy aliens. Any protests to this internment were rebuked with claims that Swiss neutrality was itself suspect (in part because of Switzerland's proximity to Germany and Austria-Hungary).[109] Where, in Germany at the start of the war, businesses actively recruited workers from neighbouring neutral countries for their essential industries, after 1915, municipalities started repatriating these workers (and other residents from neutral countries) when they lost their jobs or their German-born soldier husbands. Without the means to survive or support the German war effort, these 'useless eaters' from 'suspect' countries were not supported like German-born residents.[110] Similarly, through 1915 more than 150,000 workers from neutral China travelled on the Trans-Siberian Railway to take up jobs in essential Russian war industries. Increasingly, their presence exacerbated social tensions and heightened fears among the Russians that these neutral foreigners were German spies or saboteurs.[111] Through the course of 1915, then, the value of neutrality became suspect.

Yet a non-belligerent's war experience could be as profoundly transformative and traumatic as that of any soldier.[112] Whether as a neutral or belligerent civilian, a refugee or interned individual, child or adult, the personal experience of war inspired new questions and reflections.[113] It also brought the most unlikely combinations of people in contact with each other: be it a New Zealand X-ray technician working among the array of multi-national soldiers fighting for the French and British on the Salonika front in Greece, or her Canadian nurse counterpart stationed on the Mediterranean island of Lemnos;[114] be it a German soldier captured during the siege of Tsingtao, who spent the rest of his war years in a Japanese internment camp or a journalist from neutral Latin America reporting the war straight from the western front; be it a Turkish prisoner of war captured on the Anatolian front with Russia, interned in Siberia and finally repatriated back to Turkey in 1922 out of the Pacific Ocean port of Vladivostok;[115] or be it Mukherji's compatriot, Sisir Prasad Sarbadhikari, an orderly working for the Bengal Ambulance Corps who served in a hospital in Aleppo and witnessed the slaughter of the Armenians. Santanu Das describes Sarbadhikari's wartime memoirs, which were published in 1957 under the title *Abhi le Baghdad* ('So much for taking Baghdad'), as '*All Quiet on the Western Front* turned upside down – from a noncombatant, non-white and non-Western Front perspective'.[116] Sarbadhikari's memoirs speak of the horror of the battlefield, the terror experienced by the wounded, and the personal friends and enemies made in the melting-pot of a wartime hospital site, where individuals from all over the globe unexpectedly met and asked new questions of themselves and each other. As Sarbadhikari retrospectively framed his conversations with wounded Ottoman soldiers:

> We spoke of our lands, our joys and sorrows ... One thing that they always used to say was, 'This war that we are fighting – what is our stake in this? Why are we slashing each others' throats? You stay in Hindustan, we in Turkey, we do not know each other, share no enmity, and yet we became enemies overnight because one or two people deemed it so'.[117]

What Sarbadhikari's experiences highlight, above all, was that the loyalties expected of subjects and citizens in total war were not only hard to maintain but also shifted in response to the actual experience of war. The escalation of violence through the course of 1915 – this 'world in itself' – reflected how vital the dynamics of loyalty and distrust were in belligerent and neutral communities. As we will see in the next few chapters, those dynamics were mercurial, prone to change with the shifting sands of the war and with shifting perceptions of 'what is this war about?' and 'what does it mean for me?'[118] As the war dragged on into a seemingly endless test of endurance through the course of 1916, many of the loyalties it initially inspired shifted. Belligerent and neutral governments found it increasingly difficult to sustain or coerce the support of their subjects and citizens in the face of mounting casualty rates, rationing and inflation.

6

The test of endurance: Rethinking the war in 1916

When Léon Daudet first used the term *guerre totale* (total war) in a 1916 editorial, he did so to describe his anxieties about the seemingly endless nature of the war.[1] As a staunch monarchist, Daudet was no stranger to controversy. He had gained renown in France for his spy stories and anti-German polemics.[2] In this editorial, however, his main concern was to acknowledge that 'the war' had transformed into a brutal, inescapable and all-encompassing reality.[3] The editorial emphasized how the war forced dire 'life-or-death' choices on soldiers and civilians alike. Its brutality infiltrated every French person's life.[4] When in 1918, Daudet subsequently expanded his definition of 'total war' as a struggle of 'political, economic, commercial, industrial, intellectual, legal and financial domains', he did so to give historical form to these collective war experiences.[5]

This chapter focuses on the year 1916 as a fulcrum of the condition of total global war that developed through the course of 1915. For while the 'mutual siege' between the major belligerents did not ease in 1916, and would not ease for almost two more years after that, the willingness of ordinary people to accept and accommodate 'the war' in their lives started to shift, sometimes in radical ways. War weariness was a global phenomenon. In the face of this weariness and as they experienced ever greater economic deprivations, many questioned the existing narratives as to why this war was being fought or why their neutrality needed to be upheld. In growing numbers, they began to push-back against the authorities who were asking them to sacrifice even more. In this contentious interplay between state and society about what the total war demanded of each of them lay the root cause of enormous social and political instability.

Despite engaging in some extremely destructive military campaigns and suffering enormous casualty counts, neither set of belligerents made a decisive strategic breakthrough between January and December 1916. In one of the most devastating days of the entire war, the British empire lost

57,000 soldiers during the first twenty-four hours of its Somme offensive. The battle for the Somme in the summer of 1916 caused more than a million casualties altogether.[6] The French empire too 'bled white' its army, losing 351,000 troops defending the Verdun salient from a German attack. The Germans lost an almost equal number of casualties.[7] Russia's 1916 Brusilov offensives may have been the 'greatest victory seen on any front' and enabled Russia to re-occupy Galicia, yet they failed to collapse the Austro-Hungarian front by the onset of winter.[8] These Galician campaigns resulted in more than 1.2 million military casualties, including the capture of 300,000 Austro-Hungarian prisoners of war.[9] It also exhausted Russia's and Austria-Hungary's armies to the point of open rebellion. The campaigns fought in central Africa in and around Cameroon and the Congo and in south-east Africa in 1916 resulted in tens of thousands of deaths, especially among the African-born carrier corps.[10] Strategic stasis in 1916, much as it had done in 1915, involved an incredible amount of human endeavour, violence, grief and suffering.

The continuity of total war strained the global economy to breaking point as well. While the situation worsened in 1917 and 1918, during 1916 the economic war fought at sea caused a massive loss of shipping. The longer the war dragged on, the more intense its impact became on global supply chains. Consider, for example, the impact of the inability to get essential fertilizer chemicals from Latin America to farms in Europe, Africa, Asia and Australasia. Without adequate fertilizers, crop production declined. As crop production declined, so did the amount of food available for human and animal consumption. As human eaters were prioritized, cattle were culled (offering only temporary relief).[11] Without cattle, however, a source of natural fertilizers declined, reducing the ability of farmers to grow future food crops. The harvests of 1916 were smaller than usual. Even the neutral United States suffered from shortages that year, increasing the cost of food by an average of 46 per cent.[12] In combination with the massive war loans taken out by the belligerent powers, these distribution issues caused spiralling inflation, a global rise in the cost of living and heightened unemployment in non-essential industries.[13] Social and economic distress was a global phenomenon through 1916 in ways that far exceeded the stresses of the first two years of war.

In Russia, Germany, Austria-Hungary and the Ottoman empire, the declining availability of food and fuel stuffs had dire consequences. Even before the start of what came to be known in Germany as the 'turnip winter' of 1916–17, supplies of essential goods deteriorated drastically. By this time, Austro-Hungarians were eating a third less grain than they had in 1913. The Ottoman empire's deficit sat at 229 per cent of its GDP that year, most of which was spent on its military needs and not in alleviating the enormous shortages facing its civilian population.[14] In Germany, the lack of food resulted in the average adult weight dropping from 60 kg in 1914 to 49 kg in 1917, while German children were documented to be anywhere between

3 and 5 cm shorter than their pre-war peers.[15] In December 1916, the Russian secret police reported that in many towns and cities, 'children are starving in the most literal sense of the word'.[16]

These belligerent metropoles were not alone. In eastern Africa, the repeated requisitioning of the Wagogo's people, cattle and food by the German and British armed forces decimated their communities' social cohesion. In Nyasaland and Malawi too, the British military appropriated entire crops and cattle stocks in 1916 (and again in 1917), causing starvation, the spread of disease and social collapse.[17] In neutral Spain, a skewed balance of trade in 1916 (massively favouring exports over imports) helped to bolster inflation and resulted in what locals called a *crisis de subsistencias* (subsistence crisis).[18] When bakers in Chicago doubled bread prices in August 1916 due to the rising cost of wheat, angry delegates of the National Housewives' League protested to Congress and demanded that the White House protect domestic consumption over the profits that could be gained by selling to the warring powers.[19] In the Austro-Hungarian occupation zone of the neutral territory of Albania, the 329 residents of the small mountain-top village of Mallakastër fled into Italy or turned to begging in the nearby town of Fier to escape starvation. By 1918, only seventy-nine residents were left in the village.[20] Even Koreans experienced rice shortages, as the Japanese imperial authorities requisitioned rice stocks to offset the needs of their own metropole first.[21]

With hindsight, it is easy to frame 1916 as a year of 'frustration and failure' (as David Stevenson does),[22] of 'impasse' (as per Robin Prior)[23] and of 'wearing down and holding out' (according to Jörn Leonhard).[24] It certainly was a year in which universal war weariness set in and people's willingness to support their country's or empire's war efforts declined substantially.[25] Yet for those who lived through it, 1916 was experienced mostly as a process of unravelling, in which the multiple stresses of the war situation also offered up opportunities for action, to provoke changes, to resist authority and to rethink the war and its impact.

Across 1916, food riots, strikes and protest marches erupted in cities around the world, including in occupied Poland and Belgium, neutral Switzerland, Portugal and the Netherlands, war-torn Britain, France, Italy, Germany, Austria-Hungary and Russia.[26] In rural areas too, people grew increasingly tired of the suffering they had to endure. In the words of Benjamin Ziemann, the peasantry in most belligerent empires were 'continually overworked, physically exhausted and ... emotionally strained'.[27] In town and countryside alike, people became more willing to criticize their governments and to blame their neighbours and fellow citizens for not doing enough to share the burden of the war equitably. The 'enemy within' could now be one's 'less than loyal' neighbour, the person who did not ration their food or work hard enough, or the one who failed to hang out the flag, sing the national anthem or refused to volunteer for essential services. The politics of blame strained the politics of wartime loyalty through 1916, at times risking the cohesion of states and communities completely. In hindsight, 1916 can be seen as a 'tipping point for the intensification of protests, riots, uprisings and ... revolutions'.[28] It was also the year in which contemporaries, like Daudet, started to recognize that the political, economic and social structures of the pre-war era were failing.

The inability of the great power belligerents to achieve an all-important strategic breakthrough during 1916 came at a huge cost to their ability to sustainably govern their countries, their empires and the international environment in general. The careful balancing acts they had maintained in 1914 and 1915 – between inspiring the support and loyalty of their populations and coercing compliance when that support was no longer volunteered – teetered in 1916. Total war was an unsustainable condition. State violence against 'disloyal' groups and communities increased as their enthusiasm for the war weakened and as the personal and societal costs of sustaining the war effort heightened. Neutral governments too faced serious political opposition to their wartime policies, especially when shortages and rationing hit hard.

Throughout 1916, the recognition that the pre-war political order was under threat of collapse and that a post-war future would require new foundations and governance structures heightened.[29] This sense of the inevitability of change fed on both the popular and almost universal exasperation at the unending nature of the global war and grasped at the hope of enforcing a peace. The recognition that the war could lead to permanent changes within communities and empires opened up space for political activism to grow. It also intensified social unrest and political unpredictability. In 1917, the dam broke, collapsing firstly the Russian Romanov empire, followed by the Austro-Hungarian and Ottoman empires and the German *Kaiserreich*. But it is all too simplistic to describe 1916 as a precursor to the revolutionary disruptions of 1917 and 1918, as if this year of 'impasse' and collective strain necessitated the revolutionary period to follow. Rather, what the experiences of total war through 1916 highlight most of all is how contemporaries considered their options for the future as being more fluid than the rigid loyalties expected of them by their governments. They were also more tired of the war (and desirous for peace) than their governments were willing to allow them to be.

This chapter focuses on three themes to bring out the transformative impact of sustaining a 'world at total war' throughout 1916. It begins with the impact of labour shortages, military conscription and forced labour on the political management of belligerent and neutral communities. Then it turns to the rising tide of anti-imperial protests and uprisings. Finally, it explains how neutral states and communities navigated this year of 'endless war', and their recognition of the risks, threats and opportunities it engendered for their own futures.

The heart of any war effort is human endeavour. While the belligerent armed forces sought an endless supply of soldiers – particularly to recoup

their enormous military losses – their war economies also had to find new
sources of labour to replace the men and women in military service. This non-
military labour was especially important in essential industries like farming,
mining and armaments production. Inevitably, larger numbers of women
came to work in jobs previously reserved for men, including at the war fronts
in logistics, medical and technical-support roles. These gendered labour shifts
had an enormous impact on the functioning of families and communities,
and offered many women new sources of economic and political agency.[30]

The industrial needs of the war economies also caused substantial
demographic shifts. In the neutral United States, for example, the rapid
expansion of industrial production (to supply the belligerents' war needs)
helped to inspire the beginnings of what American historians call the 'great
migration'. From 1916 to 1918, more than 400,000 African American
workers (5 per cent of the entire African American population) moved
from their homes in the southern United States to the country's northern
industrial cities. The unprecedented influx of new workers augmented the
size of these northern cities and heightened social and racial tensions in
increasingly violent ways.[31] Similarly, Japanese cities also grew in size and
industrial capacity during the war. Here too the expansion of slums and
the influx of low-wage labourers caused social tensions to spill over into
political activism and popular unrest.[32]

In Europe, the labour needs of the belligerent countries were met both
by mobilizing citizens and by acquiring labour from 'elsewhere', including
from imperial outposts, neutral neighbours and occupied territories. France
not only mobilized considerable numbers of women (40 per cent of its
armaments jobs were staffed by women in 1917), its war economy also
attracted 230,000 labourers from neutral Spain and procured 135,000
workers from northern Africa, China, Vietnam and Malaga.[33] Along with an
influx of Belgian refugees, the social and demographic contours of France's
work landscape changed substantially. In an attempt to expand the size of its
armed forces, the French government promised to extend citizenship rights
to Africans who served for France on the European war fronts. This promise
helped to persuade some African leaders to actively recruit their men for
the war. What often looked like voluntary service, however, increasingly
turned into coercion. An extraordinary amount of violence was exacted in
obtaining enough African military labourers and soldiers for France.[34] More
often than not, such recruitment efforts were met with passive and active
defiance, including by men who fled their communities, went into hiding or
joined anti-imperial resistance groups.[35]

Similarly, Great Britain mobilized 1.2 million non-Europeans into its
armed forces during the war, including hundreds of thousands of military
labourers.[36] Many, but by no means all, of the men who served in the
Indian Labour Corps, the South African Labour Corps, the Canadian No.
2 Construction Battalion, the Maori Battalion, the Egyptian Labour Corps,
the British West Indies Regiment, the Macedonian Mule Corps and the

Maltese Labour Corps volunteered. India's Jailed Labour and Porter Corps, for example, was composed of inmates from India's prisons who were forced onto ships to undertake the worst cleaning and sanitation jobs for the British armies stationed in the Middle East.[37] The authorities in Egypt, for their part, never formalized conscription. To meet their labour quotas, they nevertheless kidnapped peasants from their homes and villages. By 1918, more than 230,000 Egyptians served in the Egyptian Labour Corps, aiding the British invasion of Palestine and the Middle East.[38] Many of the men in the British East African Carrier Corps were also forced into service by local authorities, which included night-time raids on their homes.[39] Altogether, this empire-wide marshalling of military labour not only set in motion notable demographic and socio-economic shifts (particularly when there was not enough domestic labour to bring in the harvest), it also inspired many to resist these measures. Wartime labour offered a potent reason for subject communities to demand greater political recognition within an empire and, when that was not on offer, to resist the empire more vociferously than ever before. As information about the horrors of the war fronts filtered 'back home', fewer men volunteered to serve.

By 1916, finding adequate numbers of volunteers had become harder in the metropoles and white settler colonies as well. War weariness and the massive casualty lists did not inspire confidence. While military service and soldiers' heroism were celebrated in all belligerent communities, often fed by a vocal pro-conscription movement, these communities also debated the communal and social costs of sending so many millions of people off to war. From 1916 on, priests and pastors in Germany preached about the moral dangers of creating a generation of delinquent children who had to cope with absent fathers (serving on a war front), absent mothers (working for the war effort) and a lack of food.[40] Evelyn Blücher, the British wife of a German who lived in Berlin, described the social costs of the war in equally stark terms in her war diary:

> Women are realising the enormous burden imposed upon them. They have to do the men's work as well as their own, and when they have earned their pay it all goes into the pockets of others who sell them food at enormous prices. Naturally they begin more than ever to say: 'Why should we work, starve, send our men out to fight? What is it all going to bring us? More work, more poverty, our men cripples, our homes ruined. What is it all for? What do we care whether we have a bit more land added to our big Germany? We have enough land. We'd rather fight for a more just division of the goods of this earth. For whether we obtain land or money for the 'Fatherland' after this war, *we* shall not see any change in our lives; the wealth will not come our way. The State which called upon us to fight cannot even give us decent food, does not treat our men as human beings, but as so many screws in the great machine of the German army.[41]

It is in no way surprising then to see a substantial increase in soldier protests and acts of resistance through 1916 as well. When soldiers protested the conditions of their service, they often did so in response to a particular issue (e.g. when they were not given enough leave or their rations were inadequate). Others deserted, favouring a life in hiding over the possibility of death or major injury on a battlefront. Despite the fact that desertion could result in a military court-martial and the death penalty, between 1916 and 1918, 250,000 soldiers deserted from the Austro-Hungarian army. The Ottoman empire counted 500,000 such lawless individuals,[42] while the Netherlands witnessed the arrival of tens of thousands of German deserters at its borders, all of whom refused to return to Germany. What to do with these 'alien Others', who could not be repatriated for fear they might be executed as traitors yet who ate up their host's scarce supplies, became a serious political issue for the neutral Dutch.[43]

Other soldier protests evolved out of a wider dissatisfaction with the war effort and its impact on society. These protests often fed on pre-existing social and political inequities. In 1914 in France, socialists had abandoned their anti-militarism when their leader, Jean Jaurès, was assassinated on the eve of war. French socialists, including a large working-class population, accepted their government's call to arms as a collective duty in defence of their nation, their homes and their livelihoods. By the middle of 1916, however, this political equilibrium was fraying fast. A year later, after another disastrous French assault at Chemin des Dames, more than half of France's army mutinied, demanding better conditions for their families on the home front and better food provisioning and leave conditions for themselves.[44] Eventually, France's soldiers returned to the trenches but they did so only to defend against a German attack. No French assault occurred on the western front until the first signs of a German general retreat in 1918. France might be at total war, as Daudet explained, but its citizens and colonial subjects were not willing to sustain that war effort needlessly with their own lives.

The British government also faced serious political resistance to its attempts to conscript men into military service during 1916. Unlike the other European armies, Britain did not have a tradition of compulsory military training or conscription. The early months of war did see a massive wave of British volunteers. By late 1915, however, those numbers declined. After the disastrous Somme offensive of 1916, they declined even further. The government recognized that it could only sustain its military efforts if it forced its citizens to serve. While it readily compelled its imperial subjects into working for the state, conscription sat uncomfortably within the British metropole. The introduction of conscription in 1916 caused a political crisis pitting liberals (who claimed Britain was no better than authoritarian Germany if it enacted conscription) against conservatives (who argued that the war must be won and every British man, woman and child needed to be made to do 'their bit' and play 'their part').[45] The Military Service Act, nevertheless, came into effect on 2 March 1916. Importantly, by the end of the year, more than a million British men had refused their conscription orders, preferring to apply for 'certificates of exemption', which allowed them to work in essential civilian industries instead.[46] Such high numbers of refusals presented a clear signal that many Britons considered the military cost of fighting the war as too high.[47]

Attempts to introduce conscription in Britain's white Dominions of Australia, New Zealand and Canada did not entirely go to plan either. In Australia, the 1916 referendum on the subject resulted in heated public debates and returned a 'no' vote. On the one hand, a growing number of Australians were unwilling to fight in a war for an empire that seemed to have abandoned them. The brutal repression of Ireland's Easter Rising (see below), the lack of British support for the economic needs of Australia's farming community as it coped with shipping shortages and the notion that any support for the war should be voluntarily given and not coerced, influenced these Australian debates.[48] In New Zealand, where conscription was introduced on 1 August 1916, the public debate around its implementation was equally prolific.[49] Canada too faced political crises throughout 1916 and 1917 when attempts to introduce conscription met with a decisive backlash from its Irish and Francophone populations.[50] At the same time, indigenous communities across the three Dominions navigated the empire's demands for their military labour in a variety of ways. Invariably, resistance was as likely as cooperation.

These subject communities were certainly in tune with the war's international developments.[51] They could read the news and were alert to moments of imperial weakness. As the organizers of the Easter Rising had it: 'England's troubles offer Ireland's opportunity'.[52] Across the British and French empires, overt acts of anti-imperial rebellion only increased during the war. They were particularly prolific during 1916. Such acts made the possibility of winning the war at the cost of losing an empire all too obvious to the great power governments. Of course, Germany lost much of its colonial empire in 1914. Its government thus felt fully justified in maximizing any and all opportunities to destabilize its enemies' empires as well. Germany funded anti-imperial propaganda, *jihadi* uprisings and offered armaments and monetary support for anti-French, anti-British and even anti-Japanese resistance groups. It often operated out of neutral territories to do so.[53]

The Singapore Mutiny that erupted during the celebrations of the Chinese New Year on 15 February 1915 was an early example of how the deterioration of soldier morale could merge with a set of pre-existing political ideas and lead to an outright rebellion.[54] The mutiny broke out when 400 Muslim troops in the Indian Fifth Light Infantry division were convinced that they would be shipped from Singapore to the Middle East to fight their co-religionists in the Ottoman empire. In protest, they rioted, attacked a munitions truck, set free a number of German prisoners of war and killed eighty-two people, before fleeing into the Malay peninsula. The uprising caught the British authorities by surprise. They scrambled to contain the situation, calling on the Singapore Volunteer Corps (a civilian militia composed of Malay and Chinese men) and arming 200 special constables from out the city's European population. Ultimately, the mutiny failed and the rioters were captured: of the 203 soldiers who were court-martialled, all but one was convicted. Of these, forty-one were executed (twenty-three in full public view) and sixty-three received life sentences. Along with the fifty-two soldiers who died during the mutiny, a quarter of the regiment was either dead or removed from service by year's end.[55] While the British authorities presented the mutiny as a unique case of misplaced soldier grievances, the global press read the situation more thoughtfully as an act of anti-imperial resistance in a long line of south and south-east Asian activism against the British crown stretching well back into the pre-war era.[56] Importantly, the mutiny was not only supported by Germany from out of neutral Siam, the Dutch East Indies (present-day Indonesia) and China, but also mobilized anti-imperial activists across the British empire.[57]

If the Singapore mutiny cracked the veneer of the idea of a 'happy British empire at war', the Easter Rising of 1916 broke it apart.[58] The armed rebellion centred in Dublin was planned as a distinct 'propaganda by the deed' by the followers of the Irish Republican Brotherhood (IRB). Funded in part by Irish Americans in the neutral United States and supported by German armaments suppliers, the IRB declared an Irish Republic on Easter Monday and besieged government offices and municipal buildings. They hoped that other Irish would rise up with them, but even if they did not, that the revolt would destabilize British control over the island and offer a decisive step towards Irish self-determination and independence.[59] The British authorities suppressed the uprising by sending 20,000 troops into Dublin, killing 260 civilians and arresting more than 3,500 people. Ninety of them were sentenced to death for treason. The most prominent among the leaders were executed in public. The extremes of violence used to suppress the rebellion highlighted just how frightened the British government was of the dissolution of its empire 'from within'. Violent repression was a distinct feature of British responses to anti-imperial protests before 1914. After 1916 it defined them. Surveillance operations against subject communities increased as well, including in India where the Defence of India Act enabled the authorities to detain hundreds of 'terrorists'.[60]

After the Easter Rising, imperial authorities across the world understood that their empires were at risk. The Easter Rising may not have succeeded in establishing an independent Ireland in 1916 (Ireland would gain its independence in 1921), but it encouraged anti-imperialists and ethnic nationalists globally.[61] In the Catalan region of Spain, for example, the Catalan independence movement was inspired by the Easter Rising to use a new level of violence to achieve its goals.[62] In Turkestan (present-day Kazakhstan), news of the Easter Rising encouraged a number of Kazakh and Kirgiz groups, who were themselves increasingly frustrated at the Romanov empire's rule over their people and lands. In August 1916, armed rebellions broke out in the region, bringing various anti-imperial agents together. Some were protesting the empire's new conscription laws, others baulked at the rising cost of food, the profiteering and corruption of local authorities and the seizure of *steppe* lands by a new generation of Russian settlers. A prominent sub-group of well-educated socialists also found their voice in these rebellions, and 'drew implicit and explicit parallels between the plight of Russia's minorities and that of colonized groups around the world [including the Irish]'.[63] The Russian empire repressed these rebellions with extreme force, much as they had done other 'suspicious' communities during the war.[64]

With hindsight, 1916 presented as a distinctly global anti-imperial moment, one which pitched imperial authorities against its rebels in decidedly violent ways, but also one which saw the belligerent powers mobilize anti-imperial sentiments to their advantage. At the same time, the global war offered subject communities an opportunity to fight back.[65] The Ottoman sultan's declaration of *jihad* in 1914 certainly helped to bolster a number of anti-British and anti-French uprisings in northern Africa including the Anglo-Sanussi war that was fought between 1915 and 1917, the Aulihan uprising between 1915–18 and the ongoing upheavals in British-controlled Nigeria.[66] In response, the British used their own anti-Turkish networks to fund and inspire anti-Ottoman opposition in the Middle East. The Arab revolt of 1916, which saw Arab communities across the Middle East rise up against the Ottoman state seeking independence, was as much an indigenous movement in opposition to Turkish rule as it was a political act that hoped to capitalize on an eventual Allied victory (and the promise of Arabian self-rule – a promise that would be broken).[67] In the moment, the revolt was brutally suppressed by the Ottoman authorities, who also publicly executed its leaders.[68] In the horn of Africa, however, Haile Selassie's armed rebellion removed the Italians from Abyssinia in one of the most successful military campaigns of the year.

These social and economic instabilities affected neutral countries and empires too. The Inter-Allied Conference of March 1916, for example, expanded Allied blockade tactics to drastically ration supplies from reaching the neutrals. From this point on, key neutrals were asked to either prioritize the supply of the Allies and to further restrict their trade with the Central Powers, or to risk all their trade being seized at sea.[69] Britain imposed harsh blacklisting rules, which resulted in companies across the neutral world being investigated and struck off if they traded with a German- or Austrian-owned firm, regardless of where that firm was located.[70] Britain sent its diplomats, other agents and spies into neutral territories to monitor compliance, with extraordinary results:

A cargo of apples from America was denied landing in Norway because it was addressed to a blacklisted firm; a Norwegian woman was refused needles for her sewing machine because her husband was on the 'black list'; and even public utilities, on demand of the British ..., were compelled to refuse service to Norwegian firms known to be in business relations with Germany.[71]

As one Norwegian pamphleteer decried on the subject: 'By the black list, England has penetrated most perniciously into our economic life'.[72]

Through the course of 1916, all the neutral governments faced serious challenges to their ability to negotiate the economic demands of the belligerents. Where Britain blacklisted companies, intercepted neutral shipping, seized blacklisted goods and forced export limits on neutrals, Germany increased its U-boat campaigns (although they did warn the ships before they were sunk). Through 1916, the loss of neutral lives at sea increased exponentially, as did the loss of neutral ships. In one twelve-day period in October 1916, thirty-three Norwegian merchant vessels succumbed to such attacks, nearly three a day with a total loss of 40,185 tonnes of goods. Two thousand Norwegians drowned thanks to the war at sea between 1914 and 1918.[73] It would seem Germany, too, was perniciously infiltrating Norway's economic and social life. The success of Allied blockade and blacklisting tactics made it easier for the German government to resume an unrestricted U-boat campaign in 1917 (including sinking ships without warning).[74] After all, if the neutrals could not supply Germany with resources, then an all-out economic war against the ships that supplied its enemies was a logical counter strike. In such a stressed world, it was no wonder that the perceived value of neutrality plummeted.

The politics of neutrality, sovereignty and wartime supply played out in fascinating ways. In the United States, as the historian Michael Neiberg describes it, the 'guilt-inducing paradox of neutrality that was both profitable and morally questionable' became a defining feature of political discourse in 1916.[75] In the face of creeping inflation, some Americans demanded that President Wilson's government revert to complete isolationism and protect domestic consumers against rampant war profiteering.[76] Others pushed the country to greater military readiness, fearing the cost of a German victory on their profit margins and the United States' place in a post-war international order. The country's financial interests were firmly tied to the Allies' war efforts, and the German war at sea targeted American shipping with impunity. As a result, many anticipated (while others feared) the possibility of an American war declaration on Germany. By the end of the year, as Neiberg also explains, 'the war in Europe was no longer just about "them" but, increasingly, about "us"' as well.[77]

The global war also informed Americans' perceptions of the attack by the Mexican revolutionary Pancho Villa and his militia on the United States border town of Columbus (New Mexico) on 9 March 1916. Villa's raid was part of a five-year-long revolutionary campaign in Mexico itself conducted on, near or across the United States frontier. On 9 March, the *Villistas* looted the town store, set fire to buildings and killed several residents. Villa had

ILLUSTRATION 6.1 *This French cartoon from 1916, by the renowned cartoonist Emile Dupuis, represented the United States as a greedy neutral, willingly trading in the lives of innocent civilians and risking the growth of German militarism for its own wealth and profit.*

Source: *Emile Dupuis, 'In the Shadow of Liberty' postcard, Visé, 1916, Library of Congress, Call Number LOT 4856.*

specific reasons to target Columbus, not least his need for money and goods and his anger at President Wilson for supporting his political rivals in Mexico. But he was also encouraged by his German agent, who lived in the United States and hoped that it would distract Americans from the global war.[78] The distraction worked, at least in part. The United States army retaliated by attacking Villa's militias in Mexico itself. These border skirmishes lasted until January 1917 and resulted in a number of embarrassing military defeats for the Americans. Yet ultimately, the Mexican situation played an important role in bringing the United States to declare war on Germany in April 1917.

More immediately in 1916, the Mexican war highlighted a series of deficiencies in the United States armed forces, and caused numerous political debates about the security of the country (including plans to increase the manufacture of artificial fertilizers).[79] These debates reached a zenith after 30 July 1916 when another group of German agents operating out of New York set the Black Tom docks ablaze causing a million pounds of ammunition to explode, shattering windows across lower Manhattan, and leaving a massive crater in its wake. Given that 75 per cent of American ammunition exports left from Black Tom and ended up in Britain or France, the New York target was deliberately chosen. The loss of six piers, thirteen warehouses and dozens of rail carriages hampered American ammunition exports for the foreseeable future. But above all, the attack was seen as a clear act of German sabotage, a signal that the war between the other great powers was very much a war in which the neutral United States played a decisive role.[80] As President Wilson acknowledged at the end of the year, the country's neutrality was paper thin. It would only take one more incident like the Black Tom explosion or another passenger-liner sinking to force his hand.[81] As Wilson further warned, this might be the 'last war' in which the United States could remain neutral. For the war of the world was America's war too.[82]

Neutrality politics dominated Spanish public life in 1916 as well. Spaniards suffered from intense shortages and financial hardships that year, which led them to question whether Spain should remain neutral, join the war or offer peculiar benefits to a belligerent. These discussions became increasingly polemical, exacerbating the marked socio-political and cultural divides that already existed in Spanish society. As the historian Francisco Romero Salvado explains, the issues were so divisive that they constituted a veritable 'civil war of words'. Across 1916, cinemas avoided screening war news, in the hope of preventing fights from breaking out between Francophile and Germanophile movie-goers.[83] As many of these politically alert Spaniards understood, the stakes in the war were such that the future of Europe and of the international environment was in play. For them, the war of the world was very much Spain's war too.

Throughout 1916, then, questions about 'the war' and its impact on communities became acute. War weariness was a global phenomenon, helping to open up the consideration of new 'power plays' at a local and global level.[84] The world of war in 1916 was also becoming more unpredictable. How would societies survive the war's inherent 'test of endurance'?[85] Such questioning revolved as much around concepts of neutrality as it did belligerency: What value did neutrality continue to have in a world of heightened belligerent power? What value did loyalty to an empire have in an environment of heightened economic and military crisis?

Because neutral countries were spaces of exile and refuge, they also became spaces for political agitation against the war. Prominent political figures, artists, thinkers and writers sought refuge in Switzerland during the war to escape the political and artistic confines of their belligerent countries. These included the Communist revolutionary Vladimir Lenin, the Austrian pacifist Alfred Fried, the anarchist Henri Guilbeaux and authors Stefan Zweig and Romain Rolland.[86] Their critiques of the war only grew as the war's destruction expanded.

The year 1916 certainly maligned nineteenth-century conceptions of neutrals as mitigating inter-state warfare. The number of countries that managed to remain neutral also declined. Much like Italy had done in May 1915, Bulgaria joined the war rather opportunistically on the side of the Central Powers in October 1915 (with an eye to expanding its territory in the Balkans after the failed Allied attack on the Dardanelles).[87] Its neighbour, Romania, declared war on the Central Powers in August 1916, hoping that the Russian, French and British would protect it from a likely Austrian-German-Bulgarian invasion.[88] By December 1916, none of the Allied promises came through and Bucharest fell.[89]

Portugal too joined the war in Europe in March 1916, after it seized German and Austrian merchant vessels in its territorial waters and reflagged them (thereby relieving its shipping shortage and enabling it to resume trading with the Allies).[90] Germany declared war on Portugal in response, citing the re-flagging as a major breach of neutrality, but also with an eye to invading Portuguese holdings in eastern Africa (especially around Delagoa Bay).[91] The Portuguese government subsequently declared its own war on Germany and sent troops to the western front, citing its actions as a consequence of its desire to remain sovereign and neutral and, like Belgium, protesting its status as a victim of the great power war. These formal war declarations sent a sharp warning to the world's remaining neutrals about the ease with they could be forced to become belligerents. The guarantees of neutrality with which they had entered the war in 1914 were disintegrating. From 1916 on, 'Portugalization' became a trope by which neutrals read the shifting sands of their status *vis-à-vis* the warring states.[92]

In response to these pressures, the remaining neutrals looked to accentuate the advantages of their neutrality in the international environment. In their capacity as intermediaries, they were particularly successful. The International Committee for the Red Cross (ICRC), which operated out of neutral Switzerland, grew into a massive organization which monitored prisoner-of-war and civilian internment camps around the world, and took responsibility for the well-being of their inmates. As such, the ICRC functioned as a powerful voice for the ongoing importance of neutral states and organizations to proffer 'good offices' and to protect the rights and interests of belligerent citizens and subjects who were caught in enemy territory. Other charitable organizations operating out of neutral countries, like the American Commission for the Relief of Belgium (CRB), were equally important. The CRB sent masses of American food through the Netherlands to feed starving Belgians.[93] It needed the neutrality of the United States and the Netherlands not only to negotiate the North Sea blockades, but also to get permission to pass through the Belgian-Dutch border, which was guarded by German troops and a deadly electric fence.[94] Many neutral governments sent ambulance units to the war fronts, negotiated agreements to enable prisoner-of-war exchanges and allowed their citizens to mobilize charitable aid for the war's many victims.[95] These neutral acts were more than charity. They helped to carve out a space for neutrals to operate and exist in a world at total war.[96]

Legal scholars and neutral propagandists alike also promoted the international value of neutrality, even if they despaired at the belligerents' growing disregard for the laws of war.[97] As an example, in Brazil, the international jurist and politician Rui Barbosa argued that humanity had regressed to its most primitive state during the war. As such, the world's governments – and especially its neutral governments – had a duty to return the international system back to the law of nations and to the laws that had been sanctified in Geneva in 1864 and 1906 and at The Hague in 1899 and 1907.[98] Of course, as Annette Becker argues, since the legal conception of neutrality presented the main source of legitimacy for neutral states and the only source of legitimacy of international humanitarian organizations like the ICRC, it is hardly surprising that they advocated so strongly for the importance of international law.[99] Their successes during the war ensured that, after the conflict, international humanitarian law came into its own as a foundational principle of twentieth-century international organization.[100]

Neutral states and neutral communities also looked to heighten their value as potential mediators and peace-makers. All manner of forward-looking internationalist endeavours evolved in neutral countries that aimed to bring the war to a judicious end and to shape a post-war global order that would protect both the principles of neutrality and international law more generally. The League of Neutral Nations, for example, was established by the Italian-Swiss internationalist E. Bignami in 1916. It aimed both to protect the rights of neutral states and people in time of war and to advance a non-aggressive cooperative policy for a post-war world order. Bignami's League drew inspiration from other transnational neutral organizations, like the Central Organisation for Durable Peace (CODP), which was established in 1915 in the Netherlands by a group of international jurists and peace activists (from neutral and belligerent countries) to promote a feasible post-war international order focussed on war avoidance, international law and international cooperation. Its list of aims ranged from the expansion of the principle of self-determination to 'open door' diplomacy, from the creation of an international court of justice to the limitation of armaments and the protection of the principle of the freedom of the seas. At the heart of the CODP's programme lay the notion that a post-war world order should not be forged by the belligerents alone and that the principles of international cooperation and law needed to be firmly embedded in that order.

Neutral communities supported these internationalist future-focused endeavours with vigour. An international women's congress, which was also hosted in The Hague in 1915, included several women who attended and helped to organise the earlier CODP event. It boldly advanced the same internationalist principles as the CODP but added the need for universal women's suffrage as a foundational concept for a post-war order.[101] The Neutral Conference for Continuous Mediation (involving members of the CODP and the 1915 women's congress) met in Stockholm in February 1916 to advance the CODP's platform and promote the message of a mediated peace around the world.[102] Within the year, more than 1,074 Swedish groups (110,000 individuals) signed up in support of the CODP's programme. The Norwegians were equally enthusiastic.[103] Importantly, these calls for the establishment of an international organization to oversee global politics and avoid future war were advanced in neutral and belligerent countries. Well before Wilson's call for a League of Nations (which he made in January 1917), the American 'League to Enforce Peace' promoted the concept and had done so since the middle of 1915.[104] In Britain, the 'Bryce Group' of academics and lawyers met regularly after November 1914, advocating for a similar set of ideas.[105] German internationalists would jump on the 'League' bandwagon from 1917 on as well, establishing the *Deutsche Gesellschaft für Völkerrecht* (German International Law Society) in the process.[106]

In an environment of heightened nationalism, 'Othering' and fear-mongering, and amidst intense economic and military distress, such peace-seeking endeavours might look marginal and irrelevant.[107] Yet out of these internationalist activities grew the movement to establish the League of Nations, which would eventually be set up in 1919. The activism also highlights how contemporaries across 1916 imagined a post-war future for themselves outside the parameters of a 'one side wins all' model. Furthermore, the activism underscored the vital importance of neutral spaces for internationalist cooperation, which were particularly significant for lawyers, academics, scientists, journalists, revolutionaries and anti-imperialists who relied on reliable cross-border interaction.[108] Perhaps most importantly, the extent of the internationalist posturing illustrates how many contemporaries felt uneasy about the social, political and moral costs of the war. After 1917, other political conceptions for the future organization of the world vied for international attention, including communism, fascism and ethnic nationalism. But during 1916, the rise in war weariness, anti-imperial agitation and the expansion of internationalist activism brought to the fore the wide array of ways in which contemporaries considered how they might move beyond the war and achieve some kind of post-war resolution that favoured them (and not the pre-existing imperial powers).

Importantly, all the belligerent governments were highly alert to the social and political costs of the war as it affected their citizens and subjects alike. By November 1916, they were also rethinking their own war aims. Britain's Prime Minister Herbert Asquith even asked his cabinet to design a workable programme for victory. His colleague Lord Landsdowne – one of the country's most reputable and distinguished politicians – responded with a lengthy document advocating for a negotiated peace. As Landsdowne explained it, even if the Allies won the war, it might cost them the British empire as well as their financial security, and the lives of an entire generation of British men. As such, as Landsdowne saw it, civilization itself was at risk of total collapse.[109]

Germany's Chancellor, Theobald von Bethmann-Hollweg, also saw an opportunity to sue for peace in December 1916. Since Germany now controlled much of Belgium, northern France, Poland and Romania, it was placed in an excellent position to negotiate.[110] Bethmann-Hollweg understood that since most Germans were tired of the war, a peace initiative could lift morale. This was particularly important as the country's largest political party, the Social Democrats (SPD), was becoming more vocal in opposition to the war.[111] His ally, Austria-Hungary was certainly motivated to end the war. With the death of the Austro-Hungarian Emperor Franz-Joseph in November, his successor, Charles, understood all too well that his empire was on the brink of collapse from within. Regardless of whether the Central Powers won the war, he needed to end the war. But he could not achieve peace without Germany's cooperation.[112]

Confronted with the German peace offer, President Wilson also faced a dilemma in December 1916. While he could not reject the opportunity to act as a neutral mediator, he could also not be seen to promote the premature end to the war while Belgium and northern France remained occupied and thereby alienate the Allies. Prevaricating, he called for the belligerents to present their war aims to the world instead. By mid-January 1917, however, he extended his call for peace as an opportunity to re-organize the international environment, establish a League of Nations and promote the principles of self-determination and democracy.[113] He knew the appeal would be popular. Internationalist organizations, like the Inter-Parliamentary Union (a transnational body of parliamentarians), had agitated for such a solution in parliamentary sessions in neutral and belligerent countries alike since early 1916.[114]

The chance to achieve a negotiated peace in 1916 or early 1917 was chimeric. The Allies judged the German peace note as insincere, and rejected the offer forthright.[115] The new British Prime Minister, Lloyd George (who took office in December 1916) banished all allusions to the possibility of a negotiated peace when he announced that Britain needed to work towards total victory by a 'knock-out blow'. Britain had hardened its resolve.[116] Even if he and many of their cabinet peers agreed with its sentiment, Lloyd George rejected Landsdowne's report, while *The Times* (London) refused to even publish it.[117] The *Daily Telegraph* would do so in November 1917, but the world would be on a new path of global destruction by then.[118] Although they could not have known it at the time, these half-hearted overtures for peace offered the last viable chance for the European belligerents to bring the war to an end and keep their empires and nations intact. The 'hunger winter' of 1916–17 sent the Austro-Hungarian, Russian and Ottoman empires into a tailspin of societal collapse. None of these empires would survive the war.

7

Nothing stays the same: Revolutionary transformations in 1917

In 1913, the Bengali poet Rabindranath Tagore won the Nobel Prize in Literature. He was the first south Asian awarded this prestigious accolade. His peers referred to him as *biswakabi* (global poet), a man who travelled the world, cared deeply about peace and wrote astoundingly beautiful works of art. Late in 1916, amidst the chaos of global war, Tagore embarked on a trans-oceanic journey taking him from India to Japan and then across the Pacific Ocean to the United States. Wherever he landed, he spoke to large crowds on the evils of the nationalism, imperialism and materialism that Europe had forced on the world and that had caused 'this war of retribution'.[1] At about the same time, another poet, Yvon Goll, who hailed from the troubled region of Alsace-Lorraine, published his own reflections on the war. As a French-German immigrant hiding in neutral Switzerland, Goll's epic poem *Requiem for the Dead of Europe* lamented the 'carnival of death' that originated in Europe and was now encircling the world spreading nationalistic hatreds like a plague.[2] Like Tagore, Goll despaired at the costs. In early 1917, both Tagore and Goll hoped for a humanist renewal, to end the destructive 'old ways' of the pre-war era and find 'new ways' forward, propelling the world towards peaceful rejuvenation. Despite their widely different backgrounds, Goll and Tagore proffered optimistic visions for the future, visions that were they to be realized would require fundamental changes to be made in the way states operated, empires ruled and people related to each other.

Where Tagore and Goll looked for peaceful revolution as a path out of the war, during 1917, an increasing number of communities turned to more violent alternatives. The socio-political stability of most countries teetered dangerously in 1917 and, in some places, failed completely. In response, people's loyalties to their state and obligations to their communities either entrenched or shifted. At times they did so in service of a grand ideal (like communism, nationalism, imperial glory, anti-imperial ambition, indigenous autonomy or greater democracy), at others in aid of pre-existing or older traditions and customs (including religious and indigenous ones). Even more people took to the streets in 1917 than in 1916 protesting the war and their government's handling of it. Some of these protests were radical endeavours that aimed at bringing the war to an immediate end. Some sought revolutionary solutions, including the establishment of new countries or the implementation of new social and political structures. At minimum, the protestors demanded that changes be made to the way food was distributed, conscription was enforced, laws were made or wages were set. What all these developments had in common was a greater willingness by ordinary people to insist that things change for the better. Across 1917, few communities escaped fundamental questioning about the war, the structures of power and governance that kept it going (and forced them to endure hardship and loss), and their own roles in it. Even fewer communities escaped the global momentum of social and political upheaval.

The historian Jay Winter describes 1917 as the 'climacteric' of the First World War, as the year in which the war not only continued as a war fought between states and empires but also transformed into a war whose violence turned inwards. In turning inwards, it provoked local and regional conflicts between competing groups about the future direction of their countries and, for some, the entire international system.[3] As a result, during 1917, the war transformed into an even more insecure and chaotic global reality than it already was in 1916. From this point on, the global conflagration had fewer clearly demarcated front lines (although the western front remained one), yet the war's chaos of military violence nevertheless expanded. Across Eurasia, east and south-east Europe and the Middle East these local and regional conflicts provoked destructive civil wars and inspired intense social and political unrest. Across much of the rest of the world, the year 1917 was experienced as equally destructive, as a time when political groups and ordinary people became more assertive in demanding change. In response, the governing elites attempted both to accommodate the least invasive of these appeals and to repress the more radical ones. Altogether then, the year 1917 was a year of waxing and waning change and violence, chaos and revolutionary uncertainty. By the end of 1917, there was no 'going back' to the way things were in 1914.

One of the key reasons why 1917 was so transformative was due to the two Russian revolutions, the first erupted in March, the second developed in November.[4] In combination these two events led to the abdication of the Tsar and the collapse of his empire, the establishment of a democratic republic and the take over of that republic by the radical socialist Bolshevik party headed by Vladimir Lenin. For the subjects of the Russian empire, the revolutions were all important. Their way of life would never be the same again. But the Russian revolutions were also global events of immense significance, not least because they set an example of how a protest 'by the people' against the authorities could force things to change. They also seemed to prove, at least to those who needed convincing, that the war itself was an unsustainable enterprise.

As such, the events in Russia in 1917 both inspired groups and communities to coordinate their anti-war protests better and caused fear among elites that their state would be the next to fall. If the revolutions did anything, they made it clear to governments that their people (including their soldiers) were dangerous, that their loyalties could not be guaranteed, and that their demands may need to be listened to more carefully. As a result, the Russian revolutions of 1917 provide a powerful lens through which to view the multitude of crises of legitimacy facing belligerent and neutral communities around the world through the course of the year.[5] Socialists and working-class groups were certainly inspired by the events in Russia to agitate for their own workers' revolutions.[6] The collapse of the Russian empire further motivated indigenous communities, anti-imperial activists and ethnic nationalists to use this moment of global imperial crisis to agitate for their own independence.[7] In this chapter we use examples from Russia, Japan, Korea, China, France, Britain, India, Australia, New Zealand, Latin America, Italy, Senegal, Spain, Volta Bani and the Dutch-controlled Indonesian archipelago to show how the intense stress of an unrelenting total war turned neutral and belligerent communities alike to political unrest and revolution in the wake of the events in Russia and in the context of the ongoing total war.

At an international level, the collapse of Tsarist Russia contributed to bringing down the (already) crumpling multi-ethnic Austro-Hungarian and Ottoman empires and to destabilizing the *Kaiserreich* to the point of its dissolution in 1918. It also helped to seriously disrupt the French and British 'blue water' empires. Much like the French Revolution of 1789, the successes of the Russian revolutions of 1917 preyed on the anxieties and fears of ruling elites and those who professed their loyalties to these elites. In the longer term, the establishment of a potentially powerful Bolshevik regime in Russia hampered the chance of founding a well-functioning international system and of returning to an 'open seas' system of global trade and capitalism after the war. Most importantly, the Russian Revolutions of 1917 marked a shift to a new era of revolutionary violence which ensured that, while the First World War would formally end with the armistice of 11 November 1918, the expansion of civil strife and political unrest defined the post-war period. The world beyond 1917 was a world of 'anarchy, dying empires and rising nation states',[8] a world where competing ideologies redefined the distinctions many contemporaries made between 'Us' and 'Them' and heightened political and cultural animosities everywhere.

This inflamed new world demanded that changes be made, at times in radical directions. After 1917, as the historian Robert Gerwarth shows, the First World War became 'endless', its repercussions reverberating

across the globe.[9] When historians boldly assert that the First World War
brought the contours of the twentieth century into being, they do so by
giving primacy to the 1917 revolutions, the Russian Civil War that followed,
the establishment of the Soviet Comintern in 1919 and the creation of
the Union of Soviet Socialist Republics (Soviet Union) in 1922. For, after
1917, not only was there no going back to the great power 'concert' system
that dominated the nineteenth-century world, there was also little chance
that a new international system could be created that would meet the
polycentric and largely oppositional needs of these varying states, groups
and ideologies.[10] In other words, by upending the stabilizing features of the
pre-war era, the 1914–17 war years awoke a range of powerful political
and emotional impulses that set many groups and communities against
the established authorities. It also set them in competition with each other
in creating new futures, new securities and new loyalties. In 1917, those
impulses came to the fore.

For those who lived through it, of course, none of these outcomes
were guaranteed or necessarily even imagined. They experienced 1917
as a year of profound crisis and change and, thus, also of opportunism
and unpredictability. In response to this spiral of competing interests and
identities, often only more violence, insecurity and dangers ensued. Or as
a Jewish Socialist leader in the city of Smolensk described his experiences
of 1917: 'All around us madness and danger rules, ... a thickening dark
cloud is gathering above us, and a great black abyss opens before us.'[11] What
these experiences of war and revolution in 1917 highlighted, most of all, is
how in the midst of intense social upheaval profound transformations could
come about unlooked for and unplanned. They also show how violence and
upheaval opened up new space for opportunistic individuals and groups to
take advantage and vie for power. It is in this sense that the historian Jean-
Jacques Becker called 1917 *l'année impossible* (the impossible year), a year
in which the needs of the belligerent states at total war pulled in opposition
to the wishes of many of their people. In the process of balancing these
demands, the year 1917 provoked profound and lasting local and global
changes.[12]

The subjects of the Russian empire were certainly no strangers to
revolutionary turmoil. Widespread opposition to the Russo-Japanese
War in 1904–5 resulted in popular unrest and important constitutional
changes in Tsarist Russia, and left a legacy of oppositional politics.[13] The
outbreak of the First World War was not universally welcomed in Russia
either. As the war lengthened, opposition to the mismanagement of the war
effort only grew in response to the conscription of subject communities,
heightened inflation and the distribution of foodstuffs and goods. The
highly decentralized nature of the empire did not help to inspire loyalty
to Russia's war cause, nor did the rumours of the 'German spy', Rasputin,
cavorting with the German-born Tsarina help to alleviate people's concerns
about the war's impact on their lives.[14] Why were they fighting the Germans

if the enemy already dined at the Tsar's table and slept in his bed? With 7 million men serving in the Russian armies in 1917, 2 million reserves and another 5.1 million casualties, 90 per cent of whom were peasants unable to work their land, the war affected all parts of the vast Romanov empire.[15] Alongside the displacement of another 6 million war refugees who needed housing, food and support, it was no surprise that the Russian avant-garde artist Nikolai Punin spoke of a looming revolution late in 1916: 'The war slowly turned to revolution. When the revolution began, we don't know: the war had no end'.[16] The 'starvation winter' of 1916–17 certainly made everything that much worse, especially in Russia's industrial cities.

Ostensibly, the first 1917 revolution began early in March (or late in February according to the Russian calendar) when in honour of International Women's Day the women of St Petersburg's Vyborg district – workers, soldiers' wives, mothers, and home-makers alike – took to the streets to protest rising prices, scarcity, the inequality in distribution, the drop in living standards, and the endless nature of the war and their own suffering.[17] They were joined by a crowd so large that the local authorities could not force it to disperse. Spontaneous violence spread over the ensuing days in the form of demonstrations, strikes, reprisal shootings, killings and lootings. They soon spread to some of Russia's other industrial centres as well. Calling on the 160,000 soldiers garrisoned in the city to help to suppress the unrest only fed its flames as more troops joined the protestors and demanded the Tsar's abdication.[18]

The first 1917 revolution may have been brewing for years – some argue ever since 1905 – but when it came, it still came as a surprise. None of the Vyborg women who turned out to march on International Women's Day were there to create a revolution from below. Nor did the soldiers who shot at protestors in the first few days of unrest recognize (at that time) that they would be joining the protestors' ranks all too soon. Nevertheless, the years of soldier and civilian grievances against the Tsarist regime ensured that the spark of revolution, once lit, spread swiftly and organically. As the leader of the Menshevik political party in the Duma, Matvei Ivanovich, recalled of his walk around St Petersburg on the eve of the regime's fall: 'Under the influence of everything I had seen earlier, I cursed at some precinct policemen: "Your brothers are executing your wives and children. Why are you shooting?" "Just wait," they replied, "tomorrow we'll show them." And, at that moment, for the first time I realized that something might happen as soon as tomorrow.'[19] That 'something' was the establishment of a Petrograd Soviet (a democratic body made up of soldiers and industrial workers in the renamed city of St Petersburg) and the capture of the city's municipal and military buildings by crowds of 'revolutionaries'. Within days, the Tsar renounced his throne, opening up a political vacuum in the heart of Russia.

The power vacuum was filled in first instance by two competing but not mutually exclusive entities: the Petrograd Soviet and the Provisional Government set up by the moderate members of the Russian parliament

ILLUSTRATION 7.1 *Alexander Kerensky, as head of Russia's provisional government, standing in front of a giant map of Russia and the Caucasus in 1917.* Source: *Wikipedia.org.*

(Duma) led by Alexander Kerensky. Neither entity had any official power, but they agreed to work together, as far as that was possible, until a democratic election could be held and a new Constituent Assembly set up.[20] That election was due to be held in November. In the meantime, Russia was still at war.

The ensuing months witnessed many extraordinary developments, which underscore the spontaneity and enthusiasm with which many individuals across the empire (and even across the world) embraced the potential for political rejuvenation. The first Russian revolution was so powerful because it inspired so many to reimagine their futures. As an example, Russian anarchist dissidents, who had fled the Romanov empire to escape its secret police after 1905, returned to Russia in 1917 to turn their ambitions into a reality. As the 'Freedom for Art' manifesto, signed by 1,500 Russian anarchist artists, proclaimed at the time:

> The great Russian Revolution calls us to act. Unite, fight for the freedom of art. Fight for the right of self-determination and autonomy. The Revolution creates freedom. ... Only in a free democratic republic is democratic art possible.[21]

Many Russian soldiers were equally inspired to advocate for their rights as soldiers and veterans. They called for the implementation of universal suffrage, monetary support for their fallen comrades' widows and a peaceful end to the war. Importantly, outside of Petrograd, Moscow and the Baltic cities, most of these soldier soviets agreed not to abandon their frontline posts. They would not fight in an aggressive capacity, but they would hold their lines against any attack that might come from the Austrian, German or Ottoman side. They had lost too many of their comrades to fail them at this hurdle.[22] This ongoing loyalty to the sacrifices made during the war highlighted that the issues at play were far more complex than a mere desire to change the government or to assert democratic rights. These soldiers wanted their war service to continue to have meaning, whichever version of Russia eventually appeared. The same can be said for Russia's other multifarious communities, many of which set up their own soviets, mobilizing industrial workers, garrisoned troops and peasant communities alike, all seeking representative democracy and recognition of their unique needs and wants. In the 'waiting space' between the collapse of the Tsarist state in March and the much-vaunted November election, the jostling for power in aid of a particular vision for the future of a democratic Russia evolved in a variety of oppositional ways. Yet almost all of these people considered their future in terms of the ongoing war and in anticipation of peace.

For the Provisional Government, for example, the revolution was already won. Kerensky fervently believed that the March revolution had achieved what most Russians desired, namely the establishment of a democratic state and their recognition as citizen-voters in it. Looking back to the French Revolution of 1789 as a point of reference, Kerensky also expected Russia's new citizen-soldiers to willingly continue fighting for their new nation-state.[23] In so doing, Kerensky (and many of his liberal supporters) failed to recognize that what brought the end of the Tsarist regime was not a universal demand for 'liberty, equality and fraternity' but rather a universal demand for 'peace, bread and a return to the land'. The war dominated ordinary Russians' expectations for change. These liberals thus also misunderstood that the stability of the European military front was a product of soldiers' willingness to wait for a formal resolution of the conflict and not an invitation to take up arms again against the enemy. When the Provisional Government insisted that these soldiers launch a new attack in Galicia in July (at the French and British governments' request to alleviate their own pressures on the western front), the uneasy equilibrium that existed between the working-class soviets and the bourgeois Provisional Government broke down.[24] Pandemonium ensued, its maelstrom offering multiple opportunities for even greater political radicalization to occur.

From July 1917 on, Russia descended into chaos. Hundreds of thousands of soldiers deserted their front-line posts in protest. When the Galician offensive failed, '[m]illions of brutalized, politically unmoored and armed peasant-soldiers struggled to make sense of it all'.[25] They travelled home or joined brigand groups working for local warlords who set up their own personal fiefdoms. The Russian state collapsed even further. Warlordism returned to Russia's hinterlands, including in the borderlands of Russia's fast collapsing European front, splintering the empire into a 'mosaic of under-governed statelets awash with violence and dominated by men in uniform'.[26] Popular protests against the Provisional Government reinflamed unrest in Russia's industrial cities as well, where demands that 'all power' be transferred to the soviets sounded louder and louder. Many of these protests were unorganized, opportunistic and abusive. As the writer Maxime Gorki reflected in October:

> What is going on now is not a social revolution, but a pogrom of greed, hatred and vengeance .... An unorganized crowd, hardly understanding what it wants, is crawling out into the street, and, using this crowd as cover, adventurers, thieves and professional murderers will soon 'write the history of the Russian Revolution'.[27]

The optimism and collaborations of March were replaced by fear, chaos and suffering.

Not only had Kerensky's government underestimated the soldiers' (and many civilians') desire for peace, they had overestimated the loyalties of Russia's numerous subjects to the state. Kerensky expected that the Tsar's many subjects would be excited to become the willing citizens of a new democratic Russian empire, a state that would, in the words of the historian Joshua Sanborn, 'retain its sites of power in central Russia, would use Russian as its language of state, and would remain within its current boundaries'.[28] The collapse of Russian armies in July 1917, however, inspired a number of ethnic and indigenous groups – in Finland, the Ukraine, the *steppes* and the Caucasus – to declare their independence from Russia. Meanwhile, other groups strived to take over central power of the Russian state. The first of these attempted coups, orchestrated by a group of Russian generals, failed when the Petrograd Soviet mobilized in support of the Provisional Government and formed into a militia to defend the city. The second – an attempted coup by Lenin's Bolshevik party – succeeded.

Like many other European dissidents, Lenin lived in neutral Switzerland at the start of 1917. As a well-known Marxist, Lenin advocated that the war offered an ideal opportunity for its worker-soldiers to reject the terms of the 'imperial conflict' and incite a worker revolution from below. It was Lenin's renown as a radical that inspired Germany's military leadership to use him to their advantage. In the wake of the March revolution, the Germans offered Lenin free passage to Russia and a train to travel in, hoping that his radical agenda might destabilize Russia and take the country out of the war completely.[29] In this ambition, they eventually succeeded. At first, however, Lenin's chances seemed bleak. He arrived in Petrograd in April, spoke fervently against the moderate aims of the Petrograd Soviet, fomented unrest and proclaimed the need for a working-class revolution that would inspire the entire world to communism.

Lenin's ideas were initially so unpopular (even among other socialists) that he fled Petrograd soon after his arrival. He only returned in November after a loyal band of Bolsheviks had gained power in the Petrograd and Moscow Soviets. Lenin's initial inability to inspire his fellow socialists to embrace a radical communist future was telling. It illustrated how many Russians hoped that a democratically elected government would both recognize the collective sacrifices they made in the war and call the Tsar and his 'old order' to account for continuing the war. It also underscored their deep desire for peace. But Lenin's lack of success also spoke to the ambiguous realities of the March–November period. Other than getting rid of the Tsar (a decidedly radical outcome), few Russians in March 1917 wished for the Russian state itself to fail. It was largely due to Kerensky's insistence that Russia continue fighting the First World War that the collapse of the Russian state became more likely. And it was only in the wake of the chaos of the July 1917 days that a political coup orchestrated by the Bolsheviks was made possible.

In the end, the Bolshevik take over in November 1917 was relatively peaceful. It did not involve large crowds clamouring for change, nor did it hinge on the emotive power of the moment. The second revolution was not a revolution 'of the people' like the first. Where after March 1917, many ordinary Russians accepted and applauded the Tsar's fall, whom they roundly renounced and denigrated,[30] the November 1917 take over was less obviously necessary. Its legitimacy rested on the soviets' claim to represent the people better than the liberal politicians of the Duma.[31] As a result, Lenin's declaration of an immediate demobilization was immensely popular, as was the formal armistice his government signed with Germany and Austria-Hungary on 15 December. What was far less clear, however, was what giving 'all power to the soviets' would entail going forward. Most importantly, while the Bolsheviks' promises of 'peace, land and bread' were persuasive, they did not persuade Russia's peasants, including many of its soldiers, to vote for the Bolshevik revolutionaries in the November constitutional elections (which were still held).[32] These voters preferred their own radical (but non-Bolshevik) peasant representatives in the Social Revolutionary Party of Russia. In many ways, then, the Bolshevik revolution of 1917 was considered transitory and opportunistic by many who watched it unfold.

The Bolshevik revolution became decisive when the Social Revolutionary Party won the majority of the November vote and Lenin declared the result invalid. Now all bets were off. The Bolsheviks mobilized the soldier-controlled soviets to their cause and declared that Russia had become a one-party workers' state.[33] But 'what was Russia?' now was harder to discern and whether this new state could rule its people was even less clear. Across the collapsed Romanov empire, groups and communities challenged these developments. Various warlord generals rallied their own loyal soldiers in the name of 'White Russia' to counter the Bolshevik revolutionaries and soldier soviets, some in the name of the Tsar, many in the name of liberal democracy. Other groups and communities mobilized their own loyalties, including ethnic and religious ones, to break free from Russian and Bolshevik control completely and establish their own independent states.

Everywhere, the chaos deepened. For not only had the Russian state failed (and collapsed the functioning of every-day amenities, from postal services to healthcare, food distribution and schools) but in the fight to establish a new social-political order, be it Bolshevik or something else, all sense of security disappeared. Neighbours feared each other and all strangers. Corruption, tyranny, pogroms and death were the order of the day. Ultimately, while Russia was not a belligerent in the First World War any longer, its people became embroiled in a civil war that was more destructive than anything they had witnessed between 1914 and 1917. This new civil war pitted 'White Russians' (loyal to pre-Bolshevik Russia) against 'Red Russians' (loyal to the Bolshevik and soviets' causes). It involved various communities across eastern Europe and Eurasia demanding statehood, autonomy and independence. By late 1918, it brought in the armies of a number of foreign countries (including Japan, Britain, France and the United States) all seeking the collapse of the Bolshevik state – a deeply suspicious political organization in their eyes – and the possible expansion of their own imperial interests.

In all, the Russian Civil War that waged until 1923 was a powerful by-product of the revolutionary turn taken by the Russian people in 1917. That turn came in direct response to their suffering in the First World War, even if its revolutionary dynamics were determined more by local than global developments. Just as importantly, however, the Russian revolutions of 1917 were also experienced globally. They deeply affected neutral and belligerent perceptions of the war. The 'message of worker and peasant power' inspired political groups around the world to foment change.[34] The revolutions also forced governments to think carefully about how they should respond to the acts of protest and anti-war resistance that were carried out by their subjects and citizens.

That the army-wide French mutiny in May 1917 occurred in the wake of the first Russian revolution is particularly significant. For not only did France's soldiers declare – much like their Russian counterparts had done a few weeks' earlier – that they 'were France' and that only with them could France hope to come out of the war intact, they also exacted real accommodations of these demands from their government. As representatives of democratic country, the French military leadership could not suppress this revolt as they might have done at an earlier time, for they needed to be seen to be working for their people and not against them.[35]

In Britain, too, the recognition that soldiers' declining morale and industrial workers' increasing demands might lead to dangerous results led the government to increase police surveillance and censorship measures. It also looked for opportunities to alleviate legitimate grievances.[36] To this end, the government took the briefing by the country's Chief Censor in November 1917 (at the time of the second Russian revolution) very seriously:

> A year ago, men seemed to be sublimely unconscious of political considerations. They were out simply to 'do their bit'. They rarely mentioned and never discussed political questions .... Now, they are ceasing to some extent to possess their corporate personality and to reassert individuality of opinion.[37]

These 'opinions' could, as Britain's ruling elite saw it, lead the country down dangerous paths. The outbreak of a three-week long industrial strike involving 200,000 workers in forty-five towns and cities in May 1917 heightened these fears.[38] Their response, much like in France, was to monitor public opinions more closely, and to expand their own propaganda messages of inclusivity and sacrifice for the greater good.

Thus, even though the repression of labour movements, trade unions and socialist organizations increased in Britain and elsewhere, governments also asserted the legitimacy of their own democratic foundations to promote loyalty to the state and the enduring war.[39] Lessons in civics became part of soldier training in Britain and Germany alike.[40] More widely, many neutral and belligerent countries extended their suffrage through constitutional changes implemented in 1917 or by promising that after the war more men and women would be given the vote in recognition of their wartime service.[41] For similar reasons, subject communities were enticed with promises of greater self-rule or the extension of citizenship once the war finished. In August 1917, for example, the British government promised the gradual expansion of self-governance in India.[42] It also suspended the practice of indentured migration from India to the plantation economies of places like Fiji and Trinidad, in order to placate many Indians' demands for the practice to stop.[43] These attempts to court the people aimed at sustaining their loyalties to the state at a time when the impact of the war heightened their suffering and opened up opportunities to challenge its power. In other words, they were promised that their wartime sacrifices would not be futile and that their futures would be better within the empire rather than in opposition to it.

Yet these promises of post-war rewards were hard to reconcile in the face of escalating socio-economic deprivations and military sacrifices. Throughout 1917, the number of strikes, demonstrations and political uprisings against governments and local authorities only expanded, affecting belligerent and neutral countries and empires alike. Some of these protests took direct inspiration from the Russian revolutions. Some protestors even reinterpreted Bolshevism as a powerful example of taking maximum power for the people (as opposed to agitating for a global workers' revolution, to which Lenin aspired).[44] In neutral Argentina and Brazil, for example, 'maximalist' anarchists demanded that their governments accept their 'local' versions of a 'maximal' (Bolshevik) programme and established their own soviets to parry for the cause.[45] In the city of Sao Paulo, where real wages had dropped by as much as 70 per cent since 1914, a general strike erupted in July 1917 in which participants 'explicitly associated their claims with the war and called for peace'.[46]

In neutral Spain, the political ruptures of 1917 were almost as confronting as they were in Russia. The various political factions – be it socialist labourers, militarists, nationalists, liberals or monarchists – mobilized in oppositional ways. Food shortages resulted in intense distress across the agricultural regions, leading to a flood of unemployed workers looking for work in the booming industrial cities, like Barcelona and Madrid, where bankers and industrialists were growing vastly wealthy selling their manufactured wares to the belligerents. Much like in Japan and the United States, the working-class suburbs of these cities exploded in size and misery. When the inflationary pressures could not be abated, and food supplies remained perilously low, food riots, strikes and political agitation followed. These became particularly intense in the wake of the first Russian revolution, which inspired many industrial workers to take more radical action. In Barcelona, seventy people died when soldiers loyal to the government shot at striking workers who had barricaded city streets.[47]

What had been a 'civil war of words' in 1916 (see Chapter 6) now threatened to become a real civil war. It caused enduring schisms between the various factions. The rich industrialists favoured a 'do-nothing' policy of neutrality, but 'doing nothing' had life-and-death consequences for Spain's industrial and agricultural communities. After the Spanish government fell in April 1917 (when it threatened to join the war in support of the Allies), the oppositional pull between the policies of a pro-neutrality government (who favoured the profits that could be made from the war) and the demands for change by radicalizing socialist and peasant communities would keep Spain in turmoil for years to come.[48] For Spaniards, then, 1917 marked a turning point. It was one of so many 'regional versions of the general crisis' that affected the world in the context of the Russian revolutions and First World War.[49]

In Australia's eastern cities, mines and ports, 1917 also witnessed a series of crippling industrial strikes, which locals still refer to as the 'Great Strike of 1917'. These strikes and protests involved more than 100,000 workers who protested the rising cost of living and the industrial demands placed on them by their government at war. Inspired in part by the success of the Russian revolution, this Australian strike action merged social distress with other wartime issues – including the second conscription referendum – to polarize Australian politics. The strikes and the second 'no' vote in the referendum exposed how the First World War helped to radicalize labour politics. It also brought out how the experience of the war made many Australians less willing to accept their government's or their empire's requests for service and sacrifice.[50] Australia showed that professing loyalty to an empire at war was not unconditional.

In New Zealand, the formation of the country's Second Division in January 1917, made up of its first cohort of military conscripts, led to a more subtle – yet equally powerful – demand for political accommodation. In setting up the Second Division League, which quickly grew into the country's most subscribed patriotic organization, the organization's leaders both asserted the importance of all New Zealanders supporting the men who were forced to fight for King and empire, and created a political forum to make sure that their sacrifice was recognized and duly compensated in the political arena. The League became an important voice wading into debates on 'equality of sacrifice' issues including who should be made to work for the war or who should receive dispensation. In so doing, the League was much more than a patriotic association blindly supportive of the empire at war. Rather, it used the state's desperate need for soldiers and war workers as a way to achieve short- and long-term gains. As the historian Steven Loveridge argues, this 'conditional commitment' to the war defined New Zealand politics in the years 1917 and 1918.[51] Significantly, veteran organizations would continue to have a disproportionately powerful voice on post-war politics in societies that mobilized troops during the war, including neutral and imperial ones.[52]

As the 'July troubles' hit Russia in 1917, the largest political party in Germany, the Social Democratic Party (SPD), which had clear socialist and anti-war leanings, also called for an immediate suspension of the war. In the midst of serious food shortages, demonstrations and anti-war protests, the conservative Catholic politician, Matthias Erzberger, passed a motion in the *Reichstag* asking for all the belligerents to agree to a peace treaty 'without victors or vanquished' (echoing the demands of Russia's soldier soviets in the process).[53] The motion passed with a majority of parliamentarians voting in its favour. Many of Germany's politicians were tired of war and recognized that their voters were equally exhausted.[54] They looked for a legitimate way out for their country, an 'out' that would sustain the political system. In the face of what was happening in Russia, many of these politicians feared what might happen if the people took to the streets demanding more drastic solutions. The people, in turn, were ready for something to change.

In contrast, Germany's military leadership was euphoric that July. As they witnessed the complete collapse of the Russian front and their own occupation of Poland and the Ukraine, they considered that victory was within their grasp. As a result, they dismissed the *Reichstag*'s motion as pacifist pessimism and defeatism orchestrated by a swathe of internal and 'unpatriotic' enemies of the German nation. They used the parliamentary crisis as a reason to take full control of the powers of state and assured all Germans that they need not worry, that they only needed to hold on just a little bit longer. Victory was in sight. In support of these measures, in September 1917, a new political party established itself in Germany – the Fatherland Party. Its membership grew at a phenomenal rate to 300,000 in February and 800,000 by July 1918. Its policies resisted 'democratization' and socialism and bound its supporters to the promotion of a 'strong peace' led by a victorious Germany.[55] From this point on, Germans divided themselves more rigidly between those who swore unwavering allegiance to a militarily strong and belligerent 'fatherland' and those who sought alternate futures for Germany, including distinctly socialist and social-democratic ones.

In Italy, the news of the second Russian revolution came in the wake of the rout of the Italian armies at Carporetto, which resulted in more than 300,000 Italian casualties, including 265,000 prisoners of war. The immense losses experienced on the Italian side heightened already intense social and political tensions across the country. The political divides that existed between the 'neutralists' and the 'interventionists' in 1914 and 1915 (which the 'interventionists' at the time won) turned into protests, demonstrations, strikes and calls for governmental change. The Russian revolutions inspired many here too. Italy's women were particularly active protestors. In September 1917, as Simonetta Ortaggi's history shows, women in one village took to the streets shouting 'Down with the war, we want our husbands back, otherwise we will make a revolution!' In the Po valley, other women refused to work the harvest, while in Polesine and Milan they attacked factories so that the armies would go without supplies and end the fight.[56] Police repression of these protests only accentuated the bitter rivalries between the various camps. Yet Italy's leaders also attempted to improve morale and buy-in by extending promises for reform and advocating for Italian patriotism and an ongoing involvement in the war.[57]

The 1917 war year cleft the Italian political arena apart into bitter rivalries pitting nationalists against socialists. The battlefield experiences of one Italian soldier-cum-journalist named Benito Mussolini helped to birth a new era of Italian ultra-nationalism, which he named 'fascism'. In his newspaper, *Il Popolo d'Italia* (The People of Italy), Mussolini fought against the Italian Socialist Party and the Bolshevik revolution, which he feared would lead to a global communist take over. In his words:

> It is not a time for angels, it is a time for devils. It requires ferocity, not humility .... It requires a long sword and a great deal of fire .... Either that or defeat. Either that or Russia.[58]

The future of Italy, according to Mussolini, lay in a soldier technocracy. Those who had fought the war ought to run the state, and all Italians should be grateful.[59]

What all these 1917 crises highlight is just how polemic and extreme the political stakes around the war had become. Whether as subjects or citizens of a neutral or belligerent country or empire, the war invoked potent and increasingly antagonistic responses for and against a government's wartime policies, and for and against the war itself.[60] In the process, those who were 'for' maintaining the status-quo and keeping their country or empire at (or neutral in) the war starkly differentiated themselves from those who sought an immediate end to the conflict. These inclinations inspired new political schisms to appear, and provoked polemical allegiances to ideas, identities and political visions for the future, which would have a decisive impact on the post-war era.

Perhaps the most significant impact of the Russian revolutions of 1917, then, was the inspiration they also offered to anti-imperial resistors, indigenous groups seeking autonomy and ethnic nationalists everywhere. In many ways, while Lenin did not manage to arouse the workers of the world to unite against the capitalist empires that kept them all at war, his Bolshevik revolution nevertheless encouraged many anti-imperial groups to agitate even more vociferously against their own empires. It was not that these communities did not seek autonomy earlier, or that they needed Lenin as a point of inspiration, but rather that the weaknesses that the Russian revolutions exposed in the Russian empire offered a powerful example that might be replicated. If an end to empire was not possible in 1917, then when?

As we have seen in the previous chapters, the First World War was experienced as highly transgressive by most indigenous and subject communities, not least because it further exposed the radicalizing and repressive nature of industrial and colonial imperialism. So, while the war offered plenty of opportunities for subjects to profess their loyalty to the state (usually with an eye to achieving greater political representation and racial equality within the empire), it also presented fresh opportunities to challenge and resist. Across 1916 and 1917, especially, the experiences of the war and of wartime imperial rule inspired some indigenous communities to agitate for more autonomy and others to break free completely. Consider, for example, the impact of the French government's demands that its colonized African subjects 'volunteer' for military service. To make the offer more persuasive, the French government offered incentives for chiefs to persuade their people to 'go to war'. If some chiefs were persuaded, many of their people were not and saw these demands as a reimposition of slavery. As one Senegalese veteran, Kande Kamara, recalled of his embarkation to Europe:

> A lot of people spread the rumour that we would never come back, that we are going to be sold as slaves .... So some people were trying their charms to take them back ... and some were saying, if the ships sinks, who gives a damn we're going to die anyway .... So people were beating their hands against the ship and screaming and yelling and screaming.[61]

Resistance to France's mobilization demands existed from the outset of the war. During 1917, however, the resistance to empire and the concomitant demands for independence grew in intensity across the French colonial empire. In response, the French state became more controlling and repressive of its colonial subjects. For example, the authorities in Volta Bani (present-day Burkina Faso and Mali) finally ended two years of armed resistance waged by the local people by resorting to 'scorched earth' methods: sacking villages, destroying farmlands, killing civilians and forcing their displacement. The military occupation of the region resulted in severe population loss, population displacement, a decline in agricultural production and widespread starvation.[62] Much like the Wagogo people in east Africa, the Volta Bani region and its people would never be the same. In 1919, the colonial authorities divided the region into two (Mali and Burkina Faso), aiming at a 'divide and conquer' policy to prevent any future unrest. As Michelle Moyd argues, 'the multilayered consequences of the anticolonial war reverberated well past the war, transforming regional politics, though not in the ways the Volta-Bani peoples had hoped when they went to war against the French empire [in 1915].'[63] This severe turn to state violence mirrored colonial regimes in the pre-war era. In this sense, France's suppression of Volta Bani was more than a product of the global war, yet its extremes also recognized the immense fears that the French authorities had of losing control over the empire, its people and resources. In turn, the 1914–17 war years proved a powerful fertilizer for anti-imperial forces, ethnic nationalist campaigning and anti-colonial politics in Volta Bani and many other colonial spaces.[64]

The French government understood all too well that its belligerency in the First World War endangered its tenuous hold on the empire. That realization both legitimated the use of more violence and repression and necessitated that the French government find ways of persuading local African authorities and autochthonous social organizations to see the value of supporting the empire and supplying France's war needs.[65] Here the contours of Becker's *l'année impossible* idea offer a useful lens to explain the tensions: for where the future stability of the French empire might have been better served by keeping its subject communities out of the war, its total war effort could not keep the state from forcing its imperial subjects to fight and supply the war.

Some of the persuasion worked. As the Senegalese-French politician and newly appointed Commissioner to Senegal, Blaise Diagne, promised his people: 'Those who fall under [German] fire, fall neither as whites nor as blacks; they fall as Frenchmen and for the same flag.'[66] This promise of citizenship enabled France to raise 60,000 new recruits in Senegal in 1917 and 1918.[67] The rhetoric of imperial loyalty may have persuaded some Senegalese elites (especially those who were profiting from their relationship with the French authorities in other ways). But, as Kande Kamara's quote (above) highlights, what the local chiefs and authorities looked for in this colonial exchange was rarely what their people freely gave. Their service to the empire at war was highly conditional and often not a service to empire at all, but rather to themselves, their communities and families. Importantly, these Senegalese veterans (much like veterans across the world) would become a powerful force for political advocacy against the empire and for local autonomy in the post-war years.[68]

The politics of conditional loyalty to an empire during the First World War played out in equally powerful ways across the neutral Dutch-controlled Indonesian archipelago. The Dutch East Indies consisted of an array of islands and various ethnic and religious communities, including a very large Muslim population. The people who lived on these islands played an important role in fostering anti-imperial sentiment in the belligerent empires during the war, including during the Singapore Mutiny of 1915. Yet across the archipelago, the politics of wartime neutrality mixed uncomfortably with Dutch colonial rule. While many colonial leaders proclaimed that Dutch rule was better than that of any other imperial power (rather ironically given the extremes of violence that sustained the Dutch empire in the decades leading up to 1914), many Indonesian communities and intellectuals mobilized themselves in response to the tumult of the global war to advance their own local anti-imperial agendas.[69] In response, the Dutch government both mobilized the politics of inclusion and political rights and imposed repressive measures 'to keep order'.

In the aftermath of the first Russian revolution, for example, the Dutch revolutionary socialist, Henk Sneevliet, wrote a jubilant and supportive editorial for the Dutch-language newspaper in Java: *De Indiër* (which roughly translates as 'The Indonesian'). Translated into Malay by a Javanese journalist, Darnakoesoemo, so it would reach a wide audience, the article did not call for a revolution against the Dutch colonial authorities *per se*, but did link what was happening in Russia to the Dutch East Indies. Sneevliet was arrested by the colonial authorities, but was eventually acquitted (which in itself raised the ire of the local population, whose non-white resisters had never received lenient sentences). After the Bolshevik revolution, however, Sneevliet became a rallying point for anti-imperial resistance across the islands, including by locals serving in the Dutch colonial army. Sneevliet was forcibly returned to the Netherlands, and his party repressed.[70]

Because 1917 witnessed greater social distress across the Dutch East Indies, due to food shortages and sky-rocketing inflation, the willingness of locals to protest against the colonial authorities increased. Some were drawn to the rapidly growing Sarekat Islam movement, others to nationalist, traditionalist or socialist groups, all of which opposed the Dutch colonial regime in some vital way. As strikes and demonstrations erupted in towns and cities, these groups demanded equal pay and an end to the labour practice of favouring certain ethnicities over others. Crowds attacked sugar plantations and racial tensions between Javanese and Chinese workers spilled over into violence. In various places, soldiers' and workers' soviets were established proclaiming democratic rights. In response, the newly appointed Governor-General, Johan van Limburg Stirum, both looked to accommodate some of these local grievances, and stepped up repression measures.[71] Much like in French-controlled Volta Bani, the Dutch colonial elite scrambled madly to keep control over a rapidly expanding social movement that demanded serious change.

Altogether, the various Indonesian communities' responses to the First World War, their neutrality in that war, the example of the Russian revolutions, the anti-imperial opportunism offered by Marxism and Islam and the colonial measures imposed by the Dutch state, offered powerful examples to internalize and re-mobilize at a later date. These experiences proved vitally significant for shaping the future of Indonesian resistance to the Dutch empire, not least because it mobilized individuals and groups in ideologically powerful ways.[72]

The twenty-year-old Sumatran student Tan Malaka, who happened to reside in the Netherlands in 1917, offers a telling example. Malaka witnessed the war as a subject of a neutral empire, far away from his home. During 1917 his responses to the war, to the actions of the colonial authorities in the Dutch East Indies and to the question 'what should the future look like?' altered drastically. Malaka understood all too well the vulnerabilities of 'subjecthood' in a repressive empire and how those vulnerabilities were heightened by the relative weakness of the Netherlands as a neutral empire caught in a web of a total global war. Malaka's perspectives on what the future could hold for the world, for the Dutch empire and for colonial communities like his own Minangkabau people shifted repeatedly. In searching for meaningful solutions, he moved from working for options within empire (he liked the French imperial model of offering the possibility of citizenship to imperial subjects), to embracing revolutionary socialism (inspired by Lenin), to seeking and asserting indigenous autonomy and ending the repressive capitalist and nationalist structures that sustained international society.[73] While none of Malaka's shifting ideas affected the harsh realities of Dutch imperial rule in Sumatra in 1917, they would have a powerful impact on the evolution of anti-colonial resistance across the Indonesian archipelago in the years to come. While the Dutch colonial elite may have thought they were 'educating' a loyal subject of empire, Malaka's war experiences in the Netherlands only radicalized his anti-imperialism.

The Russian revolutions also had a powerful impact on the politics of empire across the belligerent Japanese empire. In Japan, the first Russian revolution was welcomed as a positive step, one that was taking Russia away from autocratic 'old world' ways and towards modernization, much like the Meiji restoration had done in 1868.[74] Most Japanese, however, did not respond well to the Bolshevik revolution which they described as an accidental product of power-hungry militant opportunists. The Bolsheviks' cancellation of the Romanov's war debts in December 1917 only worsened these assessments (this was also true in other neutral and belligerent countries that had lent money to the Tsarist regime). But the most troubling element of the Russian revolutions for the Japanese was their impact on Japanese-controlled Korea and China, where the Bolsheviks' support for anti-imperial revolution helped to bolster protest actions against the Japanese. Chinese labourers returning from Russia brought revolutionary thoughts and structures with them, as did the 4,000 Korean expats who fought for the Russian armies and returned home in 1917 and 1918. Altogether, the Russian revolutions inspired the Japanese government to entrench its conservatism and heighten its own imperial ambitions. It used the context of the collapse of the Russian empire to extend its control over Manchuria and the east Asian mainland and suppressed rising anti-imperial resistance movements in Korea and China.[75] As Tatiana Linkhoeva argues, it was not the American President Wilson's support for global self-determination that worried the Japanese in the wake of 1917, but rather Lenin's powerful anti-imperial example.[76] Still, Wilsonian promises for a post-war international order focused on the concept of national self-determination also helped to augment anti-colonial activism in profound ways.[77]

Ultimately, the experiences of war and political change through 1917 altered contemporary expectations for the future. In the interplay between the demands of states for the loyalty of their people in an age of total war and the demands of their people for greater recognition and the alleviation of their suffering, the fabric of most societies stretched to breaking point. The 1914–18 war years also unmasked many of the claims made by the imperial elites to moral superiority, which they used to legitimate their colonial rule over subject communities.[78] Above all, the year 1917 exposed how individuals could reimagine the frameworks of legitimacy and power that framed their lives when those lives and the power structures that underpinned them became more precarious and insecure. As such, 1917 is so important as a transformative and 'climacteric' year because it inspired such deep questioning and searches for new solutions. What the Russian revolutions helped to unveil was the power of communities, when duly motivated, to take collective action and force change. Yet at the same time, the revolutionary developments in Russia also underlined the intense unpredictability that comes with unleashing the power of the people in the context of a total war. Altogether then, the revolutionary dimensions of 1917 exposed the intense unpredictability of what the world and one's own community after the war might look like. Paraphrasing Jörn Leonhard, Pandora's box had truly been opened.[79]

8

The end of neutrality? The global importance of the United States' declaration of war

The revolutionary transformations that rocked the world in 1917 were global and transnational phenomena. They did not stop at state borders or military frontlines. They disentangled the social and political cohesion of neutral and belligerent states and empires alike. This chapter focuses on neutral states and communities as they navigated the turbulence of total war during 1917. It argues that neutrals offer an excellent case study to illustrate the revolutionary consequences of total war, not least because so many of these states rejected their own neutrality and turned to belligerency in the wake of the United States' declaration of war in April 1917. Much like Britain's declaration of war in 1914 served as a vital tipping point globalizing the war, the United States' declaration of war served as a vital tipping point altering the global contours of the war and recalibrating people's expectations of what a post-war peace might entail. After April 1917, there was no 'going back' to the norms and principles that had dominated the pre-1914 international system. In the wake of President Wilson's 'fourteen points of peace' and promise to establish a League of Nations, neutrality itself had become suspect as an outdated principle. As result, no neutral country in 1917 could escape fundamental levels of questioning about its neutrality and how it might navigate a post-war world dominated by the expectations of the world's belligerent powers.

In neutral Argentina, like much of Latin America, these questions were particularly urgent. From the war's very beginnings, Argentina was fully entangled as a neutral state. News about the war dominated Argentina's public media landscape. Until the social and political convulsions of 1917, the war was almost always presented as a 'cataclysmic' event in which Argentina did well to uphold its neutrality.[1] Even as neutrals, however, the diverse migrant and expat communities in Argentina advocated for and against the various belligerents' causes, having internalized the war as part of their own political and national identities.[2] Their newspapers mobilized these biases in oppositional ways, while the tensions between the groups sometimes spilled over into the public sphere.[3] Others lamented the intense violence of the war and worried about the end of what they called 'European civilization'.[4] Many underlined their neutral identity by supporting charitable enterprises that provided aid to the war's many victims, particularly those in Belgium. For Argentina, the 1914–17 war years were fraught with political and economic insecurity.

It is highly significant then, as María Inés Tato shows, that most Argentinians experienced the year 1917 as a decisive turning point.[5] In combination with the intense economic distress they experienced that year, the Russian revolutions of March and November, the resumption of Germany's unrestricted U-boat campaigns in February and the American declaration of war on Germany in April, fundamentally altered how Argentina's many communities considered their neutrality and the course of the war. Like so many other groups and communities around the world, Argentinians became more assertive in taking public political action during this year. They demanded that their government lead the country in a specific direction, either in favour of joining the war against Germany, or for adopting an equally anti-German but pro-Argentine course of neutrality.[6] The 'rupturists' demanded war. The 'neutralists' mobilized themselves against joining this 'foreign war' that offered few advantages for the country, even if they also acknowledged that a policy of strict neutrality was untenable given Germany's military attacks on their neutral ships.[7] So, while public opinion in general galvanized against Germany and Germans – resulting in public protests and physical attacks on German legations, clubs, shops and the boycott of German goods and businesses – most Argentinians disagreed on what should happen next to the country's neutrality and its roles in the war. In response to these local and global pressures, their government had to make some stark choices.

The rupturists and neutralists clashed in parliament, in newspaper editorials and in everyday life. These clashes were only augmented by the expanding socio-economic crises they faced in 1917. In large crowds, some counting as many as 60,000 people at a time, Argentinians repeatedly took to the streets demanding one course of action over the other. After April 1917, the government adapted Argentina's neutrality policies to accommodate the demands of the newly belligerent United States and to punish Germany for its U-boat campaigns. In contrast to a number of other neutral Latin American countries including Brazil, Guatemala, Costa Rica, Haiti, Honduras, Nicaragua and Panama, however, Argentina did not declare war on Germany in 1917 or 1918. It also did not sever its diplomatic relations with Germany, unlike Bolivia, Uruguay, Paraguay and Peru, which did.[8] Argentina remained one of only a few Latin American states that held on to its formal neutrality through the course of 1917 and

1918. Yet it did so under immense political, economic and diplomatic strain. Like the other states that remained formally neutral – a group that steadily decreased in number through 1917 and 1918 – Argentina walked an even more precarious tightrope of diplomatic negotiation and socio-economic and political instability in the last two years of the global war.[9]

The year 1917 was a year of intense political and revolutionary unrest, a year in which ordinary people around the world took to the streets to force something to change or, as Jörn Leonhard phrases it, in search of 'alternative models'.[10] While their political activism developed out of fear or anger, they also aimed at post-war reconstruction or rejuvenation. Many of them understood that if the 'old ways' of the pre-war era were gone or fading, then the 'new way' forward might favour one's own hopes and ambitions. For neutral countries like Argentina, it seemed that neutrality, as an international principle steeped in nineteenth-century legal rights and obligations, was fast becoming one of these outdated norms. This realization was highly unsettling. How could their security be protected if it was not embedded in an international system that recognized and valued neutrality?

This chapter analyses the ways in which the shifting sands of global war and revolution in 1917 affected how contemporaries reconsidered their neutrality. It uses examples from a range of countries that were still neutral at the start of this year, including in the United States, China, Siam (Thailand), the Latin American states, Liberia and the Netherlands, to argue that 1917 not only transformed socio-political realities across the world but also transformed how neutral communities and their governments considered their immediate futures in the war and their intermediate futures in an imagined post-war world. It argues that the transformations experienced by neutrals of their neutrality were as much signals of the 'climacteric' of 1917 as the violent revolutions that shocked the world. It also shows that these (former) neutrals were as focused on developing a sense of security for themselves in the rapidly expanding global war as they were on looking beyond it to a post-war international system in which they hoped to take part.

The relevance of neutrality shifted radically after Germany unleashed its unrestricted U-boat campaign on 1 February and the United States responded two days later by suspending its diplomatic relations with the belligerent. Both these acts doomed neutrality as a viable foreign policy choice. For while Germany did not declare war on the United States or any other neutrals, its U-boats effectively went to war with their neutral ships. And while the United States also did not declare war on Germany in February – although it would do so on 2 April – as of 3 February, it was no longer conducting itself as a neutral state according to the rights and duties expected of neutrals by international law.[11] The end of its neutrality was further signalled when President Wilson issued a directive on 26 February allowing merchant vessels flying the United States flag to arm themselves in defence against the U-boats. Wilson framed the necessity of the directive not in terms of protecting neutrality, economic security or even sovereignty, but rather as an act of humanitarianism, in defence of:

> those great principles of compassion and of protection ... [of] human lives, the lives of non-combatants, the lives of men who are peacefully at work keeping the industrial processes of the world quick and vital, the lives of women and children and of those who supply the labor which ministers to their sustenance. We are not speaking of selfish material rights but of rights which our hearts support and whose foundation is that of righteous passion for justice upon which all law, all structures alike of family, of state, and of mankind must rest.[12]

According to this rendering, Germany's U-boats were conducting a barbaric war against the whole world. As such, the United States should do all it could to defend the lives of ordinary people, even if it meant taking military action against a belligerent and, with it, potentially dragging the country into a full-blown war.

After 3 February 1917, the United States government pressured other neutrals to follow its lead. After it declared war on Germany on 2 April, the foreign policy choices of the remaining neutral states became even more extreme: either join the war as a belligerent or lose the chance to have a say in how the belligerents reshaped the international system at conflict's end. As the president of Panama, Ramón Maximiliano Valdés, explained it:

> If any other nation of the world was concerned, it would be the duty of the Republic of Panama to observe a strict neutrality, but in a conflict where the vital interests of the United States are involved ... neutrality is impossible. Our duty then, in this important moment in the history of the world, is clear and unmistakable; our duty is that of an ally whose interests and whose existence is perpetually interwoven with the United States of America, and this is the only dignified attitude that we can and must adopt.[13]

For some of these neutrals, especially those in Europe, the choice was less difficult, but the implications no less sharp. They could not go to war for it would in all likelihood mean the end of their sovereign existence (they almost certainly would have been invaded by one of the belligerents). Yet they also understood that their ongoing adherence to neutrality offered no guarantees for their short- or long-term security.

Across 1917 and 1918, more neutrals joined the inter-state war as belligerents than had done so in any year since 1914. Many others suspended their neutrality by terminating their diplomatic and economic relationships with Germany. After the United States declared war, there were no great power neutrals left. The countries that stayed formally neutral from this point on had to recalibrate their domestic and foreign policies in response.

Unsurprisingly, many contemporaries argued that the 'death of neutrality' itself was nigh and that neutrality no longer served any useful purpose in international affairs.[14] Across the neutral and belligerent world, individuals, communities and states alike altered and reconsidered their expectations in the wake of this realization.

In many ways, the political responses that the war evoked in Russia, Argentina and around much of the world in 1917 reflected the desperation of so many in the face of the enduring deprivations caused by the seemingly unending condition of total global war. That desperation also explains, in part, why the German High Command resumed its unrestricted U-boat campaigns on 1 February 1917. It well understood that this extreme act of belligerency risked the entry into the war of the world's remaining neutrals, including the United States. For a chance at victory – and in the face of the German people's desperate suffering – it was nevertheless willing to hazard the gamble.

The German government's willingness to risk going to war with the world's remaining neutrals in early 1917 was based on three precarious assumptions.[15] Firstly, the German High Command accepted the premise that since Germany was not receiving enough material advantage from the neutrals, it could afford to provoke their anger. From this perspective, if neutrals could not offer a decisive advantage to a belligerent's war effort, then there was no point in adhering to any laws that protected neutrality. At any rate, Germany's military advisors also argued that even if the United States and some of the other neutrals declared war, it would take many months before enough American troops were adequately trained to make a difference on the western front.[16] And finally, they assured the German government that Germany's sizeable fleet of U-boats could weaken Britain's supply routes so fully that it would force that country out of the war by starving it into submission before a newly belligerent United States could come to its assistance.[17] Might made right.

These assumptions ultimately proved misguided, but in the weeks that followed the 1 February 1917 U-boat declaration, Germany's gamble seemed to pay off. Its U-boats sunk an unprecedented 534,478 tonnes of shipping in and around the British Isles during March alone, and a staggering 881,207 tonnes globally, which was 500,000 tonnes more than were sunk in January 1917.[18] At this rate, Britain and France's war effort could be crippled within months.

It really was no wonder that when the news of the first Russian revolution broke in March 1917, the German leadership was euphoric. It now anticipated that within a few months, all its enemies might be forced to capitulate: Russia by dint of popular uprising and France and Britain as a result of Germany's resurgent economic warfare. In contrast, the Allied governments were despondent. Their chances of surviving the year, let alone winning the war, looked particularly bleak.[19] To have any chance at victory, they needed the Americans to join the war as belligerents and to do so as soon as possible. In the end, it was the combination of the United States' war declaration (which immediately brought more ships into Allied service), the use of military convoys (which protected ships from being 'picked off' by the U-boats) and the laying of gigantic minefields in the North Sea (which sank U-boats) that kept Germany from victory and the Allies in the war long enough to win it in 1918.[20] The idea that the Allies might actually win the war, however, was not evident to anyone in 1917.

So much of the United States' declaration of war on 2 April 1917 turned on the waning value of neutrality in a world of total war, for what value did a country's neutrality have if it could not even protect its people from militant acts like the sinking of neutral passenger ships? As Wilson explained in a public speech given on 14 June 1917: 'It is plain enough how we were forced into the war. ... The military masters of Germany denied us the right to be neutral.'[21] For other Americans, the choice for war was even more obvious given that the United States' economic involvement in the conflict as a neutral had advantaged the Allies most of all. If the Central Powers stood a chance of victory – which seemed more likely in March 1917 than at any earlier time – then these American investors would not only lose a guaranteed return, but they might also have to accept a new world order in which Germany called the shots. In this sense, as Adam Tooze argues, the United States' support of the Allied war effort made it 'too big to fail'. The Allies had to win, even if it took the United States declaring war to make that happen.[22]

The vision of a German-dominated world order frightened many Americans. By late 1916, most Americans considered Germany a direct threat.[23] In the wake of the attacks by German agents on the Black Tom docks, Germany's encouragement of the Pancho Villa raids and the resumption of U-boat warfare on merchant and passenger ships, the United States media was rife with anti-German sentiment.[24] Barring a few steadfastly pro-German publications, the idea that Germany was undermining the United States as a sovereign nation had become obvious.[25] When late in February 1917, the British released an intercepted telegram sent by the German Foreign Office to its embassy in Mexico City, offering full German support for a Mexican declaration of war on the United States (including the future annexation of Texas, New Mexico and Arizona), the outrage was swift and widespread throughout the United States.[26] As the country had already broken off diplomatic relations with Germany, going to war seemed the only real choice left.[27]

It was quite easy then for the United States government to portray the country's entry into the war as a righteous choice in defence of its territorial borders and American values more generally.[28] The first Russian revolution helped that message along, for its people's revolutionary turn to democracy in March 1917 played well in the United States (a republic with its own 'glorious revolution' to hark back to).[29] As a war fought for democracy, President Wilson could now also portray his new enemies – the German

Kaiserreich, the Habsburgs and the Ottomans – as autocratic 'old world' empires in desperate need of renewal and overhaul. Wilson thus presented the United States' declaration of war as a necessary step towards achieving peace and as a way to reform the international arena. In so doing, the United States proclaimed it was going to war to 'save the world' for a better future.

Of course, at another level, the United States' war declaration came out of a fear that whichever side won, neither would heed the United States as a neutral power in their peace negotiations. Where before 1914, neutrals were thought of as mediators and intermediaries in time of war and crisis, by 1917 that perspective had shifted. Neutrals might continue to have their uses, particularly for providing humanitarian aid, but neutral intermediaries were rarely welcomed in belligerent communities. As a result, while many Americans recognized that their non-belligerency continued to be economically advantageous, they also recognized that their neutrality might prove untenable if it was interpreted as isolationism and, thus, kept the United States out of a post-war negotiation process. So much had shifted in terms of neutral-belligerent relations since 1914 that in order to protect its global and regional interests after the war, the United States government not only felt warranted to end its own neutrality but also pressured other neutrals to do the same. As Wilson explained: 'neutrality is no longer feasible or desirable where the peace of the world is involved and the freedom of its people.'[30]

To this end, it is vitally significant that President Wilson's war declaration included several provisos. Firstly, Wilson proclaimed that the United States joined the war not as an ally of Britain and France, but rather as a co-belligerent or 'associate' power.[31] While the United States went to war to rid the world of the German menace in allegiance with the Allies, its government was not interested in achieving a military victory at any cost. Rather, Wilson asserted that his war was fought to bring about peace as quickly as possible. As such, he was open to any overture made by any belligerent to negotiate an armistice. In this way, Wilson presented the United States' belligerency as a radical new form of diplomacy, one that closed its doors on the principles that defined great power relations in the nineteenth-century world order and, instead, embraced a 'new' form of internationalism. The catch phrases of Wilson's fourteen points of peace, which he released in January 1918, were 'collective security', the 'League of Nations' and 'self-determination'.[32] According to Wilson's post-war vision, inter-state warfare would only be allowed by agreement of the whole community of 'civilized' states, who could be held collectively responsible for determining the contours of international security and affairs. The stability of the world order would not be determined by individual states declaring their neutrality when others went to war. Rather, they would agree in concert whether or not the wars of others were acceptable.

In setting up the United States' shift from neutrality to belligerency in this way, Wilson gave credence and legitimacy to an explosive set of ideas. Much as the Russian revolutions of 1917 inspired communities and groups around the world to agitate for their own versions of political change, Wilson's ideals proved an equally powerful catalyst for political activism. Between February and April 1917, many understood that the principles that sustained the pre-war world order were fast disintegrating. In the maelstrom of changes wrought at a domestic and international level during 1917, these men and women felt confident that their actions to re-shape the future (or to defend the status quo against these attacks) were appropriate and warranted. After all, if Lenin and Wilson could assert radically new visions for the future and mobilize the power of their countries to achieve them, there was real hope that their own aspirations for change might be achieved.

For the liberal internationalists discussed in Chapter 6, who had advocated for years for the adoption of many of the concepts Wilson embedded in his fourteen points of peace, the United States' entry into the war was both inspirational and concerning.[33] At one level, Wilson's proclamations confirmed their own ambitions for improving the international environment. After April 1917, then, their lobbying of neutral and belligerent governments to adopt a range of cooperative concepts expanded. These proposals included calls to extend the reach of international law (including the creation of a Permanent Court of Justice), the maximization of arbitration and mediation practices, the establishment of a League of Nations, the promotion of democratic controls over foreign policy, universal disarmament and freedom of the seas (but not anti-imperialism).[34] At another level, however, Wilson's willingness to use a declaration of war to advance a new vision for post-war relations and peace troubled these internationalists. Many of them resided in neutral countries or represented neutral or pacifist organizations. They recognized all too well that if the value of neutrality had shifted in international relations, then their positions as internationalist visionaries representing a long tradition of peace-making, mediation and humanitarianism embedded in neutral rights and duties had shifted too.

In some ways then, the internationalist scramble to create a new set of norms for the post-war world order was also a scramble by neutral governments and groups to remain diplomatically relevant. In Norway and Sweden, two countries that sustained their formal neutrality across the 1914–18 war years, the declining value of neutrality complicated their internationalist advocacy, particularly in the sciences.[35] For many years, these two Scandinavian countries considered their long-term neutrality as a potent force to promote transnational cooperation, cooperative internationalism and peace. As signals of their value as neutral states, Alfred Nobel asked for his Nobel Prizes to be awarded by committees residing in these two countries in 1895.[36] The war years complicated these international and transnational relationships, yet it did not stop a wide range of scientific organizations and internationalist groups housed in these two countries from promoting all manner of internationalist 'solutions' for the future. While they applauded many of Wilson's ideas, they were fearful of the shift to collective security and the implication that their future neutrality might not be respected or protected. Above all, they feared that their internationalist role as sites for transnational cooperation would end.[37] Through the course of 1917, the government of the neutral Netherlands recognized the dangers of its potential exclusion from a post-war global order as well. In response, it reinstituted the planning committee for the third Hague Peace Conference, which had dissolved at the outbreak of war in August 1914. In reminding the belligerent powers of its pre-war importance to international organization and law, the Dutch government hoped to promote its own post-war importance and to ensure that the existing Hague institutions and laws were not overlooked or, worse, annulled.

The United States' shift from neutrality to belligerency in 1917 also had a fundamental impact on the manner in which American internationalist groups reconceptualized their activism. Like the other neutral countries discussed above, until April 1917, the United States was a key site of internationalist and peace advocacy. Members of the League to Enforce Peace, for example, were ardent advocates of collective security (a point on which they differed from the Scandinavians).[38] Even at the inception of the League in 1915, they were extremely careful not to present their post-war ambitions as a call for peace at any cost, understanding that this message would be rejected by the belligerents as unpatriotic. Yet they also understood that American neutrality enabled them to present these ideas as an appeal to the world for peace. When Wilson adopted several of the League's key principles yet also took the United States into the war in 1917, the League readjusted its ambitions in line with the country's new-found belligerency. The war remained a war 'for peace', but one in which they were now fighting to advance a vision of 'right' backed by collective 'might'. Armed power (as opposed to non-belligerency or neutrality) would protect this general peace.[39]

For other American internationalists, however, the shift to belligerency was harder to accommodate. The former Secretary of State and international lawyer, Elihu Root, prevaricated on the dangers in a 26 April 1917 address to the Carnegie Endowment for International Peace, using the following words:

In trying to estimate the future possibilities of International Law, and to form any useful opinion as to the methods by which the law can be made more binding upon international conduct, serious difficulties are presented in the unknown quantities introduced by the great War, which is steadily drawing into its circle the entire civilized world.[40]

The American School Peace League movement was equally confronted. It had been established in the aftermath of The Hague Conferences to teach American children about the value of peace and the importance of international agreements like The Hague Conventions.[41] By 1914, the School Peace League was a powerful educational lobby group that inspired primary and secondary schools across the United States to celebrate 18 May Peace Day (the day the first Hague conference opened its doors in 1899) and to teach the message of international cooperation and war avoidance. While the United States remained neutral during the First World War, the School Peace League continued to promote its 'peace first' programme. After April 1917, however, its message had to shift in the face of denunciations by students and parents alike for what they described as an unpatriotic agenda. In response, its members moved away from the message of peace for peace's sake to promoting moralized and 'all-American' ideals like international cooperation, democracy and collective security.[42]

In many ways, the shift in the School Peace League's messaging highlights how fundamental the move to belligerency was for Americans. In declaring war, the military fronts which they had read about as neutrals now became their own war fronts on which they and their loved ones might now fight and die. After April 1917, then, Americans reworked their narratives of patriotism and duty to accommodate this new belligerent reality. Much like other belligerent societies, they 'Othered' those who did not conform to expected behaviours, be it volunteering for military service, accepting the draft, buying war bonds or conserving essential supplies.[43] They even set up internment camps for German civilians.[44] In so doing, these Americans harked back to the 'Othering' they were already engaged in as neutrals during the war as well and to the 'rape' of Belgium motif. Race, gender and class norms affected these wartime assertions of belonging and war service. As Jennifer Keene argues, the war years 'radicalized' Americans in various political directions.[45]

For the United States' many First Nations' communities, the war years were particularly invasive. Some Indigenous Americans took up the call to serve the state at war as a way to achieve greater recognition of their indigenous rights. As William Leon Wolfe of the Winnebago people explained in 1917: 'I am fighting for the rights of a country that had not done right by my people.'[46] Others were forced to serve, including as a result of police raids on their reservations. The federal government mobilized their police powers in aid of their war ambitions in a number of other ways as well, including by enforcing leaseholds on indigenous land and compelling First Nations' people to 'till the soil' in an attempt to increase wartime crop production and livestock raising.[47] To this end, the United States as an empire at war operated in much the same ways as its co-belligerents: it used the needs of its belligerency as a cover both to promote a sense of patriotism among its subject communities and to repress any opposition. As a result, when the full integration of First Nations' people as citizens (as opposed to subjects) of the United States was legislated in 1924, it looked to some as a fitting reward for the dutiful military service of 12,000 First Nations' soldiers in 1917 and 1918. But the Indian Citizen Act also ensured that the claims to sovereignty made by these First Nations' communities – many of which were guaranteed by treaties signed in the nineteenth century – were now negated.[48] In other words, they received citizenship rights but not their own country. The coercive power of the United States was thus heightened by the war.

The United States was a formidable belligerent. It went to war proclaiming full belligerent rights and generally rejected the kinds of neutrality agreements it had itself negotiated while it was a neutral.[49] While it did not sink neutral ships like the Germans continued to do, it refused to acknowledge the agreements Germany's border neutrals had previously made with the belligerents.[50] Instead, it forced neutral governments to renegotiate these agreements, aiming to gain greater favour for the United States.[51]

In the wake of these American demands and in the face of the German U-boat campaigns and Britain's blacklisting operations, almost all the remaining neutrals reconsidered what their neutrality now meant for their own interests and futures. For most of them, the stakes were acute.[52] From August 1914 on most of them suffered the economic consequences as the global economy shifted to total war. In central and south America, as European investments declined through 1915 and 1916, American investors moved in.[53] Across the 1914–17 period of pan-American neutrality (with the notable exception of Canada in the north), the United States expanded its formal and informal networks of influence, power and control over Latin America, taking full advantage of its great power rivals' pre-occupation with the war to do so. The United States militarily occupied the Caribbean territories of Haiti in 1915 and the Dominican Republic and Guatemala in 1916, ostensibly to protect its own access to the Panama canal.[54] It extended its control over Cuba and Nicaragua through the course of 1917 for similar reasons.[55] For Haitians, Cubans, Guatemalans and Nicaraguans, these occupation regimes did not formally end until many years after the First World War.[56] Yet in all these places, locals internalized their newly found belligerency as a way to gain future rights and recognition from the United States as well. As the historian Stefan Rinke explains, for some Panamanians, going to war with Germany was an act of loyalty to their 'great protector', for others it was a way to acquire 'more room to maneuver' in their relationship with the United States.[57]

There is no question that the United States expanded the size of its formal and informal empire throughout the course of the war.[58] After April 1917, it also mobilized its enormous diplomatic and economic power to pressure the other American states (as well as the world's other neutrals) to either join the war or suspend their relationships with the Central Powers. It even set up propaganda bureaus in various neutral countries to advance the message.[59] In part, Wilson needed these neutrals to renege on their neutrality in order to validate the power of his 'collective security' principle. After all, if a range of previously neutral states acknowledged that Germany was an international pariah, then 'collective security' would not only be *de facto* operational, it would also be seen as effective.

That so many of the Latin American governments either agreed to join the war or suspend their diplomatic relations with Germany is therefore significant. Some did so to placate the United States or to obtain economic advantages from this powerful state and, in so doing, extended the United States' networks of informal imperialism substantively. Others did so because it helped to placate the political demands of many of their own people to punish Germany for its U-boat campaigns. All of them mobilized the concept of a post-war international order and the promise of equal inclusion in a League of Nations as a compelling reason to either suspend their relationship with the Central Powers or to formally go to war.[60] In Brazil, for example, the neutrality-belligerency debates were as divisive as they were in Argentina. Here too the stakes revolved both around the economic distress caused by the war years and the proclaimed advantages for the country and its people of going to war in support of the Allies.[61] Significantly, the Brazilian government broke off diplomatic relations with the Central Powers on 5 April. Its pro-neutrality and pro-German Foreign Minister resigned when a German U-boat sunk the Brazilian merchant ship, the *Tijuca*, on 23 May.[62] When Germany sunk the *Macau* on 23 October, Brazil formally declared war. By this stage, its government also recognized that a formal alliance with the United States would offer Brazil a chance to have a voice in a post-war international arena.[63]

Importantly, to many contemporaries, these acts of war and pro-American diplomacy were signals of the United States' imperial expansionism. The irony of these imperial power plays by a president who also proclaimed that his country was at war to save the world from the yoke of imperialism and to advance the principles of self-determination and democracy was not lost on them. Wilson's arch-rival, the former President Theodore Roosevelt, built an entire political campaign around the hypocrisy.[64] The hypocrisy was also not lost on the United States' various subject communities, particularly in the Philippines, whose people were promised a degree of self-rule in 1916 but did not achieve independence until 1946.[65]

After April 1917, representatives of these various subjugated communities joined up with anti-imperial activists from around the world to promote their rights to autonomy and independence. They did so by lobbying the United States government directly and, after the November 1918 armistice, by travelling to Paris to promote their cause among the great power peacemakers.[66] They may not have believed that Wilson was sincere in his proclaimed ideals of the right to self-rule, but they were nevertheless determined to hold him and the rest of the great powers accountable to the promises and allusions they had repeatedly made to those ideals. In this way, they too saw 1917 as a significant turning point. The emotive power of the 'Wilsonian moment', as the historian Erez Manela describes it, was a global phenomenon.[67] But much like the emotive power of the Russian revolutions, its importance lay first and foremost in opening up space for anti-imperial ideas to be openly acknowledged as legitimate by the very governments that equally quickly and violently suppressed anti-imperial activism when it endangered the integrity of their own empires.

Outside the Americas, the United States' turn to war resulted in equally powerful challenges to neutral communities' and states' choices and perceptions of their own futures. Would they remain neutral in a world dominated by the great power belligerents? Could they remain neutral in the face of the ever-expanding demands by these belligerents? Might their futures be better served by choosing to join the war on one or other side? How should they accommodate the principles of collective security and potential membership in a League of Nations?

In neutral China, for example, these questions were pressing. Since the middle of the nineteenth century, the Qing empire had suffered from invasive incursions into its sovereign independence and economic development. By the early twentieth century, the industrial great powers had come to an uneasy agreement to neutralize China. According to the terms of this 'open door' policy, China could remain an independent state – a vast empire ruling an array of peoples and communities – but it would do so at the cost of offering up commercial, political and financial spaces and rights to the industrializing powers. By 1914, all the great power empires, including Japan, had either made substantial forays into China's Siberian and Manchurian hinterlands or obtained treaty port rights along the Chinese coastline.

At the outbreak of the First World War, these international treaty ports faced serious issues, not least in managing the rival ambitions of enemy companies, financial institutions and resident organizations situated in these cities. As the war progressed, these rivalries became more entrenched and divisive. At the same time, and much like what happened in Latin America and across the Asia-Pacific region, these ports and the rest of China witnessed a noticeable decline in European economic activity. In turn, Japanese and American enterprises expanded.[68] Through the course of 1915, the Japanese government also used the European pre-occupation with the war as a cover to expand its imperial power in China. The 'twenty-one demands', which the Chinese government felt compelled to sign in March 1915, were a particularly invasive form of Japanese informal imperial expansionism.

The Chinese government feared Japan's rising power most of all and sought out every opportunity to entice the Allied powers and the United States to protect the 'open door' equilibrium that was in operation before the war. In order to keep Britain, France, Russia and the United States on side, and to offset Japan, China needed to be seen to be offering some kind of advantage to the Allies. It also hoped that in doing so, its own status as a fully independent state, free from 'unequal' treatment, could be guaranteed after the war.[69] As a result, it agreed to send labourers to the western front to help the Allied war effort. From 1915 on, 140,000 Chinese men travelled to Europe as members of an organized labour corps sponsored by the Chinese state through a private company (so as not to breach China's neutrality).[70]

China also opened up its borders to allow hundreds of thousands of its subjects into Russia to work for the Russian war effort.

But by early 1917, the Chinese government was fearful that even these pro-Allied contributions would not protect its position in a post-war negotiation, especially if Japan demanded that its wartime gains in Tsingtao, Manchuria and Siberia were recognized by the other Allied victors.[71] Neutrality was no longer a guarantee of China's international security and might actually endanger its post-war status. As a result, Germany's resumption of unrestricted U-boat warfare in February offered the Chinese government an opportunity to legitimately join the war on the side of the Allies and demand a seat at a post-war peace conference.[72] Thus, when a U-boat sank the French passenger ship *Athos*, killing more than 540 Chinese men who were on their way to Europe as military labourers, China suspended its diplomatic relationship with Germany. From 14 March 1917 on, China was no longer a formal neutral, but a benevolent non-belligerent.[73] On 14 August, it declared war.[74] The Chinese president, Duan Qirui, issued the following statement to the world to justify its declaration, replete with numerous allusions to Wilson's post-war world order:

> What we have desired is peace; what we have respected is international law; what we have to protect are the lives and property of our own people. ... I cannot bear to think that through us the dignity of international law should be impaired, or our position in the family of nations should be undermined or the restoration of the peace and happiness of the world should be retarded. Let the people of this entire nation do their utmost in this hour of trial and hardship to safeguard and develop the national existence of the Republic of China, so that we may establish ourselves amidst the family of nations and share with all mankind the prosperity and blessings drawn from our common association.[75]

As early as March 1917, China's government doubled its efforts to entice its subjects to volunteer for military labour service in Europe, built ships for the Allies and flew military aeroplanes for France.[76] It even toyed with sending a full-fledged expeditionary force to Europe.[77]

For many Chinese, 1917 was a decisive and troubled year. For those who volunteered for war work in Europe and Russia, the shift to Chinese belligerency offered certain incentives. With an eye to making some steady money, escaping the intense food shortages, experiencing an adventure and 'seeing the world', thousands did so, especially from the Shandong region.[78] Their experiences on the western front were life-changing.[79] Anywhere up to 4,000 of these men also lost their lives to the war.[80] The ones that came home, as the historian Xu Guoqi reminds us, were particularly critical of what they had learned of so-called 'western civilization'. As one labourer noted: 'What do foreigners mean when they use such beautiful words as liberty, justice, democracy, self-determination, permanent peace? ... Now

ILLUSTRATION 8.1 *This 1917 cartoon, published in the satirical magazine* De Notenkraker *in the neutral Netherlands by the Dutch cartoonist Albert Hahn, was titled 'China in the war'. It reflected on China's abrogation of its neutrality in March 1917 as an end to its 'open door' policy. In the cartoon, a type-cast Chinese figure hangs an epidemic warning on China's now firmly closed doors. The poster reads 'Infectious disease: War plague' and implies a warning of 'do not enter'. Its caption read, 'Increasingly so, this terrible sickness expands itself'.*
Source: *International Institute of Social History, Amsterdam, BG PM1/91-76.*

that your honorable war is over, are the hearts of men at peace?'[81] In this sense, the war years offered Chinese people another space to challenge and contest the notion that 'the west' should rule the world and, with the world, the fate of China. In this way, the war and particularly the years after 1917, presented China with a 'great awakening' of political consciousness.[82] Those who ended up in Russia as war labourers brought the rhetoric of revolution and Bolshevism with them on their return to China as well.

For the millions of Chinese subjects who remained home during the war, the end of China's neutrality in 1917 also had serious repercussions. According to the British embassy in Beijing, 80 per cent of Chinese newspapers were in favour of China's proactive belligerency. As the Republican newspaper *Chung-Yuan Pao* explained: 'This is the time for action. We must range ourselves on the side of justice, humanity and international law.'[83] Still for a decisive number of Chinese, China's declaration of war registered as weakness, as a fearful act made by a subservient state in a world of great industrial powers. In the context of the many revolutions and protests 'from below' that developed across the world in 1917, it is highly significant that China witnessed the collapse of its central government, the growth of civil unrest and a return to 'warlordism' as numerous regional leaders took charge of their own regions.[84] Sun Yat-Sen, the politician and political philosopher who had been instrumental in advancing a Chinese-centric government movement in the pre-war years, even accepted German money to set up a rival central government late in 1917.[85] Founded on the 'Three Principles of the People', which Sun Yat-Sen had first published in 1907, this new government proclaimed that only by advancing the principles of *Mínzú* ('independence' from foreign domination), *Mínquán* ('rights of the people' to political representation) and *Mínshēng* ('people's livelihood' or rights to social welfare) could China move effectively into the future. Altogether, then, 1917 caused enormous destabilization in China. That destabilization was only exacerbated by its shift to belligerency.

The government of neutral Siam (Thailand) faced equally challenging choices in 1917. As an independent monarchy, yet one subjected to a range of 'unequal treaties' with the world's industrial powers, Siam's neutrality in August 1914 was all but assured. It could not afford to alienate its relationship with either set of belligerents when they all had substantial imperial and economic interests at play in Siam.[86] After 1914, neutral Siam became a key space to organize and fund anti-imperial agitation in nearby belligerent regions, including in French-controlled Indo-China and British-controlled south and south-east Asia. But in the aftermath of the United States' war declaration in 1917, Siam's position on neutrality also changed. From this point on, King Vajiradvudh saw only opportunities in joining the war on the side of the Allies. Such an act of war would present the country as a mature state fully capable of functioning in a post-war global order as an equal to all other states. It also offered the potential for the country to break free from the constraints of the various 'unequal treaties' that provided the European powers and the United States peculiar commercial privileges.[87] To confirm its belligerency, Siam sent an ambulance unit and a small expeditionary force to France in 1918, both of which arrived too late to actually engage in any fighting. Yet these acts nevertheless left a powerful symbolic impression.[88]

Of course, King Vajiradvudh understood that this unprecedented shift to war needed domestic approval, not least because it would be the first time in modern memory that Siamese soldiers would fight in a 'foreign' war. To persuade the Siamese public that he had their interests at heart, Vajiradvudh penned various (anonymous) newspaper editorials presenting Siam's position in the war as a precarious reality. In them, he made clear that Germany threatened the world and Siam directly, not only by sinking neutral ships carrying Siamese subjects and trade, but also because Germany flouted the international laws of war, the same laws that dictated how 'civilized' societies (like Siam) should conduct themselves in the world. Even the August 1914 violation of neutral Belgium featured prominently in these editorials.[89] Whether they wished it or not, Siam's security, at least as its king presented it, no longer lay in neutrality but in the act of taking a righteous side and standing up for a particular war cause.

For Liberians – the only African country that managed to proclaim and sustain a policy of neutrality between 1914 and 1917 – the war years were also extremely difficult. The onset of the global war upset Liberia's already precarious economy. Because the Allies favoured their own African ports over Liberia's neutral ones, Liberia never recovered any trade advantages. It failed to attract merchants to its ports during the war and, with the onset of Britain's blacklisting campaigns, stood on the verge of complete financial collapse. Its people suffered intensely, and popular protests against the Liberian government heightened when it imposed a Hut Tax to offset some of these losses. The war years, then, were years of intense hardship and suffering for most Liberians.

Only the neutral United States – a country with which Liberia had a long and complicated history – offered some reprieve from the economic hardship the country endured between 1914 and 1917. Once the Americans joined the war, however, there was nowhere for the Liberian government to turn for much-needed cash.[90] Its government had as good as no choice but to join the Allied war effort. It did so on 4 August 1917 and was offered a sizeable British bank loan in compensation. But it also did so proclaiming disgust at Germany's 'violation of the rights of small neutral States', which 'if allowed to, can only result in the complete subjugation ... of all small and weak states'.[91] Two hundred Liberian men subsequently served with the French army on the western front. All German residents of Liberia were arrested, put on ships and interned in camps in France. All German-owned assets were liquidated, most of them handed over to the Allies. In retaliation, a German warship shelled the Liberian port of Monrovia in April 1918, causing significant damage and killing several civilians.[92] The United States subsequently sent a warship to Monrovia to defend its waters from future German attacks. As a result of these developments, Liberia pivoted closer to Britain, France and the United States, while Germany was made to sign away any remaining economic assets in Liberia in the Treaty of Versailles. In response, Liberia was the only independent country in Africa allowed to join the League of Nations as a founding member in 1919.[93] It declared war in 1917 to protect its post-war autonomy.[94]

The Balkan state of Greece was equally confronted by the global developments of 1917. Greece's position in the war was complicated from the moment the Ottoman empire went to war in November 1914. From this point on, Greece's political elite split themselves in two: some supporting the pro-Allied and anti-Ottoman agenda of the government, the other in favour of the pro-independence neutrality stance of the country's pro-German monarch. Without agreeing to join the war as a belligerent, Greece's government nevertheless allowed the Allies to establish a military front in and around the port of Thessaloniki (Salonika) in 1915. From this point on, Greece became embroiled in a *de facto* civil war of words, pitting monarchists against pro-government supporters.

After various domestic crises, including an armed siege of Athens by a royalist paramilitary organization, the Allies blockaded southern Greece late in 1916, while the Venizelos government established a separate state in northern Greece. In the wake of widespread starvation across southern Greece in the winter of 1916–17, almost certainly due to the blockade, Constantine I abdicated in June 1917. His son, Alexander I, agreed to let his newly reunified country join the war against the Central Powers. In bringing his supporters together to support the country's new-found belligerency, Constantine I explained that Greece only stood to gain from the deal:

> By taking part in this world war alongside democracies impelled to unite in a truly holy alliance ... we shall regain the national territories we have lost; we shall reassert our national honour; we shall effectively defend our national interests at the Peace Congress and secure our national future. We will be a worthy member of the family of free nations that the Congress will organise, and hand on to our children the Greece that past generations could only dream of.[95]

While Greece's formal turn to belligerency in 1917 masked a deeply strained political environment (and one that would see Greece tumble in and out of political crises, civil warfare and coups for decades), it was sold to the Greek people as a way to 'win' in a war that cost so many so much. Much like the Liberian government, the Greek political elite felt compelled to embrace the internationalist principles of Wilson's peace plan in order to safeguard the country's long-term security. Almost by necessity, and in aid of future ambition, neutrality fell by the wayside.

Unlike China, Siam, Liberia and Greece, the neutral Netherlands did not go to war in 1917 or 1918. Its government doggedly maintained a position of formal neutrality, often by negotiating on the most desperate of terms with the two sets of belligerents.[96] Caught between the blockading might of the Allies and the military might of their immediate neighbour Germany, the Dutch were in the unenviable position that a choice for war would have guaranteed an invasion by the Germans and an end to their sovereign existence. Occupied Belgium – on the Netherlands' southern border – offered

ILLUSTRATION 8.2 *This cartoon entitled 'Greece and the war' was pub-lished in the Dutch satirical magazine* De Notenkraker *in July 1917. The Dutch cartoonist Albert Hahn depicted death getting his hands on a type-cast Greek maiden, sighing 'Finally'. Typical of Hahn's many cartoons was his despondency at the expansion of the global war. His 1917 depictions were particu-larly critical.*
Source: *International Institute of Social History, Amsterdam, BG C6/616.*

an abject example of what a turn to belligerency might look like.[97] For most Netherlanders, then, neutrality was the country's only option.

Still, their collective experiences of 1917 also changed their perspectives on what it meant to remain neutral. They understood all too well that neutrality as an international principle protected by international law was under attack and might not survive the war. They watched with anxious eyes as other neutrals succumbed to the pressure to abrogate their neutrality (Illustrations 8.1 and 8.2 highlight how attuned Dutch newspaper readers were to the global shifts in the war). They met the news of the United States' entry into the war with equally fearful eyes. Most Netherlanders worried about their own security first: could they keep out of the war and avoid a military invasion by either side? Could they survive the economic impact of an American blockade? In the face of the two Russian revolutions and growing political crisis across the continent, they also worried about the impact of a complete collapse of social order across central and eastern Europe, so much so that they feared revolution might spread to the Netherlands itself.

Lastly, they feared that the belligerents had passed the point of no return and would not be able to reign in the revolutionary developments and civil wars that were erupting in so many places, including in the Dutch East Indies.[98] Staying out of the war continued to be the Netherlands' prime objective. But what the country and its empire might look like by war's end unsettled them all.

Altogether, during 1917, the value of neutrality as a valid and viable foreign policy choice that protected neutral rights to trade and economic security was besieged by the belligerent powers. The Germans rejected neutral trade rights by sinking neutral ships caught in its warzones. The Allies rejected neutral sovereignty and trade rights by blacklisting enemy endeavours in neutral countries and blockading neutral ships that did not adhere to their own trade requirements. The newly belligerent United States upended neutrality by advocating for a post-war global order built around collective security. While neutral charitable and humanitarian activities continued to matter (and were recognized as significant by all the belligerent states), the notion that neutrality would function as it did before August 1914 faded away through the course of 1917.

Perhaps the Chilean Ambassador to the United States, Benath Mathieu, described the shift best when he carefully explained in 1920 that Chile 'complied with her duties as a neutral' both in the 'first phase' of pan-American neutrality that stretched from August 1914 to April 1917 and during the beleaguered 'second phase' of Chilean neutrality from April 1917 to November 1918. Even though Chile (like Argentina) did not declare war on Germany and while it dutifully upheld the laws of neutrality throughout the conflict, Mathieu also stressed that Chileans were not 'indifferent' neutrals. They worried incessantly about Germany's military barbarism and sympathized with the war's (and by implication Germany's) many victims. As such, Mathieu argued, 'it is not germane to speak of our material aid given to the sufferings of Europe; it is sufficient to know that Chile is the Latin-American country that contributed most to the Red Cross and other beneficent institutions.'[99] By having to advocate so strongly for neutrality as a right, Mathieu was also having to defend his country's unwillingness to abandon its neutrality in 1917 and 1918. Like the Dutch, the Scandinavians and Argentinians, Chileans too were punished by the victorious Allies for their refusal to join their side in what they continued to describe as a 'righteous' war. From this Allied perspective, any neutrals that remained neutral in 1917 and 1918 were, in effect, pro-German and could not be seen to champion 'law and justice'.[100]

As such, neutrality had become a suspect international condition. Neutrals could not be seen as the moral arbiters of war as they had been in the pre-1914 world, nor could they be trusted to take part in any peace negotiations.[101] As the German jurist, Alex Lifschütz advocated early in 1918, in future wars neutrality could only exist when neutrals behaved as truly passive observers who kept to themselves and refrained from interfering in the business or supply of the belligerents.[102] For Lifschütz and so many others, by choosing not to partake in a war, neutrals forsook any rights to have a say in international affairs. They might offer humanitarian aid but were otherwise extraneous to the future shape of international relations. The Italian expat living in the American city of Chicago, Luigi Carnovale, framed his rejection of neutrality even more harshly: '[T]he only means by which war can be prevented [in future] is by abolishing the neutrality of nations, that neutrality corresponds exactly to selfishness.'[103] In so doing, he effectively blamed neutral countries (including the United States) for keeping the war going after 1914 and for transforming it into a total global reality.

The British government was more subtle in its approaches to the international shift away from neutrality in 1917 and 1918. Nevertheless, in August 1918, its Political Intelligence Department approved a new propaganda document aimed at persuading the remaining neutrals to consider joining the war. The pamphlet entitled *Why War?* advocated for the necessity of defeating Prussian militarism, protecting the rights of small nations, international law and democracy. Above all, the war fought by Britain and France, according to the pamphlet, was a 'titanic' struggle to defend international good faith. Neutrality as an essential principle for guaranteeing a post-war peace was not mentioned.[104]

Of course, neutrality did not disappear from the international arena with the end of the First World War. It remained particularly important for the development of international humanitarian law, various international organizations and transnational scientific cooperation.[105] Some countries – like Switzerland – embraced a new form and style of neutrality after 1918 as well. But with the collapse of neutrality in the war, so too did the nineteenth-century international system disappear.[106]

9

Exit ... 1918–19

There is something profoundly unsettling in the statistic that after China declared war on Germany in August 1917, more than 1.4 billion people (out of a total world population of 1.8 billion) were formally at war with each other. Perhaps an even more unsettling realization is that during 1917 and 1918, most neutral countries also experienced a profound unravelling of social norms, political order and economic stability.[1] By the time of the signing of an armistice that brought the war between the Allies and Central Powers to an end on 11 November 1918, few people could claim that they felt safe and secure or even 'at peace' in their current situation. The war years had unbounded so many of their pre-war assumptions, norms and expectations about the communities in which they lived, the elites who ruled their lives and the socio-economic environments in which they interacted. Civil wars, social unrest, in some places complete social and political disintegration, alongside anarchy, hunger, starvation, inflation, a profound sense of grief and a global influenza pandemic, ensured that their lives and livelihoods remained unsettled well after November 1918.[2]

This chapter analyses the final global transformation of the First World War period, namely the shift from total global war to a condition that can loosely be defined as 'peace' in the aftermath of the November 1918 armistice. The chapter argues that while contemporaries recognized that the 'Great War' ended when the guns fell silent on Europe's western front, they also understood that the war had transformed the world. For some, understanding there was a future beyond the war was all-important. As one British officer recalled of his demobilization:

> While we were going through the formalities of disembarking a strange and unreal thought was running through my mind. I had a future. It took some getting used to, this knowledge. There was a future ahead of me, something I had not imagined for some years. I said so much to Captain Brown. He smiled at me; he was a man about forty. 'Yes', he agreed. 'You've got a future now, Dickie. And so have I. I wonder what we'll do

with it, and what it will be like. Because, you know, things are not going to be the same as they were before.'[3]

What that future might bring was unclear: too much had happened, too many horizons had shifted, too many people had died and too many expectations had been ignited in the course of this 'total global tragedy'.[4] Perhaps even more fundamentally, the war had awakened so much change and instability that finding shared paths forward that could reconcile these contested expectations let alone remedy and restore the destruction wreaked between 1914 and 1918 was a nigh-on impossible task. At any rate, too many communities remained in political flux for a workable international order to be established. They recognized the post-war world as a broken world, a world in which their search for peace and stability proved interminable.[5]

For the French Prime Minister Georges Clemenceau, Armistice Day came as a great relief. Yet he could not rejoice.[6] While France came out of the war 'victorious', very few French felt like winners. They, like Clemenceau, well understood the immense debt those who survived collectively owed to those who did not.[7] As a result, and like so much of the Allied world, France's 'culture of victory' was not built around celebratory ideals but rather around the recognition of this collective grief and understanding that France and its empire faced enormous political, social and economic challenges going forward. On 11 November 1918, Clemenceau turned to Rabindranath Tagore's *Song Offerings*, which he asked his friend, the Romanian-French feminist writer Anna the Comtesse de Noailles, to read out loud to him for inspiration.[8] Tagore's message of hope and renewal, of building a global peace by bringing humanity together was the message Clemenceau most needed on this day of mourning, reflection and anxiety.

In seeking out something hopeful in the midst of his despair, Clemenceau was not alone. When Tagore visited France in 1920 and Germany in 1921, he was widely fêted. Of these visits, he later recalled:

Following the end of the War, I went to Europe where I was received with a warmth of welcome which overwhelmed me. I could not believe that it was because of my books or my work. Then I decided that it must be that the nations of the West were looking for some new ideal from the East which would reconstruct their civilization on a better basis.[9]

In the wake of the Armistice, more Europeans than ever before acknowledged that Europe might need to change from within, in line with Tagore's ideas and Wilson's fourteen points of peace. Many of them also hailed the prospect of a more open and equitable world order and a future that embraced the motto 'never again war!'. For if the war proved that 'European civilization' had failed, that civilization needed to be rebuilt on sounder and more equitable foundations.

ILLUSTRATION 9.1 *This cartoon by the American artist Sidney Greene was published in the New York* Evening Telegram *in 1919. It depicted the 'world unrest' as a product of the many crises set off by the world war, including strikes, riots, German Reds, Bolshevism, the League of Nations, murders and Hunism (a reference to German militarism). Its caption read 'turn on the hose', implying that the signing of the peace treaties at the end of the war might douse the flames of unrest. The hose had not yet been turned on, however. By implication, the flames might just keep on spreading.*
Source: Evening Telegram, *1919, reprinted in* Literary Digest *30 August 1919, np.*

While some felt the urge to make the world a better place, to move away from the past and the suffering endured during the war, others could only imagine the continuation of horror going forward. They feared the future and fixated on the improbability that the governments who survived the war – let alone those that established new states in its wake – could satisfy the various competing demands at play within their societies or within the wider international system. The Brazilian journalist and politician Otto Prazeres, for example, reflected on the armistice in terms of the insuperable obstacles the war had created:

> Besides a loss of illusions, the war will have many additional implications. ... The mental revolutions, which result in new ways of thinking and acting, are already perceptible. Many moral, social, and political values will lose the basis upon which they were formed and be fundamentally changed. ... [T]he threatened masses will march in search of new principles.[10]

In reflecting on the meaning of the First World War for Latin America, the historian Stefan Rinke concurs, arguing that the 1914–18 war years were a decisive 'transformer that brought change from the realm of ideas to the social realities of the streets. ... It would be a legacy of the First World War that people sought answers to the question of the future ... in increasingly violent conflict.'[11] In Ireland, eastern and central Europe, Germany, Russia and much of the Middle East these violent conflicts already waged.[12] In many other places they threatened to erupt.

As we saw in Chapter 1, at the outbreak of war in July 1914, most politically alert contemporaries had clear expectations of what a European inter-state conflict should look like. By the time that inter-state war came to a formal close in November 1918, however, those expectations had been uprooted and largely surpassed. 'The war' had spawned a monster beyond anyone's prior reckoning, an insatiable leviathan that devoured with reckless abandon. This book has shown how the war transformed from a potentially manageable diplomatic crisis to a total global monstrosity. Beginning with the initial transgression of the international norms of war and neutrality by Germany in its invasion of Belgium, Luxembourg and France, the war quickly evolved from a European conflict into a global crisis when the British empire went to war in early August 1914. By December of that year, hope for a short war had evaporated leaving the fearful prospect of a long-war scenario in its wake. This 'long war' engendered a spate of new transgressions against neutrals, non-belligerents and civilians alike. By 1916, it did not matter where you lived, the war penetrated your life in some (usually significant) way. The physical, psychological and emotional toll of what seemed like an endless reality through the course of 1916, 1917 and 1918 was so intense that the bonds of social cohesion of many societies strained, breaking some of them completely. In these processes of grave unravelling that affected neutrals and belligerents alike, all manner of new expectations, ambitions, hopes and fears were unleashed.

All of these societal strains were only made so much worse when a global influenza pandemic developed through the course of 1918. The virus killed anywhere between 50 to 100 million people over an eighteen-month period.[13] Around 90 per cent of the pandemic's casualties occurred between August and November 1918, coinciding with the final months of the official fighting in the First World War.[14] As the Swiss-born French writer Blaise Cendrars evocatively recalled of a visit to his friend, the poet Guillaume Apollinaire, early in November 1918:

> We spoke of the topic of the day, the epidemic of Spanish flu which was creating more victims than the war. I have just travelled halfway across France by car, and in a Lyon suburb I watched the incineration of plague-ridden bodies piled up in the fields and sprinkled with petrol, since the city had run out of coffins. ... The trauma of the flu was all the more vivid because it happened against the backdrop of the slaughter in the last months of the war, and when there was still a ban on families recovering their dead relatives and returning them to their villages and towns for reburial. Some saw this time as one of the loss of rituals of separation and bereavement, a kind of 'decivilisation', as a result of mass death.[15]

In these immediate ways that affected almost every family in the world, the Spanish flu not only further eroded social and cultural norms and rituals, but also reminded contemporaries of 'what and who had passed' in the war itself. There was no going back to a 'simpler' pre-war pre-flu era; their loved ones were simply gone. The mass of deaths on the war fronts were now intertwined with a mass of deaths in civil society. As a result, the flu accentuated an almost universal feeling that all who survived the war and the flu were somehow experiencing a 'rupture in time', from which they could not return unharmed or unchanged.[16] Only days after Cendrars' visit, Apollinaire also died of the flu.

Despite the commonly used identifier – the 'Spanish flu' – it was quite clear to contemporaries that the pandemic did not originate in Spain.[17] The influenza only became a subject of global public discussion, however, after it hit Spain in the European summer of 1918. As a neutral country, Spain did not have the same censorship rules in place regarding public health as the belligerents. And like all war-related news at the time, news from neutral countries spread particularly fast. Still, by the time Spain was infected with the virus and reporting it, the pandemic had already raised alarm bells in the United States, France, Britain and Germany. None of these belligerent governments were initially willing to take any serious measures to contain its spread because the war was still on and their military priorities came first.[18] As a result, the flu became part of the fabric of total war.

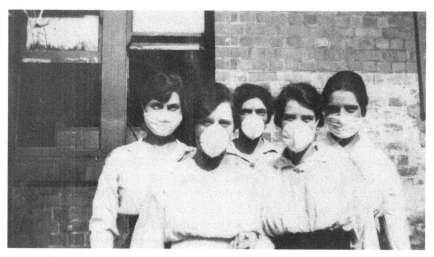

ILLUSTRATION 9.2 *A group of women in Brisbane, Australia, wearing mouth coverings to prevent the spread of the 'Spanish flu' in 1919.*
Source: *John Oxley Library, State Library of Queensland, 104332.*

The official secrecy around the pandemic certainly left ample space for belligerent communities to invent their own stories about the disease's origins and meaning. They viewed the virus as a concomitant of the war. Across Europe, for instance, many experienced the disease as treacherous: as an invisible enemy attacking their war-weakened society from within, even as a punishment sent by their god for the sins of the war. Even neutrals explained the flu in this way (see Illustration 9.3). Others suspected that their enemies had released the virus as an alarmingly effective new weapon of mass destruction. Many of them distrusted their own governments' roles in the flu's management, not least as they also understood that fighting 'the war' remained a primary priority (as opposed to combating the flu). In France, rumours abounded that the medical catastrophe facing them could not be caused by something as 'innocent' as a flu bug and that the authorities were actually trying to keep the secret that deadly cholera had returned.[19]

The virus also spread thanks to the global sinews of the war. It was carried on troop ships from home front to war front and back again. The contagion haunted soldiers as they demobilized and when they remobilized to fight new wars at home and abroad (as occurred with Japanese, American, British and French troops supporting the 'White' cause in the Russian Civil War, for example). In New Zealand, the influenza was dubbed 'the Armistice epidemic' since it arrived with the first wave of demobilized troop ships coming home.[20] The virus moved as refugees moved, as prisoners of war and internees were repatriated and as ships docked at global ports. It ravaged the population of Samoa, after the New Zealand governor allowed a ship with sick passengers to land in Apia. The loss of more than 22 per cent of

ILLUSTRATION 9.3 *This cartoon by L.J. Jordaan appeared on 26 October 1918 in the satirical Dutch magazine* De Notenkraker *(The Nutcracker). It depicted the Spanish flu as death disguised as a Spanish flamenco dancer. Its caption read: 'Now the neutrals will also get their due'.*
Source: *Institute of Social History, Amsterdam, IISG BG C6/825.*

Western Samoa's entire population to the flu (around 9,000 people in all) took an enormous toll on Samoan families and these Pacific islands' social and political order.[21] In the Middle East, the virus' toll was equally horrific not least because it came after years of famine. In Persia, famine and disease accounted for the death of anywhere between 2 and 10 million people by the end of 1919.[22] In Asia, 36 million individuals lost their lives to the pandemic, causing enormous social and emotional dislocation.[23]

In Africa, the demographic impact of the flu was similarly devastating, spreading 'inland rapidly, inserting its feverish presence into the numerous arteries of transport and communication that had been laid down to ferry supplies, soldiers and communications from the imperial metropole', as Bill Nasson explains.[24] Here too, people linked the war with the flu. When for example the East Africa campaigns came to an end on 25 November 1918 – the news of the armistice took nearly a fortnight to arrive – the British captured all 2,500 German soldiers, askari and porters and interned them in a prisoner-of-war camp. Many of them contracted the flu in the process.[25] The Wagogo's *Mtunya* was also accentuated by the losses this community suffered as a result of the flu.[26]

For Germans, the congruence of the Spanish flu with the military defeat they experienced on the western front only spurred on a revolutionary fervour. By the middle of 1918, the only geostrategic clarity that still seemed to be on offer in the war was the fighting on Europe's western front. After Germany launched an ambitious 'Spring Offensive' there in March, its troops exhausted themselves in June and July. Buoyed by the arrival of fresh troops from the United States, an Allied counterattack succeeded in breaking through the German frontlines on 8 August. From this point on, Germany could not win the war by military means.[27]

All across Germany, people responded to the realization that they were losing a war that their leaders had promised they would win by taking out their frustrations in highly public and political ways. Soldiers deserted their stations, sailors in the German Navy mutinied, workers went on strike and Germans took to the streets demanding political change and an end to their hunger and suffering. In the face of the collapse of his country and the imminent defeat of his armed forces, Kaiser Wilhelm II abdicated. A cobbled together political agreement brought a German Republic into being on 9 November 1918. On 11 November, Germany's new leaders signed an armistice agreement with the Allies. Europe's Great War had ended.[28]

For some Germans, the end of the war and the promise of political rejuvenation lifted the spirits. Lida Gustava Heymann, an active player in the women's movement and one of the driving forces behind the Women's Peace Conference in The Hague in 1915, described this feeling of expectation as follows:

Now a new life began. Looking back the following months seemed like a beautiful dream, so improbably splendid were they. The heavy burden of the war years had gone; one stepped forward elated, looking forward to the future.[29]

Yet Heyman was in the minority. Many Germans feared that their fate would mirror that of Bolshevik-ruled Russia, now engulfed in a destructive civil war, or that of Austria-Hungary, whose empire no longer existed while its former subjects engaged in all manner of violent upheavals aimed at establishing a swathe of new nation-states. The violence in Germany's streets, the abdication of the Kaiser, the demobilization of Germany's soldiers, the food shortages, the occupation of the Ruhr by Allied soldiers and the acknowledgement of their own deep grief left many Germans bereft of a sense of belonging and identity.

Various groups of Germans responded to the general uncertainty by establishing their own centres of governance, including soviets, bourgeois *Bürgerräte* (people's councils), paramilitary organizations like the *Freikorps* ('free corps') and even house-wife councils.[30] All of these groups aimed at defining a new set of rules, norms and expectations for how peace and stability might be returned to their lives and their country. Unsurprisingly, very few of these groups could agree with each other on what those rules, norms and expectations should be. Even their sense of what it was to be 'German' differed at a fundamental level. As a result, Weimar Germany's provisional government faced enormous obstacles in bringing all these competing ambitions into line in support of the republic. Ultimately, this ultra-democratic state, in which every adult citizen had the vote, would not be able to settle the political rifts that were awakened during the First World War. Germany's 1918 revolution may not have caused an all-out civil war, but the intensity of the political violence experienced in the 1918–23 period revealed the deep clefts that divided Germans and underscored the weaknesses of the new Weimar state.

In so many ways, Germany's post-war troubles also offer an excellent example of how the internalization of wartime identities and loyalties reverberated into 'peacetime'. In the wake of the war, a member of the *Freikorps*, Friedrich Wilhelm Heinz, could even claim 'the war' as his identity:

> When they told us that the war was over, we laughed, because we ourselves were the war. Its flame continued to burn in us, it lived on in our deeds surrounded by a glowing and frightful aura of destruction. We followed our inner calling and marched on the battlefields of the post-war period just as we had marched toward the front: we were singing, full of recklessness and adventurism while marching; we were grim, silent and merciless in combat.[31]

Heinz's ultra-militarism was emboldened in November 1918 by mythical discourses that Germany had not lost at all. In the context of the country's political upheavals, he could easily blame a spate of internal enemies – people who may have lived in Germany but whose loyalties were treacherous to him – for Germany's current condition. According to the myth that Heinz and so many supporters of the Fatherland Party and other nationalist groups believed, Germany was not defeated on the western front. As the main propagator of the 'stab in the back' (*Dolchstoß*) myth, the former Commander-in-Chief General Ludendorff proclaimed that Germany was defeated by an alliance of internal enemies, among whom he counted socialists, communists, Jews and all foreigners.[32] For Germany to reclaim its honour and former glory and status, these 'Others' would need to be defeated first.

In contrast, Heinz and Ludendorff's imagined enemies held to their own idealistic visions of a new Germany. Some, like the future members of the German Communist Party (KPD), hoped for a rapid working-class revolution. The socialist intellectual Rosa Luxemburg advocated for a more gradual (and less destructive) revolution by the masses. Yet precisely because Luxemburg was a woman, a socialist and an intellectual from a Polish and Jewish background, she stood out as a supreme example of the 'Other' whom militarists, traditionalists and nationalists like Heinz so despised and whom more moderate Germans feared might lead the country towards a Bolshevik future.[33] The *Freikorps* commander, Major Maercker, portrayed her as 'a female devil', one who 'can today destroy the German Empire without punishment, since there is no powerful institution in the Empire which can oppose her.'[34]

After a massive communist-inspired workers' strike broke out across Germany in January 1919, which the Weimar government only managed to suppress by asking the *Freikorps* for assistance, both Luxemburg and her KPD co-leader Karl Liebknecht were kidnapped, violently beaten and then murdered at the *Freikorps'* headquarters in Berlin. The Social Democratic newspaper *Vorwärts* proclaimed that Liebknecht and Luxemburg 'were the victims of a civil war which they themselves' had instigated.[35] The newspaper's rhetoric underlined how easily the use of extra-legal and paramilitary violence, even murder, was legitimized in the wake of the war and in aid of stabilizing Germany's republic. The report also highlighted how easily groups and individuals could continue to demonize each other as 'enemies of the state'. The Spartacist uprising of January 1919 sparked a spate of political murders, including of some of Weimar's leading politicians like Matthias Erzberger and Walter Rathenau. The regime's instability led to various attempted military coups and numerous working-class strikes. These reactionary and highly violent acts made it impossible for Weimar's government to establish stable democratic foundations for their new state. They also illustrate how well-ensconced the instinct to mobilize one's identity to advocate for a cause had become, particularly when it justified the use of violence against a perceived alien 'Other'. In this way, Germany offers a particularly poignant example of how difficult it proved to demobilize the cultures of belonging and 'Othering' that evolved during the war.

The intense difficulties facing Germans in re-establishing order and social stability in the aftermath of the First World War were mirrored around the world, in large part because so much was unsettled and made insecure but also because the war had unleashed a host of irreconcilable expectations about the future. In some respects, the war years heightened people's expectations of what their governments ought to do for them once peace returned. At the very least, many of them expected that they would be compensated for the sacrifices they had made during the war.

As an example, the many colonial soldiers from the French empire, who had fought for France in Europe, brought a new mentality of citizenship and wartime sacrifice home with them. Their expectation, that their newly confirmed status as French citizens would end the racial denigration they had experienced in the past, carried some weight. Demba Mboup, a veteran from Senegal who had served in the French army since 1915, demobilized in 1919. He recounted that when a white man on board the troop ship taunted the Senegalese veterans with racial slurs, they beat up the offender, who ended up:

> crying and said he would never do it again. ... So what happened [then]? Nothing! We were within our rights, because discrimination between people [was no longer tolerated] at that time, [and] we were French citizens like anybody else. ... [But], if the same thing had happened before the war, [we] would not have done the same thing. Because we had less power then, and [we] were treated badly like this by the French all the time.[36]

Mboup certainly believed that his wartime service could lead to an improvement in French rule in Senegal. Many of his soldier colleagues across Africa and in Indo-China soon realized there was very little evidence of that. For them the war altered very little in the imperial imbalance of power or in the treatment they received from white colonists.[37] Yet what Mboup's demobilization recollections highlight above all is the expectation that things ought to have changed had entrenched.

Mboup's gritty hope highlights two important things about the transformations evoked by the First World War in the racial dynamics of the world's industrial empires, including those of the United States and Japan. Firstly, the war helped to solidify and legitimize anti-colonial, anti-western and anti-imperial resistance movements and ideas. For many, 1914–18 registered as a great destabilizing moment for the world's empires that also helped to unsettle some of the racial norms which underpinned the industrial imperial system. As such, the First World War helped to accentuate a global 'shift away from empire' as a defining feature of the twentieth-century international era. The language of independence, autonomy, statehood, self-determination, suffrage and racial equality pervaded global and local politics after 1918. The establishment of the Soviet Union in 1922 and its foundational anti-capitalist and anti-imperial rhetoric further helped to undermine the legitimacy of imperialism as a valid means of governance. The Soviet Union was, of course, also a product of the many revolutionary transformations occasioned by the First World War. But so were the expectations that veterans like Demba Mboup brought home with them. Among Maori soldiers returning home, the expectation was encapsulated by the concept of *tina pakanga* (ultimate encounter), which the historian Monty Soutar defines as 'the fight for survival as Maori in post-war New Zealand'. Since Maori had faithfully served the state and empire at war, they felt they deserved an equal share of the opportunities offered to New Zealand's non-Maori veterans.[38]

Yet, in response and all too importantly, the second major transformation educed during the 1914–18 war years was directly oppositional to this 'shift away from empire' and the recognition of civil rights. Across the western world, there were plenty of people (and governing elites) who hoped for a return to the familiarity of the pre-war social, racial and political order. Their ambitions to 'restore' and celebrate the pre-war past offered a powerful motivation to reimpose full imperial control and to stem the expectations for change that so many of their subjects now demanded (and Wilson and Lenin seemed to confirm). Their willingness to use state violence to exact compliance was rarely restrained, as it had not been through (or for that matter before) the war either. In this sense, the war years offered no reprieve from empire or racial inequity. After 1918, most imperial authorities' willingness to resort to state violence, including by maximizing new military technologies like aerial bombardment and gas warfare, ensured that the twentieth-century era of asymmetrical warfare ('juxtaposing high-tech white armies against low-tech non-white populations')[39] was only accentuated.

In India, for example, the 'restoration of empire' impulse led to the imposition of the Rowlatt Act (also known as the Anarchical and Revolutionary Crimes Act) of 1919, which allowed the imperial authorities to arrest anyone on the mere suspicion of 'terrorism'. It also led to the massacre of a crowd of unarmed civilians in a small public square in Jallianwala Bagh in the Punjabi city of Amritsar. The local commander feared a violent uprising and banned the celebration of the festival of Baisakhi and any congregation of individuals. Confronted with a crowd of peaceful people on 3 April 1919, he ordered his troops to block off the exits to the square before they opened fire on the crowd. According to British sources, 379 Indians were killed and another 1,200 seriously injured. Indian sources cite anywhere up to 1,000 deaths. As news of the massacre slowly spread around the world, it repulsed and shocked, but among imperial apologists in Britain and the white Dominions it was applauded as an essential act of imperial restoration.[40]

When Tagore heard the Amritsar news, he wrote to the British Viceroy in India to disavow his knighthood: 'I ... wish to stand, shorn, of all special distinctions, by the side of those of my countrymen who, for their so-called insignificance, are liable to suffer degradation not fit for human beings.' According to Tagore, Amritsar 'with a rude shock, revealed to our minds the helplessness of our position as British subjects in India.'[41] For Tagore, as for so many in the colonized world, the belief that 'if we [Indians] could sacrifice our lives—so I thought—in the same cause with the English soldiers [during the First World War], we should at once become real to them, and claim fairness at their hands ever after' was yet again shattered.[42] The war had not changed attitudes to empire or racial 'Others' all that much and had only made certain kinds of Britons all the more willing to enforce their empire's power and to do so by any means at their command.

Ultimately, what the Amritsar massacre revealed is how quickly the search for security in a deeply unsettled time could lead states and imperial authorities to mobilize familiar wartime (and pre-war colonial) patterns of governing, 'Othering', even killing and murdering. In so many ways, neither the armistice nor the peace treaties that were signed between 1919 and 1923 ended the imperial fears and animosities that existed before the war, or those that were awakened during the war. Reconciling these animosities with the promises and plans for constructive change, restituting past harms and building bridges proved extremely difficult.

As an example, the collapse of the Young Turk government in November 1918 briefly brought back Ottoman rule to the Middle East. For Grigoris Balakian, an Armenian priest living in the capitulated capital of Constantinople (Istanbul), peace and a return to Ottomanism meant he could come out of hiding. Peace also brought with it the hope that the collective horrors of the Turkish-led Armenian genocide might be recognized and punished by the new authorities. On 13 November 1918, Balakian disguised himself in a top hat and gentleman's jacket (to hide his Armenian identity from his Muslim neighbours, whom he still feared), and welcomed the Allied occupation forces to the city. In contrast to Balakian, the Muslim boatman who ferried him across the Bosphorus Strait that day was despondent and loudly lamented the 'black days we have fallen upon!' While Balakian and thousands of other non-Turkish residents cheered the occupation troops who marched past their homes, bedecked in Greek, French, British and Italian flags, Constantinople's Turkish population hid behind shuttered windows fearing retribution.[43]

The festivities in Constantinople on 13 November belied the enormous turmoil facing the reinstituted Ottoman regime. After the Young Turk government fled the country on 1 November, the many communities of the Middle East only faced more uncertainty. Some hoped that the Sultan might lead them out of the horrors of war, starvation and political violence to a revived Ottoman empire based on cooperative interaction between its multi-ethnic multi-religious populations. Others saw a welcome opportunity to break away from all imperial webs and establish their own autonomous countries and regimes. Many pinned their hopes to be awarded self-rule on the peace negotiations in Paris, not least since the British and French had made significant promises to the many Arab clans who had helped to defeat the Turks during the war. In the weeks and months to come, almost all of these expectations were dashed or left unrequited.

While the Ottoman regime made some attempt at reconciliation, including by acknowledging the Armenian genocide and sentencing eighteen prominent perpetrators to death, the wider task ahead was too difficult.[44] There were too many powerful forces at play, all of them quite willing to use violence to assert their authority. Armenia's leaders not only claimed statehood, but also sent representatives across Europe, the Caucasus and Central Asia to assassinate those members of the Young Turk government who had fled the country.[45] Kurdish communities mobilized their own soldiers to establish the state of Kurdistan. The Italians invaded Cicilia. The Greeks claimed Izmir, murdering, raping and exterminating the city's dominant Muslim population in the process.[46] During the Paris peace negotiations, the French and British divided most of the Arab areas into 'protectorates' over which they exercised exclusive administrative and economic control.

Between 1919 and 1923, then, the Middle East sunk back into a series of devastating civil wars. Some of these were targeted campaigns fought by nationalist Turkish forces led by Mustafa Kemal – the so-called 'hero of Gallipoli' in 1915. Others were rebellions 'from below' that rallied against the Allied occupying forces and their mandates.[47] Many were assertions of sovereignty and statehood against the Turks and the Allies alike. In Kurdistan, Kemal faced the 'worldly younger sons of tribal chieftains insisting that Turkish-Kurdish relations be settled on the basis of' Wilson's fourteen points of peace.[48] Across Persia, the Assyrian people were slaughtered or starved to death by both Kurdish and Turkish forces.[49] A new treaty, finally signed in 1923 between the Allies and the newly established state of Turkey, only brought uneasy peace to the region. Its terms included a 'population exchange' of Muslim Turks and Orthodox Greeks, so that neither state would need to deal with these 'enemies within' in the future.[50] Needless to say, the organized displacement and dispossession of millions of people did not bode well for the region's internal cohesion. A similar reality applied to the new nation-states established in central and eastern Europe as well. Displacement became a permanent feature of the twentieth-century world and another powerful legacy of the First World War.[51]

The 1923 treaty also marked the final end of the Ottoman empire, an empire which had ruled the Middle East and much of southern Europe for more than 600 years. In its wake, the Middle East remained destabilized facing a litany of competing claims to sovereignty, 'mandated' imperial rights (and claims to various oil installations), independence, religious autonomy and self-rule. All in all, the First World War politically rewired the entire region so that it remained at the forefront of international crises for decades to come.[52]

For the representatives of the victorious Allies who met in Paris in 1919, the scale of the global peacemaking task was also insurmountable. The sheer range of expectations and agendas that demanded accommodation was unprecedented. It seemed like the whole world had come to Paris expecting recognition and compensation.[53] Meanwhile, the Allied governments could barely agree on their own priorities, let alone on conceding rights and privileges to external parties or their former enemies. On the one hand, the peace process was publicly infused with the enthusiasm and expectation of President Wilson's fourteen points of peace, particularly his assertions of the rights of ethnic communities to self-determination.[54] On the other, the text of the peace agreements gave very little credence to Wilsonian idealism, non-European groups' claims to statehood or even to the promise given to Germany in November 1918 that its peace treaty would be one 'without victors or vanquished'. The negotiators in Paris could not do justice to all the competing claims in play, in part, because their own populations demanded that the enemy be 'made to pay' for the suffering they had endured during the war and in part because their own agendas were oppositional.[55] In the end, the victors' demands came first. The Allies claimed enormous sums of money from their former enemies as reparations. They reclaimed land, reimposed their own imperial power and asserted administrative control over former German and Ottoman territories and people through an international 'mandate' system supervised by the League of Nations. They also looked to re-establish economic dominance over the seas and highways of global trade. Unsurprisingly, the peace treaties left few fully satisfied.

Wilson's other peace platform – the League of Nations – did come to fruition during the peace negotiations of 1919. It seemed to provide the world with an accessible set of internationalist principles and a solid institutional structure so governments could discuss issues, negotiate agreements, mediate conflicts and work collectively towards an elusive and lasting peace. In many places, the League was very popular because it offered a new framework to cling to.[56] It was also remarkably successful in setting up an array of transnational bureaucratic initiatives coordinating humanitarian aid, scientific and medical exchanges and economic interaction.[57] In so doing, the League of Nations helped to bring a new era of internationalist interaction into being, one in which greater numbers of individuals, communities and non-government organizations played key roles.[58] Importantly, its creation reaffirmed a global commitment to a range of pre-war norms, including adherence to western concepts of international law, statehood and even the premise of internationalist cooperation. In this way the League hoped to return the international arena back to a familiar and predictable order. Yet the League's establishment also recognized how fundamentally the 1914–18 war years had unmoored the nineteenth-century premise of 'limited war', not least the use of neutrality as a functional tool to protect the world from war.[59] In place of neutrality, the League embraced the premise of 'collective security'.

The League was not a universally popular or even universally workable organization. On the one hand, it excluded too many states and governments.

Neither the Soviet Union, which was not recognized as a state by most countries, nor Germany was offered membership to begin with, the former because it refused to accept Tsarist Russia's debt and obligations, the latter because it was held responsible for the First World War's outbreak.[60] Many of the neutral states that had maintained their neutrality through the war also had trouble reconciling their desire for neutrality with the League's demands that all decisions regarding the legality of an inter-state conflict be made collectively.[61] Japan and China – both victors in the war – were incensed at the European powers' unwillingness to include a 'racial equality' clause in the League's mandate.[62] Italy, though one of the victors, gained little of what it had been promised in 1915 for its sacrifice. Once the United States Congress refused to ratify the League's covenant, even Wilson's government took no further formal part in the organization (although the United States would cooperate with many of the internationalist endeavours organized by the League in the 1920s and 1930s). Without the involvement of three of the most potentially powerful states on the planet – the United States, Germany and the Soviet Union – the League of Nations had to overcome some sizeable obstacles and would never function as an effective ballast to stabilize the crisis-torn post-war world in the way that the 'concert of Europe' had helped to stabilize the nineteenth-century world order.

At another level, while the League opened up opportunities for a range of new countries and communities to take full part in international relations, including the former British dominions, it largely failed to satisfy the demands of most colonized peoples to take part on equal terms. As such, the League was criticized for the grave inequities it continued to allow, the imperialism it continued to facilitate and the normative assumptions about western exceptionalism (and western capitalism) it continued to justify. Tan Malaka, the young Indonesian student discussed in Chapter 7, expressed his own version of these contradictions when in 1919 he responded to a Dutch commentator who proclaimed that the people subjected to Dutch colonial rule were not ready for independence. According to the commentator, colonized communities needed first to be properly educated as to what a 'nation-state' was before they could join the 'civilized world' and the League of Nations. With bitter sharpness, Malaka retorted that western concepts of 'states', 'borders' and 'property rights' sat at the heart of all the world's problems. Europeans had brought industrial imperialism, racism, the extermination of indigenous people and endless warfare and violence into the world. These same Europeans had caused the world to succumb to the tragedy that was the First World War. Instead of lecturing colonized communities, Malaka suggested the Dutch author might be better served learning about what colonialism and imperialism involved. Furthermore, he might also like to reconsider the implications of his wish that subject communities become as greedy, nationalistic and violent as their colonial rulers already proved to be.[63]

From the vantage point of November 1918, it was quite clear that the First World War had opened Pandora's box.[64] Its many transformations unmoored the principles of global and imperial governance that had enabled the world's industrial great powers to thrive in the nineteenth century. All too ironically, these same great powers were clearly responsible for the destruction they unleashed on the world. They collectively failed to prevent the war from breaking out in 1914 and their wartime policies enabled its evolution from a manageable inter-state conflict into an unrelenting monolith of total global violence. In the process, these same powers also helped to unbound the inherent inequalities embedded in the nineteenth-century world. In the war's aftermath, these inequalities were more visible and globally connected than ever before. They were now also infused with the grief and anger that the violence of the war had unleashed on the world. Sadly, many of these unbounded issues continue to plague the world today, be it in the experience of racial inequality, capitalist exploitation, the exercise of national and state prerogatives over humanitarian need or even in coordinating communities and governments to deal with a global pandemic so that as few people as possible die. The total global tragedy that evolved between 1914 and 1918 created an international environment of unsettledness that reverberates to our present. As such, the First World War is not ancient history but very much part of our collective living past.[65]

NOTES

Introduction

1 Cf Dick Stegewerns, 'The End of World War One as a Turning Point in Modern Japanese History' in Bert Edström, ed., *Turning Points in Japanese History* Japan Library, 2002, pp. 138–40; Carl Strikwerda, 'World War I in the History of Globalization' *Historical Reflections* 42, 3, 2016, p. 112; Kai Evers, David Pan, 'Introduction' in Kai Evers, David Pan, eds, *Europe and the World: World War I as Crisis of Universalism* Telos Press, 2018, pp. ix–xi; David Reynolds, *The Long Shadow: The Great War and the Twentieth Century* Simon & Shuster, 2013; Eric Hobsbawm, *Age of Extremes: The Short Twentieth Century 1914–1991* Penguin, 1994.

2 Annette Becker, 'The Great War: World War, Total War' *International Review of the Red Cross* 97, 900, 2015, p. 1029; Mustafa Aksakal, 'The Ottoman Empire' in Jay Winter, ed., *Cambridge History of the First World War* Volume 1, Cambridge University Press, 2014, p. 459.

3 Cf Alan Kramer, *Dynamic of Destruction: Culture and Mass Killing in the First World War* Oxford University Press, 2007.

4 Tim Stapleton, 'The Impact of the First World War on African People' in John Laband, ed., *Daily Lives of Civilians in Wartime Africa* Greenwood, 2007, p. 123.

5 Stapleton, 'Impact' pp. 123–4.

6 Santanu Das, *India, Empire and First World War Culture* Cambridge University Press, 2018, pp. 6–8.

7 Stephen Broadbery, Mark Harrison, 'The Economics of World War 1: An Overview' in Stephen Broadbery, Mark Harrison, eds, *The Economics of World War 1* Cambridge University Press, 2005, pp. 6–7, 10.

8 Aksakal, 'Ottoman Empire' p. 459.

9 L.T. Fawaz, *A Land of Aching Hearts: The Middle East in the Great War* Harvard University Press, 2014, p. 82.

10 Paul K. Saint-Amour, *Tense Future: Modernism, Total War, Encyclopedic Form* Oxford University Press, 2015, p. 58.

11 Léon Daudet, *La Guerre Totale* Nouvelle Librairie Nationale, 1918, p. 8.

12 Daudet, *Guerre Totale* p. 12.

13 Cf Kramer, *Dynamic*.

14 With grateful thanks to Annalise Higgins.

15 Trevor Wilson, *The Myriad Faces of War: Britain and the Great War 1914–1918* Faber & Faber, 1987.

16 Cf Heather Streets-Salter, *World War One in Southeast Asia: Colonialism and Anticolonialism in an Era of Global Conflict* Cambridge University Press, 2017,

p. 5; Melvin E. Page, 'Introduction: Black Men in a White Men's War' in Melvin E. Page, ed., *Africa and the First World War* Palgrave MacMillan, 1987, p. 1.

17 David Stevenson, *1914–1918: The History of the First World War* Penguin, 2004, p. 3.

18 Cf John Horne, 'End of a Paradigm? The Cultural History of the Great War' *Past & Present* 242, 1, 2019, pp. 155–92; Strikwerda, 'World War I' pp. 112–32. Cf Maartje Abbenhuis, Gordon Morrell, *The First Age of Industrial Globalization: An International History 1815–1918* Bloomsbury, 2019.

19 Cf Stéphane Audoin-Rouzeau, '1915: Stalemate' in Winter, ed., *Cambridge History* Volume 1, p. 87.

20 Peter Gatrell, 'The Epic and the Domestic: Women and War in Russia, 1914–1917' in Gail Braybon, ed., *Evidence, History and the Great War* Berghahn, 2003, pp. 198–215.

21 Lawrence Sondhaus, *World War One: The Global Revolution* Cambridge University Press, 2011, p. 2.

22 Roger Chickering, Stig Förster, *Great War, Total War: Combat and Mobilization on the Western Front* Cambridge University Press, 2000; Hew Strachan, 'On Total War and Modern War' *International History Review* 2, 22, 2000, pp. 253–504; Talbot Imlay, 'Total War' *Journal of Strategic Studies* 30, 3, 2007, pp. 547–70; William J. Philpott, 'Total War' in Matthew Hughes, William J. Philpott, eds, *Palgrave Advances in Modern Military History* Palgrave MacMillan, 2006, pp. 131–52.

23 Saint-Amour, *Tense Future* pp. 55–6; Imlay, 'Total War' p. 548; Bart Ziino, 'Total War in Australia: Civilian Mobilisation and Commitment' in Kate Ariotti, James Bennett, eds, *Australians and the First World War* Palgrave MacMillan, 2017, pp. 165–82.

24 As quoted in Imlay, 'Total War' p. 556.

25 Cf Jeremy Black, *The Age of Total War, 1860–1945* Rowman & Littlefield, 2010, pp. 5–6.

26 William Mulligan, 'Total War' *War in History* 15, 2, 2008, pp. 211–21.

27 Georges Clemenceau declaration to the French Senate, 20 November 1917, in Jean Garrigues, *Le Monde Selon Clemenceau* Tallandier, 2014, p. 237.

28 Saint-Amour, *Tense Future*.

29 Cf Maartje Abbenhuis, 'On the Edge of the Storm? Situating Switzerland's Neutrality in the Context of the First World War' in Michael M. Olsansky, ed., *Am Rande des Sturms: das Schweizer Militär im Ersten Weltkrieg* Hier und Jetz, 2018, pp. 27–9.

30 Jennifer D. Keene, 'W.E.B. Du Bois and the Wounded World: Seeking Meaning in the First World War for African-Americans' *Peace & Change* 26, 2, 2001, pp. 135–52; Xu Guoqi, 'Asia' in Winter, ed., *Cambridge History* Volume 1, p. 487.

31 Maartje Abbenhuis, *An Age of Neutrals: Great Power Politics 1815–1914* Cambridge University Press, 2014.

32 Abbenhuis, Morrell, *First Age*.

33 Maartje Abbenhuis, 'A Most Useful Tool of Diplomacy and Statecraft: Neutrality and Europe in the "Long" Nineteenth Century 1815–1914' *International History Review* 35, 1, 2013, pp. 1–22.

34 Michael Geyer, 'War and the Context of General History in an Age of Total War' and Michael Howard, 'World War One: The Crisis in European History'

both in *Journal of Military History* 57, 5, 1993, pp. 145–63; John Keegan, *Intelligence in War* Pimlico, 2003, p. 369.

35 C. H. Stockton, 'The Declaration of Paris' *American Journal of International Law* 14, 3, 1920, p. 357.

36 Abbenhuis, Morrell, *First Age*.

37 Aksakal, 'Ottoman Empire' p. 462.

38 Derek Aldcroft, *The European Economy 1914–1990* Routledge, 2001, p. 20.

39 Kathleen Burk, *Britain, America and the Sinews of War 1914–1918* George Allen & Unwin, 1985; Masato Kimura, 'Securing Maritime Trade: Triangular Frictions between the Merchant Marines of the US, UK and Japan' in T. Minohara, T. Hon, E. Dawley, eds, *The Decade of the Great War: Japan and the Wider World in the 1910s* Brill, 2014, pp. 107–29.

40 Jörn Leonhard, *Pandora's Box: A History of the First World War* Belknap, 2018; Hew Strachan, *The First World War Volume 1: To Arms* Oxford University Press, 2001. Also: Stevenson, *1914–1918*.

41 Jay Winter, ed., *Cambridge History of the First World War*. Three volumes Cambridge University Press, 2014; John Horne, ed., *A Companion to World War I* Wiley-Blackwell, 2010.

42 Cf Christian Gerlach, 'Extremely Violent Societies: An Alternative to the Concept of Genocide' *Journal of Genocide Research* 8, 4, 2006, pp. 455–71.

43 Cf Christopher Barber, 'Nineteenth-Century Statecraft and the Politics of Moderation in the Franco-Prussian War' *European Review of History* 21, 1, 2014, pp. 1–17.

44 Jürgen Osterhammel, *The Transformation of the World: A Global History of the Nineteenth Century* Princeton University Press, 2014, p. 119.

45 Cf C. Paul Vincent, *The Politics of Hunger: The Allied Blockade of Germany 1915–1919* Ohio University Press, 1985.

46 John Horne in Audoin-Rouzeau, '1915' p. 87; Becker, 'Great War'.

47 Jay Winter, 'War and Anxiety in 1917' in Maartje Abbenhuis, Neill Atkinson, Kingsley Baird, Gail Romano, eds, *The Myriad Legacies of 1917: A Year of War and Revolution* Palgrave, 2018, p. 15.

48 Michael Neiberg, '1917: Global War' in Winter, ed., *Cambridge History* Volume 1, p. 130.

Chapter 1

1 Abbenhuis, Morrell, *First Age* p. 127. Also: Niels Eichhorn, 'A "Century of Peace" That Was Not: War in the Nineteenth Century' *Journal of Military History* 84, 4, 2020, pp. 1051–77.

2 Cf Oona Hathaway, Scott Shapiro, 'International Law and Its Transformation through the Outlawry of War' *International Affairs* 95, 1, 2019, pp. 45–8.

3 Abbenhuis, *Age* pp. 15–16.

4 Paul Kennedy, *The Rise and Fall of the Great Powers* Penguin, 1987, p. 150.

5 Abbenhuis, *Age* pp. 72–3.

6 Stockton, 'Declaration' p. 357.

7 For more: Jan Lemnitzer, *Power, Law and the End of Privateering* Palgrave MacMillan, 2014.

8 For more: Emily Crawford, 'The Enduring Legacy of the St Petersburg Declaration: Distinction, Military Necessity and the Prohibition of Causing Unnecessary Suffering and Superfluous Injury in IHL' *Journal of the History of International Law* 20, 4, 2019, pp. 544–66.

9 For more: Maartje Abbenhuis, *The Hague Conferences in International Politics, 1898–1915* Bloomsbury, 2019.

10 William Mulligan, 'Justifying International Action: International Law, The Hague and Diplomacy' in Maartje Abbenhuis, Christopher Barber, Annalise Higgins, eds, *War, Peace and International Order: The Legacies of the Hague Conferences of 1899 and 1907* Routledge, 2017, pp. 12–30; Daniel Segesser, '"Unlawful Warfare Is Uncivilized": The International Debate on the Punishment of War Crimes, 1872–1918' *European Review of History* 14, 2, 2007, pp. 215–34.

11 Cf James Sheehan, *Where Have All the Soldiers Gone?* Houghton Mifflin, 2008, p. 41; Michael Paris, *Warrior Nation: Images of War in British Popular Culture, 1850–2000* Reaktion, 2000.

12 Antoinette Burton, *The Trouble with Empire* Oxford University Press, 2015.

13 Martin Van Bruinessen, 'A Kurdish Warlord on the Turkish-Persian Frontier in the Early Twentieth Century: Isma'il Aqa Simko' in Touraj Atabaki, ed., *Iran and the First World War: Battleground of the Great Powers* I.B. Tauris, 2006, pp. 69–93.

14 With thanks to Charlotte MacDonald.

15 For more: Marilyn Lake, Henry Reynolds, *Drawing the Global Color Line: White Man's Countries and the International Challenge of Racial Equality* Cambridge University Press, 2012.

16 G.W. Gong, *The Standard of 'Civilization' in International Society* Clarendon Press, 1984.

17 Andrew Fitzmaurice, 'Context in the History of International Law' *Journal of the History of International Law* 20, 1, 2018, pp. 5–30.

18 John Pollock, *Kitchener: The Road to Omdurman and Saviour of the Nation* Hachete, 2013.

19 *Mataura Ensign* 579, 4 May 1899, p. 5; 'Impressions and Opinions' *Anglo-Saxon Review* 1, June 1899, pp. 244–55, quotes on p. 248.

20 For more: Abbenhuis, *Hague Conferences* esp. Chapter 1.

21 Marco Gerbig-Fabel, 'Photographic Artefacts of War 1904–1905: The Russo-Japanese War as Transnational Media Event' *European Review of History* 15, 6, 2008, pp. 629–42. With thanks to Steven Sheldon, Hemi David and Leon Ostick for sharing their research on this subject.

22 Douglas Howland, 'Sovereignty and the Laws of War: International Consequences of Japan's 1905 Victory over Russia' *Law and History Review* 29, 1, 2011, pp. 53–97.

23 *Japan Times* 5 July 1904, p. 3.

24 Howland, 'Sovereignty'; Abbenhuis, *Age* pp. 209–10.

25 Chris Williams, 'The Shadow in the East: Representations of the Russo-Japanese War in Newspaper Cartoons' *Media History* 23, 3–4, 2017, pp. 312–29.

26 Cf Simon Partner, 'Peasants into Citizens? The Meiji Village in the Russo-Japanese War' *Monumenta Nipponica* 62, 2, 2007, pp. 178–206; Rotem Kowner, 'Becoming an Honorary Civilized Nation: Remaking Japan's Military Image during the Russo-Japanese War, 1904–1905' *Historian* 64, 1, 2001, pp. 19–38.

27 David Crowley, 'Seeing Japan, Imagining Poland: Polish Art and the Russo-Japanese War' *Russian Review* 67, 1, January 2008, pp. 50–69, esp. pp. 53–5.

28 Rosa Luxemburg, 'In the Storm' 1904, quoted in Crowley, 'Seeing Japan' p. 55.

29 As exceptions see: Harold Z. Schiffring, 'The Impact of the War on China' and Guy Podoler, Michael Robinson, 'On the Confluence of History and Memory: The Significance of the War for Korea' in Rotem Kowner, ed., *The Impact of the Russo-Japanese War* Routledge, 2007, pp. 169–98.

30 E. Suk Kwon, 'An Unfulfilled Expectation: Britain's Response to the Question of Korean Independence' *International Journal of Korean History* 23, 1, 2018, p. 42.

31 Paul A. Roddell, 'Southeast Asian Nationalism and the Russo-Japanese War: Re-examining Assumptions' *Southeast Review of Asian Studies* 29, 2007, pp. 20–40.

32 With thanks to Norberto Barreto Velazquez.

33 Jon D. Carlson, 'Postcards and Propaganda: Cartographic Postcards as Soft News Images of the Russo-Japanese War' *Political Communication* 26, 2, 2009, pp. 212–37.

34 Reginald Kearney, 'The Pro-Japanese Utterances of W.E.B. Du Bois' *Contributions in Black Studies* 13, 7, 1995, pp. 1–17; Steven G. Marks, 'Bravo, Brave Tiger of the East! The Russo-Japanese War and the Rise of Nationalism in British Egypt and India' in John W. Steinberg, Bruce W. Menning, David Schimelpenninck Van Der Oye, Shinji Yokote, eds, *Russo-Japanese War in Global Perspective: World War Zero* Brill, 2005, pp. 609–28; Yitzhak Shichor, 'Ironies of History: The War and the Origins of East Asian Radicalism' in Rotem Kowner, ed., *The Impact of the Russo-Japanese War* Routledge, 2007, pp. 199–218.

35 As quoted in Marks, 'Bravo' p. 612.

36 As an example: H.F. Baldwin, *A War Photographer in Thrace* T.F. Unwin, 1913.

37 Kramer, *Dynamic* pp. 136–7.

38 Uğur Ümit Üngör, 'Mass Violence against Civilians during the Balkan Wars' in Dominik Geppert, William Mulligan, Andreas Rose, eds, *The Wars before the Great War: Conflict and International Politics before the Outbreak of the First World War* Cambridge University Press, 2015, pp. 76–91.

39 For example: *Berliner Volkszeitung* 22 October 1912, p. 1; *Altonär Nachrichten* (Hamburg) 22 October 1912, p. 1.

40 George F. Kennan, ed., *The Other Balkan Wars. A 1913 Carnegie Endowment Inquiry in Retrospect with a New Introduction and Reflections on the Present Conflict* Carnegie Endowment of International Peace, 1993.

41 *Sumatra Post* 1 July 1914, p. 2.

42 Michael Neiberg, *Dance of the Furies: European and the Outbreak of World War I* Harvard University Press, 2011. Also: Daniel Rouven Steinbach, 'Defending the *Heimat*' in Heather Jones, Jennifer O'Brien, Christian Schmidt-Supprian, eds, *Untold War: New Perspectives in First World War Studies* Brill, 2008, p. 188.

43 Pavlina Bobiç, *War and Faith: The Catholic Church in Slovenia 1914–1918* Brill, 2012, p. 15.

44 F.R. Dickinson, *War and National Reinvention: Japan and the Great War 1914–1919* Harvard University Press, 1999, p. 33.

45 For more: Michael Neiberg, *Fighting the Great War: A Global History* Harvard University Press, 2005, pp. 2–4; Neiberg, *Dance*; Catriona Pennell, *A Kingdom United: Popular Responses to the Outbreak of the First World War in Britain and Ireland* Oxford University Press, 2013; David Welch, *Germany, Propaganda and Total War, 1914–1918* Athlone Press, 2000, pp. 136–48; Joshua Sandborn, *Drafting the Russian Nation: Military Conscription, Total War and Mass Politics 1905–1925* Northern Illinois University Press, 2003, pp. 29–30.

46 Neiberg, *Dance* pp. 4–5.

47 Thomas Munro, 'The Hague as a Framework for British and American Newspapers' Public Presentations of the First World War' in Abbenhuis et al., eds, *War, Peace* pp. 155–70.

48 Cf Welch, *Germany* p. 12.

49 Welch, *Germany*, pp. 12–14; Hans F. Peterson, *Power and International Order* Skånska Centraltryckeriet, 1964, p. 3.

50 Melissa Kirschke Stockdale, *Mobilizing the Russian Nation: Patriotism and Citizenship in the First World War* Cambridge University Press, 2016, p. 15.

51 Ismee Tames, '*Oorlog voor onze gedachten*': *Oorlog, neutraliteit en identiteit in het Nederlandse publieke debat, 1914–1918* Verloren, 2006, p. 34.

Chapter 2

1 For an accessible overview: 'World War I: Declarations of War from around the Globe' Law Library, Library of Congress, https://www.loc.gov/law/help/digitized-books/world-war-i-declarations/foreign.php (accessed July 2020).

2 Holger H. Herwig, 'Through the Looking Glass' *Historian* 77, 2, 2015, pp. 290–314.

3 Paul Schroeder, *The Transformation of European Politics: 1763–1848* Clarendon Press, 1994, p. 564.

4 Cf Paul W. Schroeder, David Wetzel, Robert Jervis, Jack S. Levy, eds, *Systems, Stability, and Statecraft: Essays on the International History of Modern Europe* Palgrave Macmillan, 2004.

5 John Horne, Alan Kramer, *German Atrocities, 1914: A History of Denial* Yale University Press, 2001.

6 Stefan Rinke, *Latin America and the First World War* Cambridge University Press, 2017, p. 90.

7 Cf Isabel V. Hull, *Absolute Destruction: Military Culture and the Practices of War in Imperial Germany* Cornell University Press, 2013.

8 Isabel V. Hull, *A Scrap of Paper: Breaking and Making International Law during the Great War* Cornell University Press, 2014, p. 43.

9 Hull, *Scrap* p. 43.

10 Emily Robertson, 'Norman Lindsay and the "Asianisation" of the German Soldier in Australia during the First World War' *The Round Table* 103, 2, 2014, pp. 211–31.

11 Maartje Abbenhuis, 'Not Silent, nor Silenced: Neutrality and the First World War' in José-Leonardo Ruiz Sánchez, Immaculada Cordero Olivero, Carolina García Sanz, eds, *Shaping Neutrality Throughout the First World War* Editorial Universidad de Sevilla, 2016, pp. 17–36.

12 *De Telegraaf*, 1 August 1914, np.
13 Bruno Cabanes, *August 1914: France, the Great War, and a Month That Changed the World* Yale University Press, 2016, p. 67.
14 Cited in Cabanes, *August 1914* p. 66.
15 Cited in Cabanes, *August 1914* p. 69.
16 Horne, Kramer, *Atrocities*. Also: Kramer, *Dynamic*.
17 Sophie de Schaepdrijver, *De Groote Oorlog: Het Koninkrijk België Tijdens de Eerste Wereldoorlog* Atlas, 1997, p. 87. Cf Alberto Tuscano, '"America's Belgium": W.E.B. Du Bois on Race, Class, and the Origins of World War I' in Alexander Anievas, ed., *Cataclysm 1914: The First World War and the Making of Modern World Politics* Brill, 2015, pp. 236–57.
18 Horne, Kramer, *Atrocities*.
19 Schaepdrijver, *Oorlog* p. 69.
20 Stevenson, *1914–1918* p. 45. For more on the Schlieffen Plan: Hans Ehlert, Michael Epkenhans, Gerhard Gross, David Zabecki, eds, *The Schlieffen Plan: International Perspectives on the German Strategy for World War I* University Press of Kentucky, 2014.
21 Cited in Horne, Kramer, *Atrocities* pp. 18–19.
22 Ewoud Kieft, *Oorlogsenthousiasme: Europa 1900–1918* De Bezige Bij, 2015, p. 357.
23 Kramer, *Dynamic* p. 21.
24 Cited in Mary Fulbrook, *Dissonant Lives: Generations and Violence through the German Dictatorships* Oxford University Press, 2011, p. 33.
25 General Hans von Beseler, 23 August 1914, cited in Horne, Kramer, *Atrocities* p. 156.
26 Cited in Horne, Kramer, *Atrocities* p. 156.
27 Cited in Horne, Kramer, *Atrocities* p. 156.
28 Quoted in Elisabeth Fairman, ed., *Doomed Youth: The Poetry and the Pity of the First World War* Exhibition Catalog, Yale Center for British Art, 1999, p. 3. Cf Sophie de Schaepdrijver, 'Belgium' in *1914–1918 Online* https://encyclopedia.1914–1918-online.net/article/belgium (accessed November 2020).
29 Jan P. Ramos as quoted in Rinke, *Latin America* p. 215.
30 Cf Daniel Segesser, 'Dissolve or Punish? The International Debate among Jurists and Publicists on the Consequences of the Armenian Genocide for the Ottoman Empire, 1915–1923' *Journal of Genocide Research* 10, 1, 2008, p. 99.
31 As an example: Alexander Watson, 'Unheard-of Brutality: Russian Atrocities against Civilians in East Prussia, 1914–1915' *Journal of Modern History* 86, 4, 2014, pp. 780–825.
32 Robert Melson, 'A Theoretical Inquiry into the Armenian Massacres of 1894–1896' *Comparative Studies in Society and History* 24, 3, 1982, pp. 481–509.
33 Michael Godby, 'Confronting Horror: Emily Hobhouse and the Concentration Camp Photographs of the South African War' *Kronos* 32, 2006, pp. 34–8; Nadine Akhund, 'The Two Carnegie Reports: From the Balkan Expedition of 1913 to the Albanian Trip of 1921: A Comparative Approach' *Balkanologie* 14, 1–2, 2012, pp. 1–17.
34 Ismee Tames, '"War on Our Minds": War, Neutrality and Identity in Dutch Public Debate during the First World War' *First World War Studies* 3, 2, 2012, pp. 201–16.
35 Abbenhuis, 'Silent' p. 28.

36 Frank Trommler, 'The Lusitania Effect: America's Mobilization against Germany in World War I' *German Studies Review* 32, 2, 2009, pp. 241–66; Michael S. Neiberg, *The Path to War: How the First World War Created Modern America* Oxford University Press, 2016.

37 As examples: L. Mokveld, *De Overweldiging van België: Ervaringen, als Nederlandsch Journalist Opgedaan* np, 1916; L.H. Grondijs, *Een Nederlander in Geteisterd België* Amsterdam, 1914.

38 As an example: R. A. Reiss and Fanny S. Copeland, *Report upon the Atrocities Committed by the Austro-Hungarian Army during the First Invasion of Serbia,* 1916. Also: Sofi Qvarnström, 'Recognizing the Other: The Armenian Genocide in Scandinavian Literature' in Claes Ahlund, ed., *Scandinavia in the First World War: Studies in the War Experience of the Northern Neutrals* Nordic Academic Press, 2012, pp. 177–98.

39 Abbenhuis, *Hague* pp. 113–14.

40 Chad R. Fulwider, *German Propaganda and U.S. Neutrality in World War I* Missouri University Press, 2015.

41 Cf Fulwider, *German Propaganda*; David Welch, *Germany, Propaganda and Total War: The Sins of Omission* Athlone Press, 2000.

42 For more: Tames, *Oorlog.*

43 Tames, 'War' p. 302.

44 A. A. H. Struycken, *Oorlog en het Volkenrecht* 1915, np.

45 Tames, 'War'; Ahlund, ed., *Scandinavia.*

46 John Macdonell, 'Silent Neutrals' *Contemporary Review* 107, 1915, pp. 67–75; Abbenhuis, 'Silent'.

47 Tames, 'War'.

48 Horne, Kramer, *Atrocities* p. 198.

49 Horne, Kramer, *Atrocities* p. 201.

50 Cited in Nicoletta F. Gullace, 'Sexual Violence and Family Honor: British Propaganda and International Law during the First World War' *American Historical Review* 102, 3, 1997, p. 714.

51 Gullace, 'Violence' p. 716.

52 Horne, Kramer, *Atrocities* p. 199.

53 Eugene W. Chiu, 'The First World War and Its Impact on Chinese Concepts of Modernity' in Jan Schmidt, Katja Schmidtpott, eds, *The East Asian Dimension of the First World War* Campus, 2020, pp. 93–4.

54 Susan R. Grayzel, *Women's Identities at War: Gender, Motherhood, and Politics in Britain and France during the First World War* North Carolina University Press, 1999, p. 82.

55 On the German occupations in Eastern Europe: Vejas Gabriel Liulevicius, *War Land on the Eastern Front: Culture, National Identity, and German Occupation* Cambridge University Press, 2004.

56 Stéphane Audoin-Rouzeau, Annette Becker, eds, *14–18: Understanding the Great War* Hill and Wang, 2004, p. 9; Lina Sturfelt, 'The Call of the Blood: Scandinavia and the First World War as a Clash of Races' in Ahlund, ed., *Scandinavia* p. 199.

57 As quoted in Rinke, *Latin America* p. 89.

58 Maartje Abbenhuis, *The Art of Staying Neutral: The Netherlands in the First World War 1914–1918* Amsterdam University Press, 2006.

59 Abbenhuis, *Art.*

60 Sophie de Schaepdrijver, ed., *'We Who Are So Cosmopolitan': The War Diary of Constance Graeffe, 1914–1915* Archives Générales du Royaume, 2008.

61 Pierre Purseigle, '"A Wave on to Our Shores": The Exile and Resettlement of Refugees from the Western Front, 1914–1918' *Contemporary European History* 16, 4, 2007, pp. 427–44.

62 See for example Branden Little, 'An Explosion of New Endeavours. Global Humanitarian Responses to Industrialized Warfare in the First World War Era' *First World War Studies* 5, 1, 2014, pp. 1–16.

63 Elisabeth Piller, 'American War Relief, Cultural Mobilization and the Myth of Impartial Humanitarianism 1914–1917' *Journal of the Gilded Age and Progressive Era* 17, 4, 2018, pp. 619–35.

64 Purseigle, 'Wave'. For Russia: Peter Gatrell, *A Whole Empire Walking: Refugees in Russia during World War I* Indiana University Press, 2005.

65 Sophie de Schaepdrijver, 'The Long Shadow of the "German Atrocities" of 1914' *The British Library* 29, 2014 https://www.bl.uk/world-war-one/articles/historiography-atrocities-the-long-shadow (accessed November 2020); Sandi Cooper, 'The Guns of August and the Doves of Italy: Intervention and Internationalism' *Peace & Change* 7, 2, 1981, p. 34.

66 *The Times*, 10 September 1914, cited in Gullace, 'Violence' p. 743. For more on the complex responses to the British mobilization for war in India: Das, *India*.

67 'Belgian Flag Honored' *Poverty Bay Herald* 7 October 1914, p. 8. With thanks to Pierre Purseigle.

68 'Belgian Flag Honored' p. 8.

69 For more on the Maori war effort, see: Monty Soutar, *Whitiki! Whiti! Whiti! E! Maori in the First World War* Bateman Books, 2019.

70 Jangkhomang Guite, Thongkholal Haokip, 'Introduction' in J. Guite, T. Haokip, eds, *The Anglo-Kuki War, 1917–1919* Routledge, 2019, p. 17.

71 Guite, Haokip, 'Introduction' p. 17.

72 D. van Galen Last, *Black Shame. African Soldiers in Europe, 1914–1922* Bloomsbury, 2016, p. 36. For more on the racialization of non-European soldiers in France and Britain, see: Santanu Das, ed., *Race, Empire and First World War Writing* Cambridge University Press, 2011.

73 B. Kiernan, *Blood and Soil: A World History of Genocide and Extermination from Sparta to Darfur* Yale University Press, 2007, pp. 382–7.

74 Jeremy Silvester, Jan-Bart Gewald, eds, *Words Cannot Be Found: German Colonial Rule in Namibia: An Annotated Reprint of the 1918 Blue Book* Brill, 2003, p. 100.

75 Cf Mads Bomholt Nielsen, 'Delegitimating Empire: German and British Representations of Colonial Violence, 1918–1919' *International History Review* 42, 4, 2020, pp. 833–50.

76 Silvester, Gewald, eds, *Words* p. xxxii.

Chapter 3

1 Both quotes in Jane M. Rausch, *Colombia and World War I: The Experience of a Neutral Latin American Nation during the Great War and Its Aftermath, 1914–1921* Lexington Books, 2014, p. 26.

2   Hull, *Scrap* p. 37. Cf John W. Young, 'Emotions and the British Government's Decision for War in 1914' *Diplomacy & Statecraft* 29, 4, 2018, pp. 543–64.

3   Cf Matthew S. Seligmann, 'Failing to Prepare for the Great War? The Absence of Grand Strategy in British War Planning before 1914' *War in History* 24, 4, 2017, pp. 414–37.

4   Holger Herwig, 'Germany and the "Short-War" Illusion: Toward a New Interpretation?' *Journal of Military History* 66, 3, 2002, pp. 681–93; Jakob Zollmann, *Naulila 1914: World War I in Angola and International Law* Nomos, 2016, p. 163.

5   William Philpott, 'Squaring the Circle: The Higher Coordination of the Entente in the Winter of 1915–1916' *English Historical Review* 114, 458, 1999, pp. 875–7.

6   Cf Mark Bailey, 'Supporting the Wartime Economy: Imperial Maritime Trade and the Globalized Maritime Trade System 1914–1916' *Journal of Maritime Research* 19, 1, 2017, pp. 23–45; Virginia Haufler, *Dangerous Commerce: Insurance and the Management of International Risk* Cornell University Press, 1997, p. 34.

7   Hartmut Pogge Von Strandmann, 'The Mood in Britain in 1914' in L. Kettenacker, T. Riotte, eds, *The Legacies of Two World Wars: European Societies in the Twentieth Century* Berghahn, 2011, pp. 68–9, 72.

8   Broadberry, Harrison, 'Economics' pp. 6–7.

9   Kathryn Meyer, 'Trade and Nationality at Shanghai upon the Outbreak of the First World War 1914–1915' *International History Review* 10, 2, 1988, pp. 238–60.

10 Meyer, 'Trade' p. 238.

11 Meyer, 'Trade'.

12 Global banking systems were similarly affected: Strikwerda, 'World War I' p. 121.

13 Meyer, 'Trade'; D.K. Lieu, *The Growth and Industrialization of Shanghai* China Institute of Economic and Statistical Research, 1936, esp. pp. 11, 19, 23.

14 For an excellent overview of these global ramifications: Richard Roberts, 'A Tremendous Panic: The Global Financial Crisis of 1914' in Andrew Smith, Simon Mollan, Kevin D. Tennent, eds, *The Impact of the First World War on International Business* Routledge, 2017, pp. 121–41.

15 Martin Horn, *Britain, France, and the Financing of the First World War* McGill-Queen's University Press, 2002, p. 29; Bailey, 'Supporting' p. 28.

16 Bill Albert, *South America and the First World War: The Impact of War on Brazil, Argentina, Peru and Chile* Cambridge University Press, 1988, p. 1. Also: Abbenhuis, Morrell, *First Age* pp. 185–6.

17 Eric L. Jones, *Revealed Biodiversity: An Economic History of the Human Impact* World Scientific Publication, 2014, pp. xxix–xxx.

18 Albert, *South America*.

19 Ushisaburo Kobayashi, *The Basic Industries and Social History of Japan 1914–1918* Yale University Press, 1930.

20 Cf Roberts, 'Tremendous' p. 135.

21 'Cotton Mills in China' *Journal of the Royal Society of Arts* 9 July 1915, p. 769.

22 Akinjide Osuntokun, 'Disaffection and Revolts in Nigeria during the First World War, 1914–1918' *Canadian Journal of African Studies* 5, 2, 1971, pp. 171–81.

23 Peterson, *Power* p. 6.
24 Horn, *Britain, France* p. 26.
25 Bailey, 'Supporting' p. 29.
26 Horn, *Britain, France* p. 27. Also: Eric W. Osborne, *Britain's Economic Blockade of Germany 1914–1918* Frank Cass, 2004, p. 58.
27 Albert, *South America* p. 43.
28 Osborne, *Britain's* p. 61.
29 Marc Frey, 'Trade, Ships and the Neutrality of the Netherlands in the First World War' *International History Review* 19, 3, 1997, p. 543.
30 M. L. Sanders, Philip Taylor, *British Propaganda in the First World War 1914–1918* Macmillan, 1982, p. 19.
31 Nik Brandal, Ola Teige, 'The Secret Battlefield: Intelligence and Counter-Intelligence in Scandinavia during the First World War' in Claes Ahlund, ed., *Scandinavia in the First World War: Studies in the War Experience of the Northern Neutrals* Nordic Academic Press, 2012, p. 85.
32 Anne Samson, 'East and Central Africa' in *1914–1918 Online* doi: 10.15463/ ie1418.10851; Ingeborg Vijgen, *Tussen Mandaat En Kolonie: Rwanda, Burundi En Het Belgische Bestuur in Opdracht van de Volkenbond (1916–1932)* Acco, 2005, p. 52.
33 Richard Hough, *Falklands 1914: The Pursuit of Admiral von Spee* Periscope, 2003, p. 47; Leonhard, *Pandora's Box* pp. 173–4; Allen F. Roberts, 'Insidious Conquests: Wartime Politics along the South-Western Shore of Lake Tanganyika' in Melvin Page, ed., *Africa and the First World War* Palgrave MacMillan, 1987, pp. 193–4.
34 Vijgen, *Tussen Mandaat* p. 51.
35 Charles Stephenson, *Germany's Asia-Pacific Empire* Boydell Press, 2009, p. 100.
36 Steinbach, 'Defending the *Heimat*' pp. 179–208.
37 P.H. Ritter as quoted in Abbenhuis, *Art* p. 61.
38 Ahmad Rida, diary entry 3 August 1914, as quoted in Eugene Rogan, *The Fall of the Ottomans: The Great War in the Middle East 1914–1920* Penguin, 2015, p. 55.
39 Michelle Moyd, 'We Don't Want to Die for Nothing': Askari at War in German East-Africa, 1914–1918' in Santanu Das, ed., *Race, Empire and First World War Writing* Cambridge University Press, 2011, p. 90.
40 Bill Nasson, 'Africa', in Jay Winter, ed., *Cambridge History of the First World War* Volume 1, Cambridge University Press, 2014, pp. 445–6.
41 Alison Fletcher, 'Recruitment and Service of Maori Soldiers in World War One' *Itinerario* 38, 3, 2014, pp. 59–78.
42 Jennifer D. Keene, 'North America' in Winter, ed., *Cambridge History* Volume 1, p. 523; Guoqi, 'Asia' p. 487; Samuel Furphy, 'Aboriginal Australians and the Home Front' in Kate Ariotti, James Bennett, eds, *Australians and the First World War: Local-Global Connections and Contexts* Palgrave MacMillan, 2017, pp. 143–64; Reena N. Goldthree, 'A Greater Enterprise than the Panama Canal: Migrant Labor and Military Recruitment in the World War I-Era Circum-Caribbean' *Labor* 13, 3–4, 2016, pp. 63–4.
43 Das, *India* p. 41.

44 For example: Humayun Ansari, '"Tasting the King's Salt": Muslims Contested Loyalties and the First World War' in Hannah Ewence, Tim Grady, eds, *Minorities and the First World War* Palgrave MacMillan, 2017, pp. 33–61.

45 Streets-Salter, *World War One*.

46 Horn, *Britain, France* p. 63.

47 Antonio Salandra, October 1914, in William A. Renzi, 'Italy's Neutrality and Entrance into the Great War: A Re-Examination' *American Historical Review* 73, 5, 1968, p. 1415, fn. 7.

48 Bobič, *War* p. 47.

49 Kramer, *Dynamic* p. 50.

50 Rik Verwast, *Van Den Haag tot Geneve: België en het Internationale Oorlogsrecht 1874–1950* Die Keure, pp. 80–4.

51 Vijgen, *Tussen Mandaat* p. 72.

52 Bruinessen, 'A Kurdish Warlord' pp. 69–93.

53 S. Cronin, 'Iranian Nationalism and the Government Gendarmerie' in Touraj, ed., *Iran* pp. 43–67.

54 T. Atabaki, 'The First World War, Great Power Rivalries and the Emergence of a Political Community in Iran' and M. Ettehadiyyeh, 'The Iranian Provisional Government' both in Touraj, ed., *Iran* pp. 1–7, 9–27; Kristian Coates Ulrichsen, 'The British Occupation of Mesopotamia 1914–1922' *Journal of Strategic Studies* 30, 2, 2007, pp. 349–77.

55 Kaveh Ehsani, 'Oil, State and Society in Iran in the Aftermath of the First World War' in T. G. Fraser, ed., *The First World War and Its Aftermath: The Shaping of the Middle East* Gingko Library, 2015, pp. 191–207.

56 Dickinson, *War* p. 36.

57 J. Charles Schenking, 'The Imperial Japanese Navy and the First World War' in T. Minohara, T. Hon, E. Dawley, eds, *The Decade of the Great War: Japan and the Wider World in the 1910s* Brill, 2014, pp. 83–106; A. Morgan Young, *Japan under Taisho Tenno 1912–1926* George Allen, 1928, pp. 73–4; Wendy Matsumura, 'The Expansion of the Japanese Empire and the Rise of the Global Agrarian Question after the First World War' in Alexander Anievas, ed., *Cataclysm 1914: The First World War and the Making of Modern World Politics* Brill, 2015, p. 146.

58 John D. Meehan, 'From Alliance to Conference: The British Empire, Japan and Pacific Multilateralism 1911–1921' in Minohara et al., eds, *The Decade* p. 51.

59 Guoqi, 'Asia' p. 483.

60 Guoqi, 'Asia' p. 483.

61 Kramer, *Dynamic* p. 144.

62 Aksakal, 'Ottoman Empire' p. 473.

63 Bailey, 'Supporting' p. 29.

64 Erik-Jan Zürcher, 'Introduction' in Erik-Jan Zürcher, ed., *Jihad and Islam in World War 1: Studies on the Ottoman Jihad on the Centenary of Snouck Hurgronje's 'Holy War Made Germany'* Leiden University Press, 2016, p. 14.

65 Zürcher, 'Introduction' p. 17. Becker, 'Great War'.

66 Aksakal, 'Ottoman Empire' pp. 473–4.

67   Streets-Salter, *World War One* pp. 80–2.
68   Stapleton, 'Impact' p. 122.
69   Zürcher, 'Introduction' p. 22.
70   Bruinessen, 'A Kurdish', p. 70.
71   Kramer, *Dynamic* p. 140.
72   Gerhard Senft, 'Resistance against the War of 1914–1918' in G. Bischof, F. Karlhofer, S.R. Williamson, eds, *1914: Austria-Hungary, the Origins, and the First Year of World War* University of New Orleans Press, 2014, p. 187.
73   Stevenson, *1914–1918* p. 92.
74   Stevenson, *1914–1918* p. 96.

Chapter 4

1   Vincent, *Politics* p. 18.
2   Kennedy, *Rise* p. 262; Leonhard, *Pandora's Box* p. 192.
3   Frank Trentmann, 'Coping with Shortage: The Problem of Food Security and Global Visions of Coordination, c. 1890s–1950' in Frank Trentmann, Flemming Just, eds, *Food and Conflict in Europe in the Age of Two World Wars* Palgrave, 2006, p. 16.
4   Leonhard, *Pandora's Box* pp. 227–8; Keith Neilson, 'The Maritime Way in Munitions: The Entente and Supply in the First World War' *Journal of Military and Strategic Studies* 14, 3 & 4, 2012, p. 6.
5   Marjorie Milbank Farrar, *Conflict and Compromise: The Strategy, Politics and Diplomacy of the French Blockade 1914–1918* Martinus Nijhoff, 1974; Hew Strachan, '1915: The Search for Solutions' in John Crawford, David Littlewood, James Watson, eds, *Experience of a Lifetime: People, Personalities and Leaders in the First World War* Massey University Press, 2016, pp. 14–15.
6   Stevenson, *1914–1918* pp. 107–8; Strachan, '1915' p. 25.
7   Cf Eric Dorn Brose, *A History of the Great War: World War One and the International Crisis of the Early Twentieth Century* Oxford University Press, 2010, pp. 80–3.
8   Kennedy, *Rise* p. 262.
9   Cf Andrew Dilley, 'Trade after the Deluge: British Commerce, Armageddon and the Political Economy of Globalisation 1914–1918' in A. Smith, S. Mollan, K. D. Tennent, eds, *The Impact of the First World War on International Business* Routledge, 2017, pp. 31–2.
10   Welch, *Germany* p. 58.
11   Ulrichsen, 'British' p. 350.
12   Stevenson, *1914–1918* p. 115.
13   Strachan, '1915' p. 25.
14   Cf Stevenson, *1914–1918* p. 99.
15   Vincent, *Politics* p. 41. For a useful overview of the impact of economic warfare measures on neutrality: Stephen C. Neff, 'Disrupting a Delicate Balance: The Allied Blockade Policy and the Law of Maritime Neutrality during the Great War' *European Journal of International Law* 29, 2, 2018, pp. 459–75.

16 Farrar, *Conflict* p. 17; John W. Coogan, 'The Short-War Illusion Resurrected: The Myth of Economic Warfare as the British Schlieffen Plan' *Journal of Strategic Studies* 38, 7, 2015, pp. 1048–60.

17 Osborne, *Britain's* p. 90.

18 Cf Richard Dunley, *Britain and the Mine, 1900–1915* Palgrave MacMillan, 2018, p. 232.

19 Maartje Abbenhuis, 'Protecting Neutrality at Sea in a Global Age, 1815–1914' in David Morgan-Owen, Louis Halewood, eds, *Economic Warfare and the Sea: Grand Strategy for Maritime Powers, c. 1500–2000* Liverpool University Press, 2020, pp. 167–80.

20 Dunley, *Mine* p. 277.

21 Coogan, 'Short-War' p. 1056.

22 John W. Coogan, *The End of Neutrality: The United States, Britain, and Maritime Rights, 1899–1915* Cornell University Press, 1981, pp. 196–7; Dunley, *Mine* pp. 279–81; Vincent, *Politics* p. 40.

23 Dunley, *Mine* p. 284.

24 Farrar, *Conflict* p. 16.

25 Kramer, *Dynamic* p. 331.

26 Farrar, *Conflict* p. 18. Cf Clotilde Druelle, *Feeding Occupied France during World War I: Herbert Hoover and the Blockade* Palgrave MacMillan, 2019, p. 81.

27 T. Visser, 'De "Zaanstroom" van de Hollansche Stoomboot Maatschappij, naar Zeebrugge opgebracht 17 maart 1915' in J.H. Hoogendijk, ed., *De Nederlandsche Koopvaardij in den Oorlogstijd (1914–1918)* Van Holkema & Warendorf, 1930, pp. 87–90.

28 Elinaza Mjerne, 'World War I Shipwrecks of the Western Indian Ocean off Tanzania: Neglected Underwater Heritage Resources' in Lynn Harris, ed., *Sea Ports and Sea Power: African Maritime Cultural Landscapes* Springer Link, 2017, p. 67.

29 Samuël Kruizinga, 'Sailing in Uncharted Waters: Four Dutch Steamship Companies during the First World War, 1914–1918' *International Journal of Maritime History* 27, 2 2015, pp. 227–49. Also: Haufler, *Dangerous* p. 56; Bailey, 'Supporting' p. 33.

30 Cf Dilley, 'Trade' pp. 26, 30. For examples from the global meat industry: Richard Perren, 'Farmers and Consumers under Strain: Allied Meat Supplies in the First World War' *Agricultural History Review* 53, 2, 2005, pp. 212–28. For examples from neutral Spain: Francisco J. Romero Salvado, *Spain: Between War and Revolution* Routledge, 1999, pp. 23–6.

31 Cf Marcella Aglietti, 'Patriotism and Neutrality: The Spanish Parliament and the Great War, 1914–18' *Parliaments, Estates and Representation* 36, 1, 2016, pp. 54–70; Willem H. Van Boom, 'The Great War and Dutch Contract Law: Resistance, Responsiveness and Neutrality' *Comparative Legal History* 2, 2, 2014, pp. 303–24; Wim Klinkert, *Defending Neutrality: The Netherlands Prepares for War 1900–1925* Brill, 2013, p. 6.

32 Cf Annie Deperchin, 'The Laws of War' in Winter, ed., *Cambridge History* Volume 1, p. 615.

33 For an example from the Netherlands: Thimo de Nijs, 'Food Provision and Food Retailing in The Hague, 1914–1930', in Trentmann, Just, eds, *Food* pp. 65–87; Herman De Jong, 'Between the Devil and the Deep Blue Sea: The

Dutch Economy during World War I' in S.N. Broadberry, Mark Harrison, eds, *The Economics of World War I* Cambridge University Press, 2005, pp. 151, 157.

34 Rausch, *Colombia* p. 37.

35 Rinke, *Latin America* p. 81; Jane M. Rausch, 'Colombia's Neutrality during 1914–1918: An Overview' *Iberoamericana* 14, 53, 2014, p. 107.

36 Rausch, *Colombia* p. 33.

37 John Bassett Moore, 'The Pan-American Conferences and the Inter-American High Commission' *American Journal of International Law* 14, 3, 1920, pp. 343–55, quote on p. 343.

38 The Pan-American Union did not include the various American colonies, nor the British Dominion of Canada.

39 Rausch, *Colombia* p. 39.

40 Rausch, *Colombia* p. 111.

41 Horn, *Britain, France* p. 63.

42 Rinke, *Latin America* p. 59.

43 Rinke, *Latin America* p. 58.

44 Rinke, *Latin America* p. 81; Carolina García Sanz, María Inés Tato, 'Neutralist Crossroads: Spain and Argentina Facing the Great War' *First World War Studies* 8, 2–3, 2017, pp. 6–7.

45 Cf Phillip Dehne, 'Profiting Despite the Great War: Argentina's Grain Multinationals' in Smith, Mollan, Tennent, eds, *Impact* pp. 67–81.

46 Cf J.M. Winter, Antoine Prost, *The Great War in History: Debates and Controversies, 1914 to the Present* Cambridge University Press, 2005, p. 119.

47 Brian Black, 'Making Oil Essential: Emerging Patterns of Petroleum Culture in the United States during the Era of the Great War' in S. Daly, M. Salvante, V. Wilcox, eds, *Landscapes of the First World War* Palgrave MacMillan, 2018, p. 28.

48 Black, 'Making' p. 39.

49 Burk, *Britain*. Calculation made using the measuringworth.com's conversion tables and historic interest rates (accessed April 2019). Also: Horn, *Britain, France* p. 80.

50 Black, 'Making' p. 24.

51 Marc Frey, 'Anglo-Dutch Relations during the First World War' in Nigel Ashton, Duco Hellema, eds, *Unspoken Allies* Amsterdam University Press, 2001, pp. 59–65; Samuël Kruizinga, 'NOT Neutrality: The Dutch Government, the Netherlands Overseas Trust and the Entente Blockade of Germany 1914–1918' in Samuel Kruizinga, Johan Den Hertog, eds, *Caught in the Middle: Neutrals, Neutrality and the First World War* Amsterdam University Press, 2011, pp. 68–104.

52 Samuël Kruizinga, 'Government by Committee: Dutch Economic Policy during the First World War' in James Kitchen, Alisa Miller, Laura Rowe, eds, *Other Combatants, Other Fronts: Competing Histories of the First World War* Cambridge Scholars, 2011, p. 109.

53 D.D. Driscoll, 'Anglo-Swiss Relations 1914–1918' PhD, University of London, 1968.

54 Rinke, *Latin America* pp. 76–7; María Inés Tato, 'An Overseas Trench: Social Mobilization in Buenos Aires during the Great War' in M. Lakitsch, S. Reitmar-

Juárez, K. Seidel, eds, *Bellicose Entanglements 1914: The Great War as a Global War* LIT, 2015, p. 47.

55 Philip Dehne, *On the Far Western Front: Britain's First World War in South America* Manchester University Press, 2009, pp. 71–3.

56 Jyotirmoy Pal Chaudhuri, *Whitehall and the Black Republic: A Study of Colonial Britain's Attitude towards Liberia 1914–1939* Palgrave MacMillan, 2018, esp. Chapter 1.

57 Chaudhuri, *Whitehall* esp. Chapter 2.

58 Chaudhuri, *Whitehall* p. 58.

59 Ghassan Moazzin, 'From Globalization to Liquidation: The Deutsche-Asiastische Bank and the First World War in China' *Cross-Current: East Asian History and Culture Review* 16, 2015, p. 54.

60 Tobit Vandamme, 'The Rise of Nationalism in a Cosmopolitan Port City: The Foreign Communities of Shanghai during the First World War' *Journal of World History* 29, 1, 2018, pp. 37–64.

61 Josha A. Fogel, 'Shanghai-Japan: The Japanese Residents' Association of Shanghai' *Journal of Asian Studies* 59, 4, 2000, pp. 927–50.

62 C.W.R. Long, *British Pro-Consuls in Egypt, 1914–1929: The Challenge of Nationalism* Routledge, 2004, p. 2.

63 Valeska Huber, 'Connecting Colonial Seas: The "International Colonisation" of Port Said and the Suez Canal during and after the First World War' *European Review of History* 19, 1, 2012, pp. 148–51.

64 Charles H. Armstrong, 'Indian Trade and War' *Journal of the Royal Society of Arts* 63, 28 May 1915, pp. 650–1, 653–4.

65 Guoqi, 'Asia' p. 503; Kaushik Roy, *Indian Army and the First World War 1914–1918* Oxford University Press, 2018, p. 35; Michael Clodfelter, *Warfare and Armed Conflict: A Statistical Encyclopedia of Casualty and Other Figures, 1492–2015* McFarland, 2017, p. 374.

66 Radhika Singha, 'India's Silver Bullets: War Loans and War Propaganda 1917–1918' in M. Abbenhuis, N. Atkinson, K. Baird, G. Romano, eds, *Myriad Legacies of 1917: A Year of War and Revolution* Palgrave MacMillan, 2018, pp. 77–102.

67 Armstrong, 'Indian Trade' p. 654.

68 Armstrong, 'Indian Trade' pp. 655–6.

69 Hidemasa Morikawa, 'Japan's Unstable Course during Its Remarkable Economic Development' in Alice Teichova, Herbert Matis, eds, *Nation, State and the Economy in History* Cambridge University Press, 2003, pp. 335–6.

70 Guoqi, 'Asia' p. 503.

71 Susan C. Townsend, 'The Great War and Urban Crisis: Conceptualizing the Industrial Metropolis in Japan and Britain in the 1910s' in T. Minohara, T. Hon, E. Dawley, eds, *The Decade of the Great War: Japan and the Wider World in the 1910s* Brill, 2014 pp. 301–22.

72 Charles Shenking, 'Imperial' p. 96; Matsumura, 'Expansion' p. 147.

73 Young, *Japan* pp. 110–11.

74 Young, *Japan* p. 112.

75 Young, *Japan* pp. 93–4.

76 Young, *Japan* p. 114; Matsumura, 'Expansion' pp. 149–50.

77 Fawaz, *Land* p. 89.

78 Rogan, *The Fall* pp. 57–9.

79 Aksakal, 'Ottoman Empire' p. 475.
80 Jeffrey D. Reger, 'Lamps, Never before Dim Are Being Extinguished from Lack of Olive Oil: Deforestation and Famine in Palestine at War and in Peace under the Late Ottoman Empire and Early British Empire, 1910–1920' in Daly, Salvante, Wilcox, eds, *Landscapes* pp. 37–56.
81 Fawaz, *Land* pp. 89–115.
82 Najwa al-Qattan, 'Historicising Hunger: The Famine in Wartime Lebanon and Syria' in T. G. Fraser, ed., *The First World War and Its Aftermath: The Shaping of the Modern Middle East* Gingko Library, 2015, pp. 111–26.
83 Brose, *History* p. 81.
84 Peter Holquist, *Making War, Forging Revolution: Russia's Continuum of Crisis 1914–1921* Harvard University Press, 2002.
85 Peter Gatrell, 'Poor Russia, Poor Show: Mobilising a Backward Economy for War, 1914–1917' in Broadberry, Harrison, eds, *Economics* pp. 247, 249.
86 Cf Dirk Bönker, *Militarism in a Global Age: Naval Ambitions in Germany and the United States before World War I* Cornell University Press, 2012, p. 150; Coleman Phillipson, *International Law and the Great War* T. Fisher Unwin, 1915, p. xvii.
87 Salvado, *Spain* pp. 8–9.
88 Francis Taylor, 'Neutral Merchants and the Rights of War' *Journal of the Royal Society of Arts* 64, 12 May 1916, pp. 467–79; Harold C. Syrett, 'The Business Press and American Neutrality 1914–1917' *Mississippi Valley Historical Review* 32, 2, 1945, p. 217.
89 Rebecka Lettevall, Geert Somsen, Sven Widmalm, 'Introduction' in Rebecka Lettevall, Geert Somsen, Sven Widmalm, eds, *Neutrality in Twentieth-Century Europe: Intersections of Science, Culture and Politics after the First World War* Routledge, 2012, esp. pp. 2–3; Rinke, *Latin America* p. 88.

Chapter 5

1   Das, *India* p. 252.
2   Roy, *Indian Army* p. 258; Das, *India* p. 243.
3   See Nikolas Gardner, *The Siege of Kut-al-Amara: At War in Mesopotamia, 1915–1916* Indiana University Press, 2014, p. 156; Rogan, *The Fall* p. 242.
4   Das, *India* p. 263.
5   Rogan, *The Fall* p. 249; Das, *India* p. 263; Roy, *Indian Army* p. 270.
6   Roy, *Indian Army* p. 270.
7   Mokkhada Devi, *Kalyan-Pradeep: The Life of Captain Kumar Mukherji, I.M.S* Kolkata 1928, p. 442, cited in: Amitav Ghosh, 'Iraq 1915–16: The Siege of Kut al-Amara' 3 August 2012 in *At Home and the World in Mesopotamia*, http://amitavghosh.com/blog/?p=4356http://www.oiist.org/?q=de/node/33 (accessed January 2020).
8   Rogan, *The Fall* p. 263.
9   As quoted in Rogan, *The Fall* p. 267.
10 Rogan, *The Fall* p. 268.
11 Rogan, *The Fall* p. 272.

12 Devi, *Kalyan-Pradeep*.

13 Devi, *Kalyan-Pradeep* pp. 333–5, cited in: Amitav Ghosh, 'I Spit in the Face of Patriotism' in *At Home and the World in Mesopotamia* 27 July 2012 http://amitavghosh.com/blog/?cat=27#_edn3 (accessed November 2020). Please note: a *crore* refers to millions.

14 Das, *India* p. 262.

15 John Horne, 'Nineteen Fifteen and the Totalizing Logic of the First World War' *Thyssen Lectures IV The Great War beyond National Perspectives* Max Weber Stiftung 32 2017, http://www.oiist.org/?q=de/node/33. (accessed January 2020).

16 Gerald J. Fitzgerald, 'Chemical Warfare and Medical Response during World War I' *American Journal of Public Health* 98, 4, 2008, pp. 611–25.

17 Thomas I. Faith, 'Gas Warfare' *1914–1918 Online* https://encyclopedia.1914–1918online.net/article/gas_warfare (accessed August 2020).

18 Hugh R. Slotten, 'Humane Chemistry or Scientific Barbarism? American Responses to World War 1 Poison Gas, 1915–1930' *Journal of American History* 77, 2, 1990, pp. 476–98; R. Price, *The Chemical Weapons Taboo* Cornell University Press 1997, pp. 14–71.

19 As quoted by Willem Van Der Kloot, 'April 1915: Five Future Noble Prize-Winners Inaugurate Weapons of Mass Destruction and the Academic-Industrial-Military Complex' *Notes and Records of the Royal Society of London* 58, 2, 2004, p. 152.

20 Audoin-Rouzeau, '1915' p. 70; Yigal Sheffy, 'The Chemical Dimension of the Gallipoli Campaign: Introducing Chemical Warfare to the Middle East' *War in History* 12, 3, 2005, pp. 278–317; Leo Van Bergen, Maartje Abbenhuis, 'Man-Monkey, Monkey-Man: Neutrality and the Discussions about the "Inhumanity" of Poison Gas in the Netherlands and International Committee of the Red Cross' *First World War Studies* 3, 1, 2012, pp. 1–23.

21 John H. Morrow Jr., 'The Air War' in Winter, ed., *Cambridge History* Volume 1, pp. 353–6.

22 John Horne in Audoin-Rouzeau, '1915' p. 87.

23 Melvin Page, 'Africa's First "High Tech" War: The Technological Impact of World War One on Africans' *Journal of African Military History* 2, 1, 2018, p. 28.

24 Audoin-Rouzeau refers to the anthropologist Jean-Pierre Warnier who uses the term '"sensori-affectivo-motor" conducts'. See, for instance, Warnier's chapter 'Inside and Outside. Surfaces and Containers' in Christopher Tilley, Webb Keane, Susanne Küchler, Michael Rowlands, Patricia Spyer, eds, *Handbook of Material Culture* Sage Publications, 2006, pp. 186–95. Also: Ross Wilson, 'Strange Hells: A New Approach on the Western Front' *Historical Research* 81, 211, 2008, esp. pp. 156–63.

25 Piet Chielens, '1917 in Flanders Fields: The Seeds for the Commemorative War Landscape in Belgian Flanders', in Maartje Abbenhuis, Neill Atkinson, Kingsley Baird, Gail Romano, eds, *The Myriad Legacies of 1917: A Year of War and Revolution* Palgrave, 2018, p. 224.

26 As quoted in Page, 'Black Men' p. 2.

27 Page, 'Black Men' p. 1.

28 Guoqi, 'Asia' p. 502.

29 Ulrik Lehrmann, 'An Album of War: The Visual Mediation of the First World War in Danish Magazines and Daily Newspapers' in Claes Ahlund, ed., *Scandinavia in the First World War: Studies in the War Experience of the Northern Neutrals* Nordic Academic Press, 2012, pp. 57–84; Conny Kristel, *De Oorlog van Anderen: Nederlanders en Oorlogsgeweld, 1914–1918* Amsterdam, 2016.

30 Audoin-Rouzeau, '1915' p. 74; John Horne, 'Atrocities and War Crimes' in Winter, ed., *Cambridge History* Volume 1, p. 566.

31 As quoted in Page, 'Black Men' p. 4. Also: Soutar, *Whitiki!* p. 43.

32 Leonhard, *Pandora's Box* p. 322.

33 'Look at that Man!', recruitment poster, *The Times Press* (Bombay), 1918, Imperial War Museum, Art. IWM PST 12576, https://www.iwm.org.uk/collections/item/object/31125 (accessed August 2020).

34 'Your Chums are Fighting', recruitment poster, Central Recruiting Committee, Toronto, 1914, Art. IWM PST 12428, https://www.iwm.org.uk/collections/item/object/31011; 'If You are an Irishman, Your Place is with Your Chums under the Flags', recruitment poster, David Turner, Allen and Sons, 1914, Art. IWM PST 13657.

35 As quoted by Page, 'Black Men' p. 5.

36 Melvin E. Page, *The Chiwaya War: Malawians in the First World War* Westview, 2000, p. 215.

37 Das, *India* p. 163.

38 Cited in Das, *India* p. 87.

39 As quoted in Guoqi, 'Asia' p. 109.

40 Joshua Sanborn, *Drafting the Russian Nation: Military Conscription, Total War and Mass Politics 1905–25* Northern Illinois University Press, 2003, p. 4.

41 John Horne, 'Nineteen Fifteen and the Totalizing Logic of the First World War', Thyssen Lectures IV The Great War Beyond National Perspectives, Pera Blätter 32 Max Weber Stiftung 2017, http://www.oiist.org/?q=de/node/33.

42 Claes Ahlund, 'Rats and Anthills: The First World War in the Scandinavian Spy Novel' in Ahlund, ed., *Scandinavia* pp. 109–28.

43 Cf Douglas Pfeifer, 'The Sinking of the *Lusitania*: Wilson's Response and Paths Not Taken: Historical Revisionism, the Nyc Committee and the Ghost of William Jennings Bryan' *Journal of Military History* 79, 4, 2015, pp. 1025–7.

44 Armin Rappaport, *The British Press and Wilsonian Neutrality* Stanford University Press, 1951, p. 33.

45 John Protasio, *The Day the World was Shocked: The* Lusitania *Disaster and It Influence on the Course of World War One* Casemate, 2015, p. 130; Fulwider, *German Propaganda*, esp. pp. 65–75.

46 M.L. Sanders, P. M. Taylor, *British Propaganda during the First World War, 1914–18* Macmillan Education UK, 1982, pp. 130–1.

47 Phil Dutton, 'How a German Medallion became a British Propaganda Tool' *Imperial War Museum Review* 1, 1986, also at: https://www.iwm.org.uk/history/how-a-germanmedallion-became-a-british-propaganda-tool (accessed August 2020).

48 As an example: Christian Meurer, *Der Lusitania-fall: eine volkerrichtliche Studie* J.C.B. Mohr, 1915. Also: Fulwider, *German Propaganda* pp. 75–88.

49 Trommler, 'The *Lusitania*' pp. 241–66.

50 Neiberg, *Path to War* pp. 66–77; Rappaport, *British Press* pp. 43–53.
51 For which, see Chapter 4.
52 Trommler, 'The *Lusitania*' p. 244.
53 Panikos Panayi, 'Minorities' in Winter, ed., *Cambridge History* Volume 3, p. 227; Stefan Goebel, 'Cities' in Winter, ed., *Cambridge History* Volume 2, p. 362.
54 *Auckland Star* 14 May 1915, p. 5.
55 Eric Lohr, *Nationalizing the Russian Empire: The Campaign against Enemy Aliens during World War I* Harvard University Press, 2003, p. 148.
56 Goebel, 'Cities' p. 362.
57 Nicoletta Gullace, 'Friends, Aliens and Enemies: Fictive Communities and the *Lusitania* Riots of 1915' *Journal of Social History* 39, 2, 2005, pp. 345–67, esp. p. 352 and p. 354.
58 Cited in Gullace, 'Friends' pp. 352–3.
59 Gullace, 'Friends' p. 352.
60 Paul Thompson, 'The *Lusitania* Riots in Pietermaritzburg 13–14 May 1915' *War & Society* 36, 1, 2017, pp. 1–30.
61 As quoted in Tilman Dedering, 'Avenge the *Lusitania*: The Anti-German Riots in South Africa in 1915' *Immigrants & Minorities* 31, 3, 2013, p. 267.
62 As reported in the *Manawatu Times* 15 May 1915, p. 6.
63 *Poverty Bay Herald* 19 May 1915, p. 3.
64 Stefan Manz, Panikos Panayi, 'The Internment of Civilian "Enemy Aliens" in the British Empire' in Stefan Manz, Panikos Panayi, Matthew Stibbe, eds, *Internment during the First World War: A Mass Global Phenomenon* Routledge, 2019, pp. 25–8.
65 Manz et al., eds, *Internment*.
66 Tames, 'War' pp. 201–16.
67 Maartje Abbenhuis, 'Where War Met Peace: The Borders of the Neutral Netherlands with Belgium and Germany in the First World War' *Journal of Borderland Studies* 22, 1, 2007, pp. 53–77.
68 Panikos Panayi, *Prisoners of Britain: German Civilian and Combatant Internees during the First World War* Manchester University Press, 2012, p. 303.
69 Alexandra Ludewig, 'Visualising a Community in Incarceration: Images from Civilian Internees on Rottnest Island and in Ruhleben during the First World War' *War & Society* 35, 1, 2016, pp. 54–74.
70 Gullace, 'Friends' p. 356.
71 As examples: Steven Hyland Jr., 'The Syrian-Ottoman Home Front in Buenos Aires and Rosario during the First World War' *Journal of Migration History* 4, 1, 2018, pp. 211–35; Eirik Brazier, 'The Stranger in Our Midst: Public Discourses, Constructions and Representations of "Others" in Scandinavia, 1914–1918' Neutrals at War Conference, KNHG Conference, November 2015, available at: https://knhg.nl/wp/content/uploads/2015/08/Eirik-Brazier.pdf (accessed September 2020).
72 Cf Brian K. Feltman, 'Tolerance as a Crime? The British Treatment of German Prisoners of War on the Western Front, 1914–1918' *War in History* 17, 4, pp. 435–58. Also: Heather Jones, *Violence against Prisoners of War in the First World War* Cambridge University Press, 2014.

73 Sophie de Schaepdrijver, 'Populations under Occupation' in Winter, ed., *Cambridge History* Volume 3, p. 243.

74 Liulevicius, *War*; Schaepdrijver, 'Populations' p. 251.

75 Annette Becker, 'Captive Civilians' in Winter, ed., *Cambridge History* Volume 3, p. 257.

76 Peter Gatrell, 'Resettlement' *1914–1918 Online* https://doi.org/10.15463/IE1418.10344 (accessed May 2020).

77 Alexander Watson, *Ring of Steel: Germany and Austria-Hungary at War 1914–1918* Penguin, 2014, p. 182.

78 Alexander Watson, *The Fortress: The Great Siege of Przemyśl* Penguin, 2019, p. 52; Kramer, *Dynamic* pp. 140–4.

79 Cited in Watson, *Fortress* p. 51.

80 Watson, *Fortress* p. 70.

81 Watson, *Ring* p. 183.

82 Watson, *Ring* pp. 183–97; Watson, *Fortress* p. 138

83 Watson, *Fortress* p. 137.

84 Watson, *Ring* p. 203.

85 Watson, *Fortress* p. 122.

86 Cf Kramer, *Dynamic* p. 139.

87 Kramer, *Dynamic* p. 151; Peter Gatrell, 'The Epic and the Domestic' in Gail Braybon, ed., *Evidence, History and the Great War* Berghahn Books, 2003, p. 203.

88 Cf John H. Morrow, 'The Imperial Framework' in Winter, ed., *Cambridge History* Volume 1, pp. 417–23.

89 Aksakal, 'Ottoman Empire' p. 473.

90 Ozan Arslan, 'The "Bon Pour L'Orient" Front: Analysis of Russia's Anticipated Victory over the Ottoman Empire in World War I' *Middle East Critique* 23, 2, 2014, pp. 175–88; Bruinessen, 'A Kurdish' pp. 69–93.

91 Kramer, *Dynamic* pp. 139–40; Donald Bloxham, 'The First World War and the Development of the Armenian Genocide' in Ronald Grigor Suny, Fatma Múge Göçek, Norman A. Naimark, eds, *A Question of Genocide: Armenians and Turks at the End of the Ottoman Empire* Oxford University Press, 2011, pp. 260–75.

92 As quoted in Anna Aleksanyan, 'Between Love, Pain and Identity: Armenian Women after World War I' in Ulrike Ziemer, ed., *Women's Everyday Lives in War and Peace in the South Caucasus* Palgrave MacMillan, 2020, p. 105. See also: Katherine Derderian, 'Common Fate, Different Experience: Gender-Specific Aspects of the Armenian Genocide 1915–1917' *Holocaust and Genocide Studies* 19, 1, 2005, pp. 1–25.

93 Fawaz, *Land*.

94 Fawaz, *Land* p. 3.

95 Cf Sophie De Schaepdrijver, 'Introduction: Military Occupation, Political Imaginations and the First World War' *First World War Studies* 4, 1, 2013, pp. 1–5.

96 With thanks to David Monger. David Monger, 'Networking against Genocide during the First World War: The International Network behind the British Parliamentary Report on the Armenian Genocide' *Journal of Transatlantic Studies* 16, 3, 2018, pp. 295–316. See also: Segesser, 'Dissolve' pp. 95–110; Qvarnström, 'Recognizing' pp. 177–98; Peter Balakian, 'Photography, Visual

Culture, and the Armenian Genocide' in Heide Fehrenbach, Davide Rodogno, eds, *Humanitarian Photography: A History* Cambridge University Press, 2015, pp. 100–9.

97 Sanders, Taylor, *British Propaganda* p. 11; Heidi Tworek, *News from Germany: The Competition to Control World Communications, 1900–1945* Harvard University Press, 2019.

98 Mark Hewitson, 'A War of Words: The Cultural Meanings of the First World War in Britain and Germany' *European Review of History* 25, 5, 2018, p. 749.

99 María Inés Tato, 'A Discordant Voice from the Trenches: Juan José de Soiza Reilly's War Chronicles' *Studies in 20th & 21st Century Literature* 41, 2, 2017, pp. 5–6.

100 Sanders, Taylor, *British Propaganda* pp. 120–1.

101 Xosé Núñez Seixas, 'Catalonia and the "War of Nations": Catalan Nationalism and the First World War' *Journal of Modern European History* 16, 3, 2018, p. 385.

102 Touraj Atabaki, 'Going East: The Ottomans' Secret Services in Iran' in Atabaki, ed., *Iran*, p. 32.

103 British propaganda poster intended for a Chinese Muslim audience, np, [1918], Library of Congress Prints and Photographs Division, http://loc.gov/pictures/resource/cph.3g11304/(accessed September 2020).

104 Fulwider, *German Propaganda*.

105 *Red Book* Magazine (New York) 24, 2, December 1914, p. 207.

106 Richard Abel, 'Charge and Countercharge: "Documentary" War Pictures in the USA 1914–1916' *Film History* 22, 4, 2010, pp. 366–88.

107 Hewitson, 'A War' pp. 749–50.

108 Tato, 'Discordant Voice' quotes on pp. 7, 9.

109 Anja Huber, 'Restrictions against Swiss Nationals in England during the First World War', Neutrals at War Conference, KNHG, https://knhg.nl/wp/content/uploads/2015/08/Abstracts-Neutrals-at-War.pdf (accessed September 2020).

110 Abbenhuis, 'Where War'.

111 Olga V. Alexeeva, 'Experiencing War: Chinese Workers in Russia during the First World War' *Chinese Historical Review* 25, 1, 2018, pp. 46–66.

112 Some examples: Carolyn Kay, 'War Pedagogy in the German Primary School during the First World War' *War & Society* 33, 1, 2014, pp. 3–11; Mischa Honeck, 'Playing on Uncle Sam's Team: American Childhood during World War 1' *Journal of the Gilded Age and Progressive Era* 17, 4, 2018, pp. 677–90; María Inés Tato, 'Recording the War Effort: Immigrant Communities in Latin America and the Memory of the Great War' *Archives and Manuscripts* 48, 2, pp. 200–15.

113 Sanders, Taylor, *British Propaganda* p. 157.

114 Glyn Harper, Christine Clement, Rebecca Johns, *Fighting for King and Other Countries* Massey University Press, 2019; Andrea McKenzie, 'Our Common Colonial Voices: Canadian Nurses, Patient Relations and Nation on Lemnos' in Joachim Bürgschwentner, Matthias Egger, Gunda Barth-Scalmani, eds, *Other Fronts, Other Wars? First World War Studies on the Eve of the Centennial* Brill, 2014, pp. 92–123.

115 Mahon Murphy, 'Brücken, Beethoven und Baumkuchen: German and Austro-Hungarian Prisoners of War and the Japanese Home Front' in

Bürgschwentner et al., eds, *Other Fronts* pp. 125–45; Yücel Yanikdag, *Healing the Nation: Prisoners of War, Medicine and Nationalism in Turkey 1914–1939* Edinburg University Press, 2014, p. 1.

116 Das, *India* p. 256.
117 Cited in Das, *India* p. 269.
118 Sanborn, *Drafting* p. 204.

Chapter 6

1 Saint-Amour, *Tense Future* p. 58. For more, please return to the Introduction of this book.
2 'The War: Various Points of View' *Athaneum* 4576, 10 July 1915, p. 2.
3 Cf David Bell, Annie Crépin, Hervé Drévillon, Olivier Forcade, Bernard Gainot, 'Autour de la Guerre Totale' *Annalles Historiques de la Révolution Française* 4, 2011, p. 153.
4 Saint-Amour, *Tense Future* p. 58.
5 Daudet, *Guerre Totale* p. 8.
6 Robin Prior, 'Impasse' in Winter, ed., *Cambridge History* Volume 2, 102, 108.
7 Prior, 'Impasse' p. 98.
8 John Keegan, *The First World War* Random House, 1998, p. 306.
9 Keegan, *First World War* p. 328.
10 Stevenson, *1914–1918* pp. 123–4.
11 For the impact on meat supplies from the Red Sea region: Massimo Zaccaria, 'Feeding the War: Canned Meat Production in the Horn of Africa and the Italian Front' in Shiferaw Bekele, Uoldelul Chelati Dirar, Alessandro Volterra, Massimo Zaccaria, eds, *The First World War from Tripoli to Addis Ababa* Centre Français des Études Éthiopiennes, 2018, np.
12 Tom G. Hall, 'Wilson and the Food Crisis: Agricultural Price Control during World War I' *Agricultural History* 47, 1, 1973, p. 25.
13 Broadberry, Harrison, eds, *Economics*.
14 Max-Stephan Schulze, 'Austria-Hungary's Economy in World War I' and Sevket Pamuk, 'The Ottoman Economy in World War I' both in Broadberry and Harrison, eds, *Economics* pp. 94, 127. Also: Melanie Tanielian, 'Politics of Wartime Relief in Ottoman Beirut (1914–1918)' *First World War Studies* 5, 1, 2014, pp. 69–82.
15 Matthias Blum, 'War, Food Rationing, and Socio-Economic Inequality in Germany during the First World War' *Economic History Review* 66, 4, 2013, p. 1064.
16 Brose, *History* p. 234.
17 Stapleton, 'Impact' pp. 113–37.
18 Salvado, *Spain* pp. 23–5.
19 Hall, 'Wilson' p. 29.
20 Beryl Nicolson, 'On the Front Line in Someone Else's War: Mallakastër, Albania 1916–1918' *Region* 4, 2, 2015, pp. 247–63.
21 Guoqi, 'Asia' p. 54.
22 Stevenson, *1914–1918* p. 179.
23 Prior, 'Impasse'.

24 Leonhard, *Pandora's Box* p. 385.

25 Prior, 'Impasse'; Stevenson, *1914–1918* p. 179; Leonhard, *Pandora's Box* p. 547.

26 Iaroslav Golubinov, 'Food and Nutrition (Russian Empire)' and Maria Fernanda Rollo, Ana Paula Pires, 'Food and Nutrition (Portugal)' both in *1914–1918 Online* https://encyclopedia.1914-1918.net (accessed September 2020); Robert Blobaum, Donata Blobaum, 'A Different Kind of Home Front: War, Gender and Propaganda in Warsaw 1914–1918' in Troy Paddock, ed., *World War I Propaganda* Brill, 2014, p. 264; Regula Pfeifer, 'Frauen und Protest: Marktdemonstrationen in der deutschen Schweiz im Kriegsjahr 1916' *Schweizerische Gesellschaft für Wirtschafts- und Sozialgeschichte* 11, 1993, pp. 93–112; Giselle Nath, 'Stad in de Storm: Arbeidersvrouwen en het Hongerjaar 1916' *Handelingen der Maatschappij voor Geschiedenis en Oudheidkunde te Gent* 65, 1–2, 2011, pp. 205–27; Antoinne Prost, 'Workers' in Winter, ed., *Cambridge History* Volume 2, p. 350; Karen Hunt, 'The Politics of Food and Women's Neighbourhood Activism in First World War Britain' *International Labour and Working-Class History* 77, 1, 2010, pp. 8–26.

27 Benjamin Ziemann, 'Agrarian Society' in Winter, ed., *Cambridge History* Volume 2, p. 398.

28 As quoted in Enrico Dal Lago, Róisín Healy, Gearóid Barry, 'Globalising the Easter Rising: 1916 and the Challenges to Empires' in Enrico Dal Lago, Róisín Healy, Gearóid Barry, eds, *1916 in Global Context: An Anti-Imperial Moment* Routledge, 2019, p. 3.

29 García Sanz, Inés Tato, 'Neutralist Crossroads' p. 12.

30 Prost, 'Workers' pp. 333–5; Dirk Hoerder, 'Migrations and Belongings' in Emily Rosenberg, ed., *A World Connecting 1870–1945* Belknap Press, 2012, p. 555; Gatrell, 'Epic' pp. 198–215.

31 Carole Marks, 'Lines of Communication, Recruitment Mechanisms and the Great Migration of 1916–1918' *Social Problems* 31, 1, 1983, pp. 73–83; Cecelia Hartsell, 'The Great American Protest: African Americans and the Great Migration' in Dal Lago, et al., eds, *1916* pp. 49–61.

32 Townsend, 'The Great War' pp. 301–22.

33 Leonhard, *Pandora's Box* p. 326.

34 Joe Lunn, 'Remembering the "Tirailleurs Sénégalais" and the Great War: Oral History as a Methodology of Inclusion in French Colonial Studies' *French Colonial History* 10, 2009, p. 140.

35 Michelle Moyd, 'Ordeal and Opportunity: Ending the First World War in Africa' *Fletcher Forum of World Affairs* 43, 1, 2019, p. 147; James E. Genova, *Colonial Ambivalence, Cultural Authenticity and the Limitations of Mimicry in French-Ruled West Africa 1914–1856* Peter Lang, 2004, p. 31.

36 Hoerder, 'Migrations' p. 555.

37 Radhika Singha, *The Coolie's Great War: Indian Labour in a Global Conflict, 1914–1921* Oxford University Press, 2020, pp. 97, 106–7.

38 Kyle Anderson, 'The Egyptian Labor Corps: Workers, Peasants and the State in World War I' *International Journal of Middle East Studies* 49, 1, 2017, pp. 5–24.

39 See also: Donald C. Savage, J. Forbes Munro, 'Carrier Corps Recruitment in the British East Africa Protectorate 1914–1918' *Journal of African History* 7, 2, 1966, pp. 313–24.

40 Richard Bessel, *Germany after the First World War* Clarendon Press, 1993,
    pp. 1–48. For a Russian example: Aaron J. Cohen, 'Flowers of Evil: Media,
    Child Psychology and the Struggle for Russia's Future during the First World
    War' in James Martin, Robert Coles, eds, *Children and War: A Historical
    Anthology* New York University Press, 2002, pp. 38–49.

41 As quoted in Richard Blom, *Hunger: How Food Shaped the Course of the First
    World War* Wilfred Laurier University Press, 2019, p. 177 (italics in original).

42 Alexander Watson, 'Morale' in Winter, ed., *Cambridge History* Volume 2,
    p. 180.

43 Abbenhuis, *Art* pp. 111–12. For more: Susanne Wolf, *Guarded Neutrality:
    Diplomacy and Internment in the Netherlands during the First World War*
    Brill, 2013.

44 Leonard V. Smith, 'Mutiny' in Winter, ed, *Cambridge History* Volume 2,
    pp. 202–3.

45 Leonhard, *Pandora's Box* p. 439.

46 Caroline Moorhead, *Troublesome People: Enemies of War, 1916–1986* Hamish
    Hamilton, 1987, pp. 3–80; Leonhard, *Pandora's Box* p. 440.

47 Leonhard, *Pandora's Box* p. 447.

48 Daniel Segesser, 'To be Avoided at all Hazards – Rebel Irish and Syndicalists
    Coming into Office: The Easter Rising, Climatic Conditions and the 1916
    Australian Referendum on Conscription' in Dal Lago et al., eds, *1916*
    pp. 146–56.

49 Joan Beaumont, 'Similar, Yet Different: The Conscription Issue in Australia and
    New Zealand 1916–17' *Journal of New Zealand Studies* 27, 2018, pp. 2–15.

50 Charles-Philippe Courtois, 'Echoes of the Rising in Quebec's Conscription
    Crisis: The French Canadian Press and the Irish Revolution between 1916 and
    1918' in Dal Lago et al., eds, *1916* pp. 31–48.

51 Cf Aaron Retish, *Russia's Peasants in Revolution and Civil War* Cambridge
    University Press, 2008, p. 25.

52 Timothy D. Hoyt, 'The Easter Rising and the Changing Character of the
    Irregular War' in Dal Lago et al., eds, *1916* pp. 18–19.

53 Streets-Salter, *World War One*; Roy, *Indian Army* pp. 37–8; Mohammad
    Rafi, 'Kulturarbeid and Ideology in the Great War: Germany's Role in the
    Formation of Iranian Nationalism' in Kai Evers, David Pan, eds, *Europe and
    the World: World War I as Crisis of Universalism* Telos Press Publishing, 2018,
    pp. 157–79; Jennifer Jenkins, Heike Liebau, Larissa Schmid, 'Transnationalism
    and Insurrection: Independence Committees, Anti-Colonial Networks, and
    Germany's Global War' *Journal of Global History* 15, 1, 2020, pp. 61–79.

54 Tim Harper, 'Singapore, 1915, and the Birth of the Asian Underground'
    Modern Asian Studies 47, 6, 2013, pp. 1782–811.

55 Streets-Salter, *World War One* pp. 18–23.

56 With immense thanks to Bernadette How for her research on this point. Also:
    Ansari, 'Tasting' pp. 33–61.

57 Streets-Salter, *World War One*, p. 17; Stephen McQuillan, 'Revolutionaries,
    Renegades and Refugees: Anti-British Allegiances in the Context of World War
    I' in Dal Lagos et al., eds, *1916*, pp. 117–30.

58 Smith, 'Mutiny' pp. 199–200.

59 Hoyt, 'Easter Rising'.

60 Kris Manjapra, 'Communist Internationalism and Transcolonial Recognition' in Sugata Bose, Kris Manjapra, eds, *Cosmopolitan Thought Zones: South Asia and the Global Circulation of Ideas* Palgrave MacMillan, 2010, p. 163; Leon Comber, 'The Singapore Mutiny (1915) and the Genesis of Political Intelligence in Singapore' *Intelligence and National Security* 24, 4, 2009, pp. 529–41.

61 Dal Lago et al., *1916*. Also: M.C. Rast, 'Ireland's Sister Nations: Internationalism and Sectarianism in the Irish Struggle for Independence, 1916–22' *Journal of Global History* 10, 3, 2015, pp. 479–501; Jérôme aan de Wiel, 'The Shots That Reverberated for a Long Time: 1916–1932: The Irish Revolution, the Bolsheviks and the European Left' *International History Review* 42, 1, 2020, pp. 195–213.

62 Xosé M. Núñez Seixas, *Catalan Nationalism and the Quest for Independence in the Twenty-First Century. A Historical Perspective* Peristyle, 2020, p. 387.

63 Danielle Ross, 'From Dublin to Turgai: Discourses on Small Nations and Violence in the Russian Muslim Press in 1916' in Dal Lago et al., eds, *1916*, pp. 131–45, quote on pp. 142–3; Alexander Morrison, 'Peasant Settlers and the "Civilising Mission" in Russian Turkestan, 1865–1917' *Journal of Imperial and Commonwealth History* 43, 3, 2015, esp. pp. 401–2.

64 Sanborn, *Drafting* pp. 35–6.

65 As examples: Juliette Honvault, 'World War I and the Perspective of a Hashemite Order in Yemen' in Bekele, et al., eds, *First World War* np; Bruinessen, 'A Kurdish' pp. 69–93; Singha, *Indian Labour* pp. 172–3.

66 Osuntokun, 'Disaffection' pp. 186, 191; Patrick Gilkes, Martin Plaut, 'Great War Intrigues in the Horn of Africa' in Bekele et al., eds, *First World War*; Jason Pack, 'The Antecedents and Implications of the So-Called Anglo-Sanussi War 1915–1917' in T.G. Fraser, ed., *The First World War and Its Aftermath* Gingko Library, 2015, pp. 41–62; George L. Simpson Jr., 'British Perspectives on Aulihan Somali Unrest in the East Africa Protectorate, 1915–1918' *Northeast African Studies* 6, 1–2, 1999, pp. 7–43; Stapleton, 'Impact' pp. 119–22; Black, *Age* pp. 72–7.

67 Haggai Erlich, 'WWI in the Middle East and Africa: Nationalist Movements in a Formative Age' in Bekele et al., eds, *First World War* pp. 12–13; Rogan, *The Fall* pp. 275–309.

68 Mark Farha, 'From Anti-Imperial Dissent to National Consent: The First World War and the Formation of a Trans-Sectarian National Consciousness in Lebanon' in Fraser, ed., *Aftermath* pp. 100–1.

69 Farrar, *Conflict* p. 26.

70 Matthias Blum, 'Government Decisions before and during the First World War and the Living Standards in Germany during a Drastic National Experiment' *Explorations in Economic History* 48, 4, 2011, pp. 556–67.

71 Paul Vigness, *The Neutrality of Norway in the World War* Stanford University Press, 1932, p. 53.

72 As quoted in Vigness, *Neutrality* p. 53.

73 Vigness, *Neutrality* p. 93.

74 Osborne, *Britain's* p. 144.

75 Neiberg, *Path to War* p. 100.

76 Cf *The War Business in the United States* American Embarge Conference, 1916, available in *The Making of Modern Law: Legal Treatises 1800–1926* database, Gale Centrage.

77 Neiberg, *Path to War* p. 103. Also: S. Marianne Johnson, Ian Isherwood, 'Gettysburg and the Great War' *War & Society* 36, 3, 2017, pp. 217–34.

78 James A. Sandos, 'German Involvement in Northern Mexico, 1915–1916: A New Look at the Columbus Raid' *Hispanic American Historical Review* 50, 1, 1970, pp. 85–8; Michael E. Neagle, 'A Bandit Worth Hunting: Pancho Villa and America's War on Terror in Mexico 1916–1917' *Terrorism and Political Violence* 2019, doi.org/10.1080/09546553.2019.1632199.

79 Alexander Barnes, 'On the Border: The National Guard Mobilizes for War in 1916' *Army Sustainment* 48, 2, 2016, pp. 66–72; Timothy Johnson, 'Nitrogen Nation: The Legacy of World War I and the Politics of Chemical Agriculture in the United States' *Agricultural History* 90, 2, 2016, p. 216.

80 Michael Neiberg, 'German Spies in New York!' *Military History* 31, 1, 2013, pp. 66–71.

81 As quoted in Michael Neiberg, 'Blinking Eyes Began to Open: Legacies from America's Road to the Great War 1914–1917' *Diplomatic History* 38, 4, 2014, p. 807.

82 Ross Kennedy, 'Peace Initiatives' *1914–1918 Online* https://encyclopedia.1914–1918-online.net/article/peace_initiatives (accessed November 2020).

83 Salvado, *Spain* pp. 5–26, quote on p. 9.

84 Black, *Age* p. 18.

85 Sanders, Taylor, *British Propaganda* p. 11.

86 Landry Charrier, 'Switzerland during the Great War: "Front of Dissidence" and Platform for Franco-German Exchanges' in Allisa Miller, Laura Rowe, James Kitchen, eds, *Other Combatants, Other Fronts: Competing Histories of the First World War* Cambridge Scholars, 2011, pp. 147–9.

87 Chris Kostov, 'Pre-War Politics and Bulgarian Public Opinion at the Outbreak of WW1 (1913–1915)' *Studia Historyczne* 4, 2014, pp. 457–72.

88 V.N. Vinogradov, 'Romania in the First World War: The Years of Neutrality, 1914–1916' *International History Review* 14, 3, 1992, pp. 441–61.

89 Michael B. Barrett, *Prelude to Blitzkrieg: The 1916 Austro-German Campaign in Romania* Indiana University Press, 2013.

90 Filipe Ribeiro de Meneses, 'Portuguese Intervention 9 March 1916: Germany Declares War on Portugal' in Alan Sharp, ed., *Sarajevo 1914 – Versailles 1919: The War and Peace That Made the Modern World* Haus, 2014, pp. 180–5.

91 Samuël Kruizinga, 'Neutrality' in Winter, ed., *Cambridge History* Volume 2, pp. 554–5. For more on the Portuguese war in East Africa: Ana Pires, 'The First World War in Portuguese East Africa: Civilian and Military Encounters in the Indian Ocean' *e-Journal of Portuguese History* 15, 1, 2017, np.

92 Vigness, *Neutrality* p. 90.

93 Thomas D. Westerman, 'Touring Occupied Belgium: American Humanitarians at "Work" and "Leisure" (1914–1917)' *First World War Studies* 5, 1, 2014, pp. 43–53.

94 Johan Den Hertog, 'The Commission for the Relief of Belgium and the Political Diplomatic History of the First World War' *Diplomacy & Statecraft* 21, 4, 2010, pp. 593–613.

95   Bent Blüdnikow, 'Denmark during the First World War' *Journal of Contemporary History* 24, 1989, pp. 683–703; Karen Gram-Skjoldager, 'Denmark during the First World War: Neutral Policy, Economy and Culture' *Journal of Modern European History* 17, 2, 2019, p. 240; Jennifer D. Keene, 'Americans Respond: Perspectives on the Global War, 1914–1917' *Geschichte und Gesellschaft* 40, 2, 2014, pp. 266–86; Elisabeth Piller, 'To Aid the Fatherland: German-Americans, Transatlantic Relief Work and American Neutrality, 1914–17' *Immigrants and Minorities* 35, 6, 2017, pp. 196–215; Caroline Reeves, 'Sovereignty and the Chinese Red Cross Society: The Differentiated Practice of International Law in Shandong, 1914–1916' *Journal of the History of International Law* 13, 2011, pp. 155–77.

96   Blüdnikow, 'Denmark'.

97   Georg Cavallar, 'Eye-Deep in Hell: Heinrich Lammasch, the Confederation of Neutral States, and Austrian Neutrality, 1899–1920' in Rebecka Letteval, Geert Somsen, Sven Widmalm, eds, *Neutrality in Twentieth-Century Europe* Routledge, 2012, p. 281.

98   Ruy Barbosa, *Le Devoir des Neutres* Félix Alcan, 1917, pp. 62–5.

99   Annette Becker, 'From the *Bulletin Internationale des Sociétés de la Croix Rouge* to the *International Review of the Red Cross*: The Great War as Revelator' *International Review of the Red Cross* 100, 907–9, 2019, pp. 97–113.

100   Bruno Cabanes, *The Great War and the Origins of Humanitarianism 1918–1924* Cambridge University Press, 2014; Keith Watenpaugh, 'The League of Nations' Rescue of Armenian Genocide Survivors and the Making of Modern Humanitarianism, 1920–1927' *American Historical Review* 115, 5, 2010, p. 1319.

101   Thomas Munro, 'The Courageous Conference: British and American Newspaper Coverage of the 1915 Women's Peace Congress at The Hague', *Australian Journal of Politics and History* 64, 3, 2018, pp. 422–35.

102   L.P. Lochner, *The Neutral Conference for Continuous Mediation* np, 1916; *Women's Manifesto. A Clear and Concise Exposition of the Inception and Development of the Plan for a Neutral Conference for Continuous Mediation* Neutral Conference for Continuous Mediation, 1916 (with thanks to the Peace Collection at Swarthmore College, Pennsylvania).

103   Karen Gram-Skjoldager, Øyvind Tønnesson, 'Unity and Divergence: Scandinavian Internationalism 1914–1921' *Contemporary European History* 17, 3, 2008, p. 309.

104   Martin Ceadel, 'Enforced Pacific Settlement or Guaranteed Mutual Defence? British and US Approaches to Collective Security in the Eclectic Covenant of the League of Nations' *International History Review* 35, 5, 2013, pp. 996–7.

105   Sakiko Kaiga, 'The Use of Force to Prevent War? The Bryce Group's "Proposal for the Avoidance of War" 1914–1915' *Journal of British Studies* 57, 2, 2018, pp. 308–32; Martin David Dubin, 'Toward the Concept of Collective Security: The Bryce Group's "Proposals for the Avoidance of War" 1914–1917' *International Organization* 24, 2, 1970, pp. 288–318.

106   Martti Koskenniemi, *The Gentle Civilizer of Nations: The Rise and Fall of International Law, 1870–1960* Cambridge University Press, 2002, pp. 220, 232, 235.

107   Cf Heather Jones, 'International or Transnational? Humanitarian Action during the First World War' *European Review of History* 16, 5, 2009, pp. 697–713.

108 Cf Sven Widmalm, 'A Superior Type of Universal Civilisation: Science as
     Politics in Sweden, 1917–1926', Robert Marc Friedman, 'Has the Swedish
     Academy of Sciences … Seen Nothing, Heard Nothing and Understood
     Nothing? The First World War, Biased Neutrality and the Nobel Prizes in
     Science' and Kenneth Bertrams, 'Caught-up by Politics? The Solvay Councils
     on Physics and the Trials of Neutrality', all in Letteval et al., eds, *Twentieth-
     Century*; Stacy Fahrenthold, 'Transnational Modes and Media: The Syrian
     Press in the *Mahjar* and Emigrant Activism during World War I' *Mashriq &
     Mahjar* 1, 1, 2013, pp. 30–54.
109 Stevenson, *1914–1918* p. 149.
110 Stevenson, *1914–1918* p. 136.
111 Kennedy, 'Peace'
112 E. Keleher, 'Emperor Karl and the Sixtus Affair: Politico-Nationalist
     Repercussions in the Reich' *Eastern European Quarterly* 26, 2, 1992,
     pp. 163–84.
113 Justus D. Doenecke, *Nothing Less than War: A New History of America's
     Entry into World War I* University Press of Kentucky, 2011, pp. 230–4.
114 *Friedensdebatte im deutschen Reichstag mit Kommentaren. Peace.
     Discussions in the House of Commons with Comments* Nederlands Anti-
     Oorlog Raad, 1916; *Governments and Parliaments on Peace Collected by
     the Nederland Anti-Oorlog Raad* Published by the Neutral Conference,
     NAOR, 1916.
115 Stevenson, *1914–1918* p. 136.
116 Cf Georges-Henri Soutou, 'Diplomacy' in Winter, ed., *Cambridge History*
     Volume 2, p. 508.
117 Daniel Larsen, 'War Pessimism in Britain and an American Peace in Early
     1916' *International History Review* 34, 4, 2012, p. 813.
118 Frank Winters, 'Exaggerating the Efficacy of Diplomacy: The Marquis of
     Landsdowne's "Peace Letter" of November 1917' *International History
     Review* 32, 1, 2010, pp. 25–46.

Chapter 7

1   Sugata Bose, *A Hundred Horizons: The Indian Ocean in the Age of Global
    Empire* Cambridge University Press, 2006, p. 247; Das, *India* p. 396;
    Mohammad A. Quayum, 'War, Violence and Rabindranath Tagore's Quest for
    World Peace' *Transnational Literature* 9, 2, 2017, http://fhrc.flinders.edu.au/
    transnational/home.html (accessed September 2020).
2   Yvan Goll, *Requiem für die Gefallenen von Europa* Rascher, 1917, p. 38
    (English translation available at: https://www.poemhunter.com/poem/requiem-
    for-the-dead-of-europe/); Maartje Abbenhuis, 'Death's Carnival: The Myriad
    Legacies of 1917' in Maartje Abbenhuis, Neill Atkinson, Kingsley Baird, Gail
    Romano, eds, *The Myriad Legacies of 1917: A Year of War and Revolution*
    Palgrave, 2018, pp. 1–2.
3   Winter, 'War and Anxiety in 1917' p. 15.
4   Because of difference in calendar use, the two revolutions are also known as
    the February and October revolutions (using the Russian calendar of the time).

5   Cf Pierre Purseigle, 'The First World War and the Transformation of the State' *International Affairs* 90, 2, 2014, pp. 261–2.

6   For a useful overview: Gerhard Besier, Katarzyna Stoklosa, eds, *1917 and the Consequences* Routledge, 2020.

7   Cf Stephen A. Smith, 'The Russian Revolution, National Self-Determination, and Anti-Imperialism' in Oleksa Drachewych, Ian McKay, eds, *Left Transnationalism: The Communist International and the National, Colonial and Racial Questions* McGill Queen's University Press, 2020, esp. p. 73.

8   David Motadel, 'Review of Robert Gerwarth, *The Vanquished: Why the First World War Failed to End, 1917–1923*' *Times Literary Supplement*, 6 January 2017.

9   Robert Gerwarth, *The Vanquished: Why the First World War Failed to End* Straus and Giroux, 2016.

10 Abbenhuis, Morrell, *First Age*, Chapter 10.

11 Solomon Grigor'evich Gurevich as quoted in Richard Bessel, 'Revolution' in Winter, ed., *Cambridge History* Volume 1, p. 126.

12 Jean-Jacques Becker, *1917 en Europe: L'Année Impossible* Complexe, 1997. Cf Jörn Leonhard, '1917 und die Revolution Steigende Erwartungen' *Journal of Modern European History* 15, 2, 2017, p. 157.

13 Sheila Fitzpatrick, *The Russian Revolution* Oxford University Press, 1994, pp. 32–5.

14 Peter Gatrell, *Russia's First World War* Routledge, 2005, p. 178.

15 Nicolas Werth, 'Russia 1917: The Soldiers' Revolution' *South Central Review* 34, 3, 2017, p. 49.

16 Quoted in Peter Gatrell, 'Tsarist Russia at War: The View from above, 1914 – February 1917' *Journal of Modern History* 87, 2015, p. 668.

17 Barbara Alpern Engel, 'Not by Bread Alone: Subsistence Riots in Russia during World War I' *Journal of Modern History* 69, 4, 1997, p. 697; Fitzpatrick, *Russian* p. 44.

18 Werth, 'Russia' p. 50.

19 Semion Lyandres, *The Fall of Tsarism: Untold Stories of the February 1917 Revolution* Oxford University Press, 2013, Chapter 10.

20 Fitzpatrick, *Russian* p. 43.

21 Quoted in Kathy Ferguson, 'The Russian Revolution and Anarchist Imaginaries' *South Atlantic Quarterly* 116, 4, 2017, pp. 747–8.

22 Werth, 'Russia' p. 52.

23 Smith, 'Mutiny' p. 208.

24 Werth, 'Russia' p. 53.

25 Smith, 'Mutiny' p. 208. Also: Joshua Sanborn, 'Russian Empire' in Robert Gerwarth, Erez Manela, eds, *Empires at War: 1911–1923* Oxford University Press, 2014, p. 102; Werth, 'Russia' p. 54.

26 Joshua Sanborn, 'The Genesis of Russian Warlordism: Violence and Governance during the First World War and the Civil War' *Contemporary European History* 19, 3, 2010, pp. 195–213, quote on p. 196.

27 Quoted in Werth, 'Russia' p. 56, fn 16.

28 Sanborn, 'Russian Empire' p. 101.

29 Catherine Merridale, *Lenin on the Train* Penguin, 2016.

30 Elizabeth Jones Hemenway, 'Nicholas in Hell: Rewriting the Tsarist Narrative in the Revolutionary Skazki of 1917' *Russian Review* 60, 2, 2001, p. 189.

31 Smith, 'Mutiny' p. 209.
32 Werth, 'Russia' p. 49.
33 Smith, 'Mutiny' p. 210.
34 Aaron B. Retish, Matthew Rendle, 'Introduction from Lenin's Overcoat? The Global Impact of the Russian Revolution' *Revolutionary Russia* 31, 2, 2018, pp. 145–51, quote on p. 146.
35 Purseigle, 'Transformation' p. 252.
36 Cf David Stevenson, 'Britain's Biggest Wartime Stoppage: The Origins of the Engineering Strike of May 1917' *History* 105, 365, 2020, pp. 268–90.
37 David Englander, 'Discipline and Morale in the British Army 1917–1918' in John Horne, ed., *State, Society and Mobilization in Europe during the First World War* Cambridge University Press, 1997, p. 139.
38 Stevenson, 'Wartime Stoppage' p. 268.
39 Purseigle, 'Transformation' p. 261; John Horne, 'Remobilizing for "Total War": France and Britain 1917–1918' in Horne, ed., *State* pp. 195–8.
40 Englander, 'Discipline' p. 140.
41 Tames, 'War' pp. 201–16.
42 George Morton-Jack, *The Indian Empire at War* Abacus, 2018, pp. 432–3; Singha, *The Coolie's* p. 321.
43 Singha, *Indian Labour* pp. 114–16.
44 Rinke, *Latin America* p. 166; Alexander Trapeznik, 'New Zealand's Perceptions of the Russian Revolution of 1917' *Revolutionary Russia* 19, 1, 2006, p. 71; P.J. O'Farrell, 'The Russian Revolution and the Labour Movements of Australia and New Zealand, 1917–1922' *International Review of Social History* 8, 2, 1963, pp. 177–97.
45 Franziska Yost, 'Glory to the Russian Maximalists! Reactions to the Russian Revolution in Argentina and Brazil 1917–22' *Revolutionary Russia* 31, 2, 2018, pp. 247–60.
46 Olivier Compagnon, 'Latin America' in Winter, ed., *Cambridge History* Volume 1, p. 545.
47 Francisco J. Romero Salvado, 'The Great War and the Crisis of Liberalism in Spain, 1916–1917' *Historical Journal* 46, 4, 2003, p. 905; Arturo Zoffmann Rodriguez, 'An Uncanny Honeymoon: Spanish Anarchism and the Dictatorship of the Proletariat 1917–22' *International Labor and Working-Class History* 94, 2018, pp. 5–26.
48 Cf Paul Preston, 'The Origins of the Socialist Schism in Spain, 1917–31' *Journal of Contemporary History* 12, 1977, pp. 101–32.
49 Gerwarth, *Vanquished* pp. 153–4.
50 Robert Bollard, 'The Great Strike of 1917 – Was Defeat Inevitable?' *Australian Journal of Politics and History* 56, 2, 2010, pp. 159–60; O'Farrell, 'Labour Movements' pp. 177–80.
51 Steven Loveridge, 'What Should Daddy Do in the Great War? The Second Division Question and Conditional Commitment to New Zealand's War Effort, 1917–1918' *Journal of New Zealand Studies* 27, 2018, pp. 16–34. Cf Adrian Gregory, *The Last War: British Society and the First World War* Cambridge University Press, 2008, p. 187.
52 John Horne, 'The Living' in Winter, ed., *Cambridge History* Volume 3, pp. 598–606; Guoqi, 'Asia', esp. Chapter 4.

53 Watson, *Ring* p. 451; William Mulligan, *The Great War for Peace* Yale University Press, 2014, pp. 212–14.

54 Horne, 'Remobilizing' p. 203.

55 Watson, *Ring* pp. 484–5.

56 Simonette Ortaggi, 'Italian Women during the Great War' in Gail Braybon, ed., *Evidence, History* pp. 216–38, quotes on p. 224.

57 Paul Corner, Giovanna Procacci, 'The Italian Experience of "Total" Mobilization 1915–1920' in Horne, ed., *State* pp. 223–32.

58 As quoted in Gerwarth, *Vanquished* p. 160.

59 Gerwarth, *Vanquished* p. 160.

60 Stephen C. MacDonald, 'Crisis, War and Revolution in Europe 1917–23' in Hans A. Schmitt, ed., *Neutral Europe between War and Revolution 1917–1923* University Press of Virginia, 1988, pp. 235–9.

61 Joe Lunn, 'Kande Kamara Speaks' in Melvin E. Page, ed., *Africa and the First World War* Macmillan, 1987, p. 36.

62 Michelle Moyd, 'Resistance and Rebellions (Africa)' *1914–1918 Online* https://encyclopedia.1914–1918-online.net/article/resistance_and_rebellions_africa (accessed September 2020).

63 Moyd, 'Resistance' p. 6.

64 Nasson, 'Africa' pp. 456–7. As an example: John Maynard, 'On the Political "Warpath": Native Americans and Australian Aborigines after the First World War' *Wicazo Sa Review* 32, 1, 2017, pp. 48–62.

65 Genova, *Colonial* pp. 33–40.

66 Cited in Lunn, 'Kamara' p. 43.

67 Cited in Lunn, 'Kamara' p. 43.

68 Anne Summers, R.W. Johnson, 'World War I Conscription and Social Change in Guinea' *Journal of African History* 19, 1, 1978, pp. 25–38; Sarah-Jane (Saje) Mathieu, 'L'Union Fait la Force: Black Soldiers in the Great War' *First World War Studies* 9, 2, 2018, pp. 230–44; B. P. Willan, 'The South African Native Labour Contingent, 1916–1918' *Journal of African History* 19, 1, 1978, pp. 61–86.

69 This was called *Ethische Politiek* (Ethical Policy) and may be regarded as a variation to the 'white man's burden' rhetoric in Britain.

70 Henk Sneevliet 'Zegepraal' *De Indiër*, 17 Marchs 1917. Also: Klaas Stutje, '"Volk van Java, de Russische Revolutie Houdt ook Lessen in Voor U": Indonesisch Socialisme, Bolsjewisme, en het Spook van het Anarchisme' *Tijdschrift voor Geschiedenis* 130, 3, 2017, pp. 427–47.

71 Kees Van Dijk, *The Netherlands Indies in the First World War* Brill, 2014, p. 591.

72 For an example: Rudolf Mrázek, 'Tan Malaka: A Political Personality's Structure of Experience' *Indonesia* 14, 1972, pp. 1–48.

73 Cf Harry A. Poeze, *Tan Malaka: Strijder voor Indonesie's Vrijheid: Levelsloop van 1897 tot 1945* Martinus Nijhoff, 1976.

74 Tatiana Linkhoeva, 'The Russian Revolution and the Emergence of Japanese Anticommunism' *Revolutionary Russia* 31, 2, 2018, p. 263.

75 Linkhoeva, 'Russian Revolution' pp. 264–6; John H. Morrow, 'Imperial Framework' in Winter, ed., *Cambridge History* Volume 1, p. 427.

76 Linkhoeva, 'Russian Revolution' pp. 270–1.

77 Leonhard, *Pandora's Box* pp. 633–5.

78 Das, *India* pp. 109–10.
79 Leonhard, *Pandora's Box.*

Chapter 8

1   Tato, 'Overseas' p. 47.
2   Sanz, Tato, 'Neutralist Crossroads' pp. 2–3.
3   Rinke, *Latin America* p. 107.
4   Compagnon, 'Latin America' p. 552.
5   Tato, 'Overseas' pp. 48–54.
6   Tato, 'Overseas' pp. 48–54.
7   Compagnon, 'Latin America' p. 550.
8   For a useful overview of Latin American states and their shifts to belligerency: Stefan Rinke, Karina Kriegesmann, 'Latin America' in *1914–1918 Online* https://encyclopedia.1914–1918-online.net/article/latin_america (accessed October 2020). Also: Compagnon, 'Latin America' p. 547; Rinke, *Latin America* pp. 108–60.
9   Rinke, *Latin America* pp. 143–52.
10 Leonhard, *Pandora's Box* p. 635.
11 John Coogan, 'Wilsononian Diplomacy in War and Peace' in Gordon Martel, ed., *American Foreign Relations Reconsidered 1890–1993* Routledge, 1994, p. 78.
12 Woodrow Wilson, Presidential Speech, 26 February 1917, available at: https:// millercenter.org/the-presidency/presidential-speeches/february-26-1917-message-regarding-safety-merchant-ships (accessed November 2020).
13 Translation of a Proclamation by the president of the Republic of Panama, Ramón Maximiliano Valdés, 7 April 1917, National Archives, Kew, ADM 116/1721. With grateful thanks to Annalise Higgins.
14 Cf Pål Wrange, *Impartial or Uninvolved? The Anatomy of 20th Century Doctrine on the Law of Neutrality* Elanders, 2007, p. 246.
15 Dirk Steffen, 'The Holtzendorff Memorandum of 22 December 1916 and Germany's Declaration of Unrestricted U-boat Warfare' *Journal of Military History* 68, 1, 2004, pp. 215–24.
16 Kathleen Burk, 'Great Britain and the United States, 1917–1918: The Turning Point' *International History Review* 1, 2, 1979, p. 234.
17 Mulligan, *Great War* pp. 189–90.
18 Stevenson, *1914–1918* pp. 321–2.
19 Brose, *History* p. 247.
20 Paul Kennedy, 'The War at Sea' in Winter, ed., *Cambridge History* Volume 1, pp. 337–43; Michael Adas, 'Ambivalent Ally: American Military Intervention and the Legacy of the World War I' in Thomas D. Zeiler, David K. Ekbladh, Benjamin C. Montoya, eds, *Beyond 1917: The United States and the Global Legacies of the Great War* Oxford University Press, 2017, pp. 89–90.
21 As quoted in Beltran Mathieu, 'The Neutrality of Chile during the European War' *American Journal of International Law* 14, 3, 1920, p. 324.
22 Adam Tooze, *The Deluge: The Great War and the Remaking of the Global Order* Penguin, 2014, p. 39.

23 Neiberg, *Path to War*. Also: Neiberg, 'Blinking Eyes' pp. 801–12.

24 J. Bennett, M. Hampton, 'World War I and the Anglo-American Imagined Community' in J.H. Wiener, M. Hampton, eds, *Anglo-American Media Interactions* Palgrave MacMillan, 2007, p. 167.

25 Fulwider, *German Propaganda*.

26 Gerhard Krebs, 'German-Japanese-United States Mutual Perceptions and Diplomatic Initiatives over Mexico: New Perspectives on the Zimmerman Telegram' in Jan Schmidt, Katja Schmidtpott, eds, *The East Asian Dimension of the First World War* Campus Verlag, 2020, pp. 247–67.

27 Tooze, *Deluge* pp. 65–7.

28 Mulligan, *Great War* p. 194.

29 Tooze, *Deluge* pp. 68–9.

30 President Woodrow Wilson, 2 April 1917 speech, as quoted by Quincy Wright, 'The Present Status of Neutrality' *American Journal of International Law* 34, 3, 1940, p. 391.

31 Tooze, *Deluge* p. 67.

32 Alan Sharp, 'The Genie That Would Not Go Back into the Bottle: National Self-Determination and the Legacy of the First World War and the Peace Settlement' in Seamus Dunn, T. G. Fraser, eds, *Europe and Ethnicity: World War I and Contemporary Ethnic Conflict* Routledge, 1996, p. 11.

33 Cf Nadine Aklund-Lange, Stéphane Tison, eds, *En Guerre pour la Paix: Correspondance Paul d'Estournelles de Constant – Nicholas Murray Butler 1914–1919* Alma, 2018, esp. pp. 23–4.

34 Maartje Abbenhuis, 'International Law and the "Peace through Law" Movement in the Age of Empire, 1870–1920' in Randall Lesaffer, Stephen Neff, eds, *Cambridge History of International Law. Volume IX: Global International Law in the Age of Empire* Cambridge University Press, forthcoming.

35 For an excellent body of work on this subject: Letteval et al., eds, *Neutrality*.

36 Vidar Enebakk, 'Nobel Science of Peace: Norwegian Neutrality, Internationalism and the Nobel Peace Prize' in Letteval et al., eds, *Neutrality* p. 299.

37 Marta Stachurska-Kounta, 'Norway's Legalistic Approach to Peace in the Aftermath of the First World War' in Maartje Abbenhuis, Christopher Barber, Annalise Higgins, eds, *War, Peace and International Order? The Legacies of the Hague Conferences of 1899 and 1907* Routledge, 2017, pp. 171–88.

38 Stachurska-Kounta, 'Norway's' p. 172.

39 As an example: Oscar Straus, *Preparedness against the Rebarbarization of the World* League to Enforce Peace, 1916/1917.

40 *The Effect of Democracy on International Law.* Carnegie Endowment for International Peace Pamphlet no. 30, 1917.

41 Abbenhuis, *Hague* p. 139; Honeck, 'Playing' p. 680.

42 Honeck, 'Playing' p. 680.

43 Daniel T. Rodgers, *Atlantic Crossings: Social Politics in a Progressive Age* Harvard University Press, 1998, p. 285.

44 Christopher Capozzola, 'Legacies for Citizenship: Pinpointing Americans during and after World War I' in Zeiler, ed., *Beyond* p. 110.

45 Jennifer Keene, 'A "Brutalizing" War? The USA after the First World War'
    Journal of Contemporary History 50, 1, 2015, p. 79. Also: Keene, 'W. E. B. Du
    Bois' pp. 135–52; Jennifer Keene, 'Deeds Not Words: American Social Justice
    Movements and World War I' *Journal of the Gilded Age and Progressive Era*
    17, 4, 2018, pp. 704–18.
46 As quoted in Capozzola, 'Legacies' p. 116.
47 Keene, 'North' p. 523; David L. Wood, 'American Indian Farmland and the
    Great War' *Agricultural History Society* 55, 3, 1981, pp. 249–65.
48 Capozzola, 'Legacies' pp. 115–18.
49 Osborne, *Britain's* pp. 167–8.
50 Frey, 'Anglo-Dutch' p. 67.
51 Farrar, *Conflict* pp. 159–62; Vigness, *Neutrality* pp. 124–63; Frey, 'Anglo-
    Dutch' pp. 59–84; Blüdnikow, 'Denmark' pp. 683–703.
52 For an excellent overview of the impact of Uboat warfare on neutral shipping:
    Javier Ponce, 'Commerce Warfare in the East Central Atlantic during the First
    World War: German Submarines around the Canary Islands, 1916–1918'
    Mariner's Mirror 100, 3, 2014, pp. 335–48. Also useful: Rolf Hobson, Tom
    Kristiansen, Nils Arne Sørensen, Gunnar Åselius, 'Scandinavia in the First
    World War' and Gjermund F. Rongved, 'Money Talks: Failed Cooperation over
    the Gold Problem of the Scandinavian Monetary Union during the First World
    War' both in Claes Ahlund, ed., *Scandinavia in the First World War* Nordic
    Academic Press, 2012, pp. 31–5, 39–40, pp. 240–2.
53 Although they did not disappear completely: Dehne, 'Profiting' pp. 67–86.
54 Adam Burns, *American Imperialism: The Territorial Expansion of the United
    States 1783–2013* Edinburgh University Press, 2017, p. 138; M.W. Shannon,
    Jean Price-Mars, the Haitian Elite and the American Occupation 1915–1935
    Palgrave, 1996, p. 7.
55 Irene Fattacciu, 'Central America, the Caribbean and the First World War' in
    Alan Sharp, ed., *Sarajevo 1914 – Versailles 1919: The War and Peace That
    Made the Modern World* Haus, 2014, p. 220.
56 Rinke, *Latin America* p. 124.
57 Rinke, *Latin America* pp. 126–7.
58 Emily Rosenberg, 'The Great War, Wilsonianism and the Challenges to a
    United States Empire' in Zeiler, ed., *Beyond* pp. 213–31.
59 As an example: José Antonio Montero Jiménez, 'Images, Ideology and
    Propaganda: The Works of the American Committee on Public Information
    in Spain c. 1917–1918' *Hispania* 68, 2008, pp. 211–34. Also: Rinke, *Latin
    America* p. 118.
60 Edoardo Braschi, 'In the Grasp of the United States' in Sharp, ed., *Sarajevo*
    p. 227.
61 Rinke, *Latin America* pp. 129–38.
62 Edoardo Braschi, 'The Wavering Road 26 October 1917: Brazil Declares War
    on Germany' in Sharp, ed., *Sarajevo*, pp. 242–6.
63 Braschi, 'Wavering' pp. 242–6.
64 Rosenberg, 'Great War' p. 213. Cf Lloyd E. Ambrosius, 'The Great War,
    Americanism Revisited, and the Anti-Wilson Crusade' in Serge Ricard, ed., *A
    Companion to Theodore Roosevelt* Blackwell, 2011, pp. 468–84.
65 Burns, *American Imperialism* p. 101.
66 Rosenberg, 'Great War' pp. 219–20.

67 Erez Manela, *The Wilsonian Moment: Self-Determination and the International Origins of Anticolonial Nationalism* Oxford University Press, 2007.

68 Jack Patrick Hayes, 'The Political and Natural Eco-Footprint of the First World War in East Asia: Environments, Systems Building and the Japanese Empire 1914–1923' in Richard P. Tucker, Tait Keller, John Robert McNeill, Martin Schmid, eds, *Environmental Histories of the First World War* Cambridge University Press, 2018, pp. 152–72; Wu Lin-chin, 'The First World War and Chinese-American Economic Networks' in Jan Schmidt, Schmidtpott, eds, *East Asian* pp. 231–46

69 Guoqi, 'Great War' p. 107.

70 Xu Guoqi, *Strangers on the Western Front: Chinese Workers in the Great War* Harvard University Press, 2011, pp. 1, 17.

71 Stephen G. Craft, 'Angling for an Invitation to Paris: China's Entry into the First World War' *International History Review* 16, 1, 1994, p. 1.

72 Craft, 'Angling' p. 16.

73 Craft, 'Angling' p. 15.

74 Jonathan Clements, 'Labourers in Place of Soldiers' in Sharp, ed., *Sarajevo* p. 240.

75 As quoted in Guoqi, 'Great War' p. 119.

76 Guoqi, 'Asia' p. 31.

77 Guoqi, 'Great War' p. 124.

78 Zhang Yan, 'The British Recruitment Campaigns of the Chinese Labour Corps during the First World War and the Shandong Workers' Motives to Enrol' in Schmidt et al., eds, *East Asia* p. 389.

79 Guoqi, *Strangers*.

80 Guoqi, 'Great War' p. 116.

81 As quoted in Guoqi, *Strangers* p. 221.

82 Xu Guoqi, 'The Year 1919 and the Question of "What Is China?"' *International Politics* 55, 6, 2018, pp. 754–5.

83 As quoted by Tooze, *Deluge* p. 98.

84 Mulligan, *Great War* pp. 198–9.

85 Clements, 'Labourers' p. 241.

86 Streets-Salter, *World War One* pp. 142–68.

87 Gregory V. Raymond, 'War as Membership: International Society and Thailand's Participation in World War I' *Asian Studies Review* 43, 1, pp. 132–47.

88 Andrew Dalby, 'Why on Earth Was Siam a Participant in the First World War?' in Sharp, ed., *Sarajevo* pp. 234–6; Raymond, 'Membership' 132–3.

89 Raymond, 'Membership' pp. 137–40.

90 Mariella Hudson, 'Why Did Liberia Enter the First World War?' in Sharp, ed., *Sarajevo* pp. 247–9.

91 As quoted in William Gillispie, 'Colonialism in Global Conflict: Liberia's Entry and Participation in World War One' *First World War Studies* 9, 1, 2018, p. 119.

92 Gillispie, 'Colonialism' pp. 111, 120–1.

93 Jyotirmoy Pal Chaudhuri, *Whitehall and the Black Republic: A Study of Colonial Britain's Attitude towards Liberia 1914–1939* Palgrave MacMillan, 2018, Chapter 3; Hudson, 'Why?' p. 249.

94 Gillispie, 'Colonialism' p. 122.

95   Andrew Dalby, 'Greece and the First World War' in Sharp, ed., *Sarajevo* pp. 228–33, quote on p. 233.
96   Abbenhuis, *Art* esp. Chapter 12.
97   Tames, *Oorlog* p. 114.
98   Tames, *Oorlog* pp. 118–19.
99   Mathieu, 'Neutrality' pp. 319–42, last quote on p. 342.
100 Cf Rinke, *Latin America* pp. 150–3; Tames, 'War' p. 205.
101 Tames, 'War' p. 211.
102 In Abbenhuis, 'Not Silent' p. 35.
103 Quoted in Abbenhuis, *Age of Neutrals* p. 11.
104 As described in Hull, *Scrap* pp. 1–2.
105 Letteval et al., *Neutrality*.
106 Cf Stephen C. Neff, *The Rights and Duties of Neutrals: A General History* Manchester University Press, 2000, p. 168.

Chapter 9

1   Rinke, *Latin America* pp. 256–7; Schmitt, ed., *Neutral Europe*.
2   Watson, *Ring* p. 505.
3   Lieutenant R.G. Dickson, as quoted in David Stevenson, *With Our Backs to the Wall: Victory and Defeat in 1918* Harvard University Press, 2011, p. 509.
4   Becker, 'Great War' p. 1029.
5   Cf Raymond Sontag, *A Broken World 1919–1939* Harper & Row, 1971; Sally Marks, *The Illusion of Peace: International Relations in Europe 1918–1933* Palgrave MacMillan, 2003.
6   Stevenson, *Backs* p. 1.
7   John Horne, 'Defending Victory: Paramilitary Politics in France, 1918–1926: A Counter-Example' in Robert Gerwarth, ed., *War in Peace: Paramilitary Violence in Europe after the Great War* Oxford University Press, 2013, p. 218. Cf Peter Jackson, *Beyond the Balance of Power: France and the Politics of National Security in the Era of the First World War* Cambridge University Press, 2013, pp. 79–80.
8   Das, *India* p. 385.
9   Cited in Ramachandra Guha, 'Travelling with Tagore' 2012, available at: http://ramachandraguha.in/archives/traveling-with-tagore-penguin-classics.html (accessed November 2020).
10   As quoted in Rinke, *Latin America* p. 258.
11   Rinke, *Latin America* p. 262.
12   Gerwarth, ed., *War in Peace*.
13   P.A. Niall, A.S. Johnson, Juergen Mueller, 'Updating the Accounts: Global Mortality of the 1918–1920 "Spanish" Influenza Pandemic' *Bulletin of the History of Medicine* 76, 1, 2002, p. 114.
14   Anne Rasmussen, 'The Spanish Flu' in Winter, ed., *Cambridge History* Volume 3, p. 336.
15   Cited in Rasmussen, 'Spanish Flu' pp. 350–1.
16   al-Qattan, 'Historicising' p. 126.

17 Mark Osborne Humphries, 'Paths of Infection: The First World War and the Origins of the 1918 Influenza Pandemic' *War in History* 21, 1, 2013, pp. 55–81.

18 Rasmussen, 'Spanish Flu' pp. 337–8.

19 Rasmussen, 'Spanish Flu' pp. 339–43.

20 Geoffrey Rice, *Black November: The 1918 Influenza Pandemic in New Zealand* Canterbury University Press, 2005.

21 Michael Tyquin, 'Problems in Paradise: Medical Aspects of the New Zealand Occupation of Western Samoa, 1914–1918' *Journal of Military and Veterans' Health* 20, 2, 2012, p. 9; Sandra M. Tomkins, 'The Influenza Epidemic of 1918–19 in Western Samoa' *Journal of Pacific History* 27, 2, 1992, pp. 181–97.

22 Fawaz, *Land* p. 61.

23 Niall et al., 'Updating' p. 112.

24 Nasson, 'Africa' p. 442. Also: Leonhard, *Pandora's Box* p. 825.

25 Michelle Moyd, 'Radical Potentials, Conservative Realities: African Veterans of the German Colonial Army in Post-World War I Tanganyika' *First World War Studies*, 10, 1, 2019, p. 94.

26 Stapleton, 'Impact' p. 123.

27 For a useful overview: Mulligan, *Great War* pp. 255–7.

28 For a useful history: Stevenson, *Backs* pp. 514–28.

29 Helen L. Boak, 'Women in the German Revolution' in G. Kets, J. Muldoon, eds, *The German Revolution and Political Theory* Springer, 2019, p. 40.

30 Boak, 'Women' p. 31.

31 Smith, 'Mutiny' p. 212.

32 For more: George Vascik, Mark Sadler, *The Stab-in-the-Back Myth and the Fall of the Weimar Republic* Bloomsbury, 2016, pp. 1–3.

33 Boak, 'Women' p. 38.

34 As quoted in Boak, 'Women' p. 36.

35 As quoted in Boak, 'Women' p. 39.

36 Joe Lunn, 'France's Legacy to Demba Mboup? A Senenalese Griot and His Descendants Remember His Military Service during the First World War' in Santanu Das, ed., *Race, Empire and First World War Writing* Cambridge University Press, 2011, pp. 108–24, quote on p. 116.

37 Lunn, 'Mboup' p. 117.

38 Soutar, *Whitiki!* p. 493.

39 Morrow, 'Imperial' p. 432.

40 Yusuf Meherally, *The Price of Liberty* Sneha, 1948; Rohan Dhabade, *Something about Jallianwala Bagh and the Days of British Empire* Evince, 2019, p. 169.

41 Kalyan Sen Gupta, *The Philosophy of Rabindranath Tagore* Ashgate, 2005, p. 3.

42 Simon Featherstone, 'The School Play and the Murder Machine: Nationalism and Amateur Theatre in the Work of Patrick Pearse and Rabindranath Tagore' *Journal of Postcolonial Writing* 53, 5, 2017, p. 574.

43 Rogan, *The Fall* pp. 385–7. Also: Daniel-Joseph MacArthur-Seal, 'Intoxication and Imperialism: Nightlife in Occupied Istanbul, 1918–1923' *Comparative Studies of South Asia, Africa and the Middle East* 37, 2, 2017, pp. 299–313.

44 Rogan, *The Fall* pp. 387–8.

45 Rogan, *The Fall* p. 389.

46 Mulligan, *Great War* p. 315.

47 Rogan, *The Fall* pp. 390–5; Leonhard, *Pandora's Box* p. 841.
48 Tooze, *Deluge* p. 233.
49 Mohammad Gholi Majd, *The Great Famine and Genocide in Persia 1917–1919* University Press of America, 2003.
50 Umut Özsu, *Formalising Displacement: International Law and Population Transfers* Oxford University Press, 2014.
51 Peter Gatrell, *The Making of the Modern Refugee* Oxford University Press, 2015.
52 Fawaz, *Land*.
53 Gerwarth, *Vanquished* pp. 171–86; Mulligan, *Great War* pp. 267–301.
54 Manela, *Wilsonian*.
55 Cf Marcus Payk, 'What We Seek Is the Reign of Law: The Legalism of the Paris Peace Settlement after the Great War' *European Journal of International Law* 39, 3, 2018, p. 815.
56 Helen McCarthy, *The British People and the League of Nations: Democracy, Citizenship and Internationalism c. 1918–1945* Manchester University Press, 2011; Thomas R. Davies, 'Internationalism in a Divided World: The Experience of the International Federation of League of Nations Societies, 1919–1939' *Peace & Change* 37, 2, 2012, pp. 227–52.
57 Patrica Clavin, *Securing the World Economy: The Reinvention of the League of Nations* Oxford University Press, 2010; Patricia Clavin, 'The Austrian Hunger Crisis and the Genesis of International Organization after the First World War' *International Affairs* 90, 2, 2014, pp. 265–78.
58 Daniel Gorman, *The Emergence of International Society in the 1920s* Cambridge University Press, 2012.
59 Maartje Abbenhuis, 'This Is an Account of Failure: The Contested Historiography of the Hague Peace Conferences of 1899, 1907 and 1915' *Diplomacy & Statecraft* 3, 2, 2021, pp. 1–30.
60 Klaus Schwabe, 'Woodrow Wilson and Germany's Membership of the League of Nations, 1918–1919' *Central European History* 8, 1, 1975, pp. 3–22.
61 Michael Olsansky, 'Under the Spell of the League of Nations: Different Notions of Neutrality in the Swiss Military Elite at the End of the First World War' 2015, https://knhg.nl/wp/content/uploads/2015/08/Michael-Olsansky.pdf (accessed November 2020).
62 Xu Guoqi, *China and the Great War* Cambridge University Press, 2005, pp. 244–77; Stevenson, *1914–1918* pp. 508–10.
63 Tan Malaka, 'Is er een "Koloniaal Probleem?"' *Bijdragen aan Hindi Ja Poeh Tra* 1, 1918–1919, pp. 161–164.
64 Cf Leonhard, *Pandora's Box*.
65 Cf Akira Iriye, 'The Historiographic Impact of the Great War' in T.W. Zeiler, D.K. Ekbladh, B.C. Montoya, eds, *Beyond 1917: The United States and the Global Legacies of the Great War* Oxford University Press, 2017, p. 34.

SELECT BIBLIOGRAPHY

Please find here a curated list of readings in English on the global history of the First World War, listed by general readings and chapter-specific themes. To avoid duplication, we have only listed each reference once.

General Histories of the First World War

1914–1918 Online: International Encyclopaedia of the First World War Freie Universität Berlin, http://www.1914–1918-online.net

Brose, Eric Dorn, *The History of the Great War: World War One and the International Crisis of the Early Twentieth Century* Oxford University Press, 2010

Horne, John, ed., *A Companion to World War I* Wiley-Blackwell, 2010

Leonhard, Jörn, *Pandora's Box: A History of the First World War* Belknap, 2014

Stevenson, David, *1914–1918: The History of the First World War* Penguin, 2004

Strachan, Hew, *The First World War Volume 1: To Arms* Oxford University Press, 2001

Winter, Jay, ed., *Cambridge History of the First World War*, Three Volumes, Cambridge University Press, 2014

Regional and Thematic Histories of the First World War

Ahlund, Claes, ed., *Scandinavia in the First World War: Studies in the War Experience of the Northern Neutrals* Nordic Academic Press, 2012

Albert, Bill, *South America and the First World War: The Impact of War on Brazil, Argentina, Peru and Chile* Cambridge University Press, 1988

Anievas, Alexander, ed., *Cataclysm 1914: The First World War and the Making of Modern World Politics* Brill, 2015

Atabaki, Touraj, ed., *Iran and the First World War: Battleground of the Great Powers* I.B. Tauris, 2006

Audoin-Rouzeau, Stephane, Annette Becker, *Understanding the First World War* Hill & Wang, 2003

Braybon, Gail, ed., *Evidence, History and the Great War* Berghahn, 2003

Broadberry, Stephen, Mark Harrison, eds, *The Economics of World War 1* Cambridge University Press, 2005

Daly, Selena, Martina Salvante, Vanda Wilcox, eds, *Landscapes of the First World War* Palgrave MacMillan, 2018

Das, Santanu, *India, Empire and First World War Culture* Cambridge University Press, 2018

Das, Santanu, ed., *Race, Empire and First World War Writing* Cambridge University Press, 2011

Dehne, Phillip, *On the Far Western Front: Britain's First World War in South America* Manchester University Press, 2009

Dickinson, F.R., *War and National Reinvention: Japan and the Great War 1914–1919* Harvard University Press, 1999

Ewence, Hannah, Tim Grady, eds, *Minorities and the First World War* Palgrave MacMillan, 2017

Fawaz, Leila Tarazi, *A Land of Aching Hearts: The Middle East in the Great War* Harvard University Press, 2014

Fraser, T.G., ed., *The First World War and Its Aftermath: The Shaping of the Middle East* Gingko Library, 2015

Gatrell, Peter, *Russia's First World War: A Social and Economic History* Routledge, 2005

Grayzel, Susan, *Women's Identities at War: Gender, Motherhood and Politics in Britain and France during the First World War* University of North Carolina Press, 1999

Guoqi, Xu, *Asia and the Great War: A Shared History* Oxford University Press, 2016

Holquist, Peter, *Making War, Forging Revolution: Russia's Continuum of Crisis 1914–1921* Harvard University Press, 2002

Jones, Heather, Jennifer O'Brien, Christoph Schmidt-Supprian, eds, *Untold War: New Perspectives in First World War Studies* Brill, 2015

Keene, Jennifer, Michael Neiberg, eds, *Finding Common Ground: New Directions in First World War Studies* Brill, 2011

Kitchen, James E., Alisa Miller, Laura Rowe, *Other Combatants, Other Fronts: Competing Histories of the First World War* Cambridge Scholars, 2011

Kruizinga, Samuël, Johan Den Hertog, eds, *Caught in the Middle: Neutrals, Neutrality and the First World War* Amsterdam University Press, 2011

Lakitsch, M., S. Reitmar-Juárez, K. Seidel, eds, *Bellicose Entanglements 1914: The Great War as a Global War* LIT, 2015

Lettevall, Rebecka, Geert Somsen, Sven Widmalm, eds, *Neutrality in Twentieth-Century Europe: Intersections of Science, Culture and Politics after the First World War* Routledge, 2012

Manz, Stefan, Panikos Panayi, Matthew Stibbe, eds, *Internment during the First World War: A Mass Global Phenomenon* Routledge, 2019

Minohara, Tosh, Evan Dawley, Tze-ki Hon, eds, *The Decade of the Great War: Japan and the Wider World in the 1910s* Brill, 2015

Mulligan, William, *The Great War for Peace* Yale University Press, 2014

Page, Melvin E., *Africa and the First World War* Palgrave MacMillan, 1987

Rinke, Stefan, *Latin America and the First World War* Cambridge University Press, 2017

Rogan, Eugene, *The Fall of the Ottomans: The Great War in the Middle East 1914–1920* Penguin, 2015

Schmidt, Jan, Katja Schmidtpott, eds, *The East Asian Dimension of the First World War* Campus, 2020

Smith, Andrew, Simon Mollan, Kevin Tennent, eds, *The Impact of the First World War on International Business* Routledge, 2017

Streets-Salter, Heather, *World War One in Southeast Asia: Colonialism and Anticolonialism in an Era of Global Conflict* Cambridge University Press, 2017

Tucker, Richard P., Tait Keller, J.R. McNeill, Martin Schmid, eds, *Environmental Histories of the First World* War Cambridge University Press, 2018

Watson, Alexander, *Ring of Steel: Germany and Austria-Hungary at War, 1914–1918* Penguin, 2014

Zollmann, Jakob, *Naulila 1914: World War I in Angola and International Law: A Study in (Post-)Colonial Border Regimes and Interstate Arbitration* Nomos, 2016

Introduction: A Total Global Tragedy

Abbenhuis, Maartje, 'On the Edge of the Storm? Situating Switzerland's Neutrality in the Context of the First World War' in Michael M. Olsansky, ed., *Am Rande des Sturms: das Schweizer Militär im Ersten Weltkrieg* Hier und Jetz, 2018, pp. 27–9

Becker, Annette, 'The Great War: World War, Total War' *International Review of the Red Cross* 97, 2015, pp. 1029–45

Compagnon, Olivier, Pierre Purseigle, 'Geographies of Mobilization and Territories of Belligerence during the First World War' *Annales (English Edition)* 71, 1, 2016, pp. 37–60

Gatrell, Peter, 'The Epic and the Domestic: Women and War in Russia, 1914–1917' in Gail Braybon, ed., *Evidence, History and the Great War* Berghahn, 2003, pp. 198–215

Horne, John, 'End of a Paradigm? The Cultural History of the Great War' *Past & Present* 242, 2019, pp. 155–92

Keene, Jennifer D., 'W.E.B. Du Bois and the Wounded World: Seeking Meaning in the First World War for African-Americans' *Peace & Change* 26, 2, 2001, pp. 135–52

Kramer, Alan, *Dynamic of Destruction: Culture and Mass Killing in the First World War* Oxford University Press, 2007

Mulligan, William, 'Total War' *War in History* 15, 2, 2008, pp. 211–21

Saint Amour, Paul K., *Tense Future: Modernism, Total War, Encyclopedic Form* Oxford University Press, 2015

Stapleton, Tim, 'The Impact of the First World War on African People' in John Laband, ed., *Daily Lives of Civilians in Wartime Africa* Greenwood, 2007, pp. 113–38

Stockton, C.H., 'The Declaration of Paris' *American Journal of International Law* 14, 1920, pp. 356–68

Strikwerda, Carl, 'World War I in the History of Globalization' *Historical Reflections* 42, 3, 2016, pp. 112–32

Chapter 1: A World of War before 1914

Abbenhuis, Maartje, *An Age of Neutrals: Great Power Politics 1815–1914*
    Cambridge University Press, 2014
Abbenhuis, Maartje, *The Hague Conferences in International Politics 1898–1915*
    Bloomsbury, 2019
Abbenhuis, Maartje, 'A Most Useful Tool for Diplomacy and Statecraft: Neutrality
    and Europe in the "Long" Nineteenth Century 1815–1914' *International
    History Review* 35, 1, 2013, pp. 1–22
Abbenhuis, Maartje, Gordon Morrell, *The First Age of Industrial Globalization:
    An International History 1815–1914* Bloomsbury, 2019
Burton, Antoinette, *The Trouble with Empire* Oxford University Press, 2015
Crawford, Emily, 'The Enduring Legacy of the St Petersburg Declaration:
    Distinction, Military Necessity and the Prohibition of Causing Unnecessary
    Suffering and Superfluous Injury in IHL' *Journal of the History of International
    Law* 20, 4, 2019, pp. 544–66
Eichhorn, Niels, 'A "Century of Peace" That Was Not: War in the Nineteenth
    Century' *Journal of Military History* 84, 4, 2020, pp. 1051–77
Geppert, Dominik, William Mulligan, Andreas Rose, eds, *The Wars before the
    Great War: Conflict and International Politics before the Outbreak of the First
    World War* Cambridge University Press, 2015
Gerbig-Fabel, Marco, 'Photographic Artefacts of War 1904–1905: The Russo-
    Japanese War as Transnational Media Event' *European Review of History* 15, 6,
    2008, pp. 629–42
Gong, G.W., *The Standard of 'Civilization' in International Society* Clarendon
    Press, 1984
Howland, Douglas, 'Sovereignty and the Laws of War: International Consequences
    of Japan's 1905 Victory over Russia' *Law and History Review* 29, 1, 2011,
    pp. 53–97
Kowner, Rotem, ed., *The Impact of the Russo-Japanese War* Routledge, 2007
Lake, Marilyn, Henry Reynolds, *Drawing the Global Color Line: White Man's
    Countries and the International Challenge of Racial Equality* Cambridge
    University Press, 2012
Mulligan, William, *The Origins of the First World War* Second Edition, Cambridge
    University Press, 2018
Neiberg, Michael, *Dance of the Furies: European and the Outbreak of World War
    I* Harvard University Press, 2011
Osterhammel, Jürgen, *The Transformation of the World: A Global History of the
    Nineteenth Century* Princeton University Press, 2014
Partner, Simon, 'Peasants into Citizens? The Meiji Village in the Russo-Japanese
    War' *Monumenta Nipponica* 62, 2, 2007, pp. 178–206
Segesser, Daniel, '"Unlawful Warfare Is Uncivilized": The International Debate on
    the Punishment of War Crimes, 1872–1918' *European Review of History* 14, 2,
    2007, pp. 215–34
Steinberg, John W., Bruce W. Menning, David Schimelpenninck Van Der Oye,
    Shinji Yokote, eds, *Russo-Japanese War in Global Perspective: World War Zero*
    Leiden, Brill, 2005

Chapter 2: Germany's Invasion of Belgium and the Expectations of Civilized War

Cabanes, Bruno, *August 1914: France, the Great War, and a Month That Changed the World* Yale University Press, 2016

Chiu, Eugene W., 'The First World War and Its Impact on Chinese Concepts of Modernity' in Jan Schmidt, Katja Schmidtpott, eds, *The East Asian Dimension of the First World War* Campus, 2020, pp. 93–4

Fulbrook, Mary, *Dissonant Lives: Generations and Violence through the German Dictatorships* Oxford University Press, 2011

Galen Last, D. van, *Black Shame: African Soldiers in Europe, 1914–1922* Bloomsbury, 2016

Guite, J. and T. Haokip, eds, *The Anglo-Kuki War, 1917–1919* Routledge, 2019

Gullace, Nicoletta F., 'Sexual Violence and Family Honor: British Propaganda and International Law during the First World War' *American Historical Review* 102, 3, 1997, p. 714

Horne, John, Alan Kramer, *German Atrocities, 1914: A History of Denial* Yale University Press, 2001

Hull, Isabel V., *A Scrap of Paper: Breaking and Making International Law during the Great War* Cornell University Press, 2014

Liulevicius, Vejas Gabriel, *War Land on the Eastern Front: Culture, National Identity, and German Occupation* Cambridge University Press, 2004

Nielsen, M. B., 'Delegitimating Empire: German and British Representations of Colonial Violence, 1918–1919' *International History Review* 42, 4, 2020, pp. 833–50

Purseigle, Pierre, '"A Wave on to Our Shores": The Exile and Resettlement of Refugees from the Western Front, 1914–1918' *Contemporary European History* 16, 4, 2007, pp. 427–44

Schaepdrijver, Sophie de, ed., *'We Who Are So Cosmopolitan': The War Diary of Constance Graeffe, 1914–1915* Archives Générales du Royaume, 2008

Soutar, Monty, *Whitiki! Whiti! Whiti! E! Maori in the First World War* Bateman Books, 2019

Tames, Ismee, '"War on Our Minds": War, Neutrality and Identity in Dutch Public Debate during the First World War' *First World War Studies* 3, 2, 2012, pp. 201–16

Tuscano, Alberto, '"America's Belgium": W.E.B. Du Bois on Race, Class, and the Origins of World War I' in Alexander Anievas, ed., *Cataclysm 1914: The First World War and the Making of Modern World Politics* Brill, 2015, pp. 236–57

Watson, Alexander, 'Unheard-of Brutality: Russian Atrocities against Civilians in East Prussia, 1914–1915' *Journal of Modern History* 86, 4, 2014, pp. 780–825

Welch, David, *Germany, Propaganda and Total War: The Sins of Omission* Athlone Press, 2000

Chapter 3: Short-War Ambitions

Ansari, Humayun, '"Tasting the King's Salt": Muslims Contested Loyalties and the First World War' in Hannah Ewence, Tim Grady, eds, *Minorities and the First World War* Palgrave MacMillan, 2017, pp. 33–61

Bailey, Mark, 'Supporting the Wartime Economy: Imperial Maritime Trade and the Globalized Maritime Trade System 1914–1916' *Journal of Maritime Research* 19, 1, 2017, pp. 23–45

Frey, Marc, 'Trade, Ships and the Neutrality of the Netherlands in the First World War' *International History Review* 19, 3, 1997, pp. 541–62

Goldthree, Reena N., 'A Greater Enterprise Than the Panama Canal: Migrant Labor and Military Recruitment in the World War I-Era Circum-Caribbean' *Labor* 13, 3–4, 2016, pp. 57–82

Horn, Martin, *Britain, France and the Financing of the First World War* McGill-Queen's University Press, 2002

Meyer, Kathryn, 'Trade and Nationality at Shanghai upon the Outbreak of the First World War 1914–1915' *International History Review* 10, 2, 1988, pp. 238–60

Moyd, Michelle, 'We Don't Want to Die for Nothing': Askari at War in German East-Africa, 1914–1918' in Santanu Das, ed., *Race, Empire and First World War Writing* Cambridge University Press, 2011, pp. 90–107

Osuntokun, Akinjide, 'Disaffection and Revolts in Nigeria during the First World War, 1914–1918' *Canadian Journal of African Studies* 5, 2, 1971, pp. 171–81

Pennell, Catriona, *A Kingdom United. Popular Responses to the Outbreak of the First World War in Britain and Ireland* Oxford University Press, 2013

Rausch, Jane M., *Colombia and World War I: The Experience of a Neutral Latin American Nation during the Great War and Its Aftermath, 1914–1921* Lexington Books, 2014

Roberts, Richard, 'A Tremendous Panic: The Global Financial Crisis of 1914' in Andrew Smith, Simon Mollan, Kevin D. Tennent, eds, *The Impact of the First World War on International Business* Routledge, 2017, pp. 121–41

Sanders, M. L., Philip Taylor, *British Propaganda in the First World War 1914–1918* MacMillan, 1982

Young, John W., 'Emotions and the British Government's Decision for War in 1914' *Diplomacy & Statecraft* 29, 4, 2018, pp. 543–64

Zollmann, Jakob, *Naulila 1914: World War I in Angola and International Law* Nomos, 2016

Chapter 4: Long-War Realities

Aglietti, Marcella, 'Patriotism and Neutrality: The Spanish Parliament and the Great War, 1914–18' *Parliaments, Estates and Representation* 36, 1, 2016, pp. 54–70

Boom, Willem H. van, 'The Great War and Dutch Contract Law: Resistance, Responsiveness and Neutrality' *Comparative Legal History* 2, 2, 2014, pp. 303–24

Burk, Kathleen, *Britain, America and the Sinews of War 1914–1918* George Allen & Unwin, 1985

Chaudhuri, Jyotirmoy Pal, *Whitehall and the Black Republic: A Study of Colonial Britain's Attitude towards Liberia 1914–1939* Palgrave MacMillan, 2018

Coogan, John W., *The End of Neutrality: The United States, Britain, and Maritime Rights, 1899–1915* Cornell University Press, 1981

Coogan, John W., 'The Short-War Illusion Resurrected: The Myth of Economic Warfare as the British Schlieffen Plan' *Journal of Strategic Studies* 38, 7, 2015, pp. 1048–60

Dilley, Andrew, 'Trade after the Deluge: British Commerce, Armageddon and the Political Economy of Globalisation 1914–1918' in A. Smith, S. Mollan, K. D. Tennent, eds, *The Impact of the First World War on International Business* Routledge, 2017, pp. 25–46

Farrar, Marjorie Milbank, *Conflict and Compromise: The Strategy, Politics and Diplomacy of the French Blockade 1914–1918* Martinus Nijhoff, 1974

Huber, Valeska, 'Connecting Colonial Seas: The "International Colonisation" of Port Said and the Suez Canal during and after the First World War' *European Review of History* 19, 1, 2012, pp. 148–51

Kruizinga, Samuël, 'Government by Committee: Dutch Economic Policy during the First World War' in James Kitchen, Alisa Miller, Laura Rowe, eds, *Other Combatants, Other Fronts: Competing Histories of the First World War* Cambridge Scholars, 2011, pp. 99–124

Kruizinga, Samuël, 'Sailing in Uncharted Waters: Four Dutch Steamship Companies during the First World War, 1914–1918' *International Journal of Maritime History* 27, 2 2015, pp. 227–49

Neff, Stephen C., 'Disrupting a Delicate Balance: The Allied Blockade Policy and the Law of Maritime Neutrality during the Great War' *European Journal of International Law* 29, 2, 2018, pp. 459–75

Neilson, Keith, 'The Maritime Way in Munitions: The Entente and Supply in the First World War' *Journal of Military and Strategic Studies* 14, 3–4, 2012, pp. 1–18

Nijs, Thimo de, 'Food Provision and Food Retailing in The Hague 1914–1930' in Frank Trentmann, Flemming Just, eds, *Food and Conflict in Europe in the Age of Two World Wars* Palgrave, 2006, pp. 65–87

Osborne, Eric W., *Britain's Economic Blockade of Germany 1914–1918* Frank Cass, 2004

Reger, Jeffrey D., 'Lamps, Never before Dim Are Being Extinguished from Lack of Olive Oil: Deforestation and Famine in Palestine at War and in Peace under the Late Ottoman Empire and Early British Empire, 1910–1920' in Selena Daly, Martina Salvante, Vanda Wilcox, eds, *Landscapes of the First World War* Palgrave MacMillan, 2018, pp. 37–56

Singha, Radhika, 'India's Silver Bullets: War Loans and War Propaganda 1917–1918' in M. Abbenhuis, N. Atkinson, K. Baird, G. Romano, eds., *Myriad Legacies of 1917: A Year of War and Revolution* Palgrave MacMillan, 2018, pp. 77–102

Townsend, Susan C., 'The Great War and Urban Crisis: Conceptualizing the Industrial Metropolis in Japan and Britain in the 1910s' in T. Minohara, T. Hon, E. Dawley, eds, *The Decade of the Great War: Japan and the Wider World in the 1910s* Brill, 2014, pp. 301–22

Vandamme, Tobit, 'The Rise of Nationalism in a Cosmopolitan Port City: The Foreign Communities of Shanghai during the First World War' *Journal of World History* 29, 1, 2018, pp. 37–64

Vincent, C. Paul, *The Politics of Hunger: The Allied Blockade of Germany 1915–1919* Ohio University Press, 1985

Weinreb, Alice, 'Beans Are Bullets, Potatoes Are Powder: Food as a Weapon during the First World War' in Richard p. Tucker, Tait Keller, J.R. McNeill, Martin Schmid, eds, *Environmental Histories of the First World War* Cambridge University Press, 2018, pp. 19–37

Chapter 5: The Barbarian Next Door

Abbenhuis, Maartje, 'Where War Met Peace: The Borders of the Neutral Netherlands with Belgium and Germany in the First World War' *Journal of Borderland Studies* 22, 1, 2007, pp. 53–77

Alexeeva, Olga V., 'Experiencing War: Chinese Workers in Russia during the First World War' *Chinese Historical Review* 25, 1, 2018, pp. 46–66

Audoin-Rouzeau, Stéphane, '1915: Stalemate' in Jay Winter, ed., *Cambridge History of the First World War*, Volume 1, Cambridge University Press, 2014, pp. 65–88

Bergen, Leo van, Maartje Abbenhuis, 'Man-Monkey, Monkey-Man: Neutrality and the Discussions about the "Inhumanity" of Poison Gas in the Netherlands and International Committee of the Red Cross' *First World War Studies* 3, 1, 2012, pp. 1–23

Bloxham, Donald, 'The First World War and the Development of the Armenian Genocide' in Ronald Grigor Suny, Fatma Múge Göçek, Norman A. Naimark, eds, *A Question of Genocide: Armenians and Turks at the End of the Ottoman Empire* Oxford University Press, 2011, pp. 260–75

Gatrell, Peter, *A Whole Empire Walking: Refugees in Russia during World War I* Oxford University Press, 2000

Gullace, Nicoletta, 'Friends, Aliens and Enemies: Fictive Communities and the *Lusitania* Riots of 1915' *Journal of Social History* 39, 2, 2005, pp. 345–67

Horne, John, 'Nineteen Fifteen and the Totalizing Logic of the First World War' *Thyssen Lectures IV The Great War beyond National Perspectives* Max Weber Stiftung 32, 2017, http://www.oiist.org/?q=de/node/33

Hyland Jr., Steven, 'The Syrian-Ottoman Home Front in Buenos Aires and Rosario during the First World War' *Journal of Migration History* 4, 1, 2018, pp. 211–35

Jones, Heather, *Violence against Prisoners of War in the First World War* Cambridge University Press, 2014

Lohr, Eric, *Nationalizing the Russian Empire: The Campaign against Enemy Aliens during World War I* Harvard University Press, 2003

Page, Melvin, 'Africa's First "High Tech" War: The Technological Impact of World War One on Africans' *Journal of African Military History* 2, 1, 2018, pp. 24–61

Panayi, Panikos, ed., *Minorities in Wartime: National and Racial Groupings in Europe, North America and Australia during the Two World Wars* Berg, 1993

Protasio, John, *The Day the World Was Shocked: The Lusitania Disaster and Its Influence on the Course of World War One* Casemate, 2015

Roy, Kaushik, *The Indian Army and the First World War 1914–1918* Oxford University Press, 2018

Slotten, Hugh R., 'Humane Chemistry or Scientific Barbarism? American Responses to World War 1 Poison Gas, 1915–1930' *Journal of American History* 77, 2, 1990, pp. 476–98

Tato, María Ínes, 'A Discordant Voice from the Trenches: Juan José de Soiza Reilly's War Chronicles' *Studies in 20th & 21st Century Literature* 41, 2, 2017, np

Thompson, Paul, 'The *Lusitania* Riots in Pietermaritzburg 13–14 May 1915' *War & Society* 36, 1, 2017, pp. 1–30

Trommler, Frank, 'The *Lusitania* Effect: America's Mobilization against Germany in World War I' *German Studies Review* 32, 2, 2009, pp. 241–66

Ulrichsen, Kristian Coates, 'The British Occupation of Mesopotamia 1914–1922' *Journal of Strategic Studies* 30, 2, 2007, pp. 349–77

Watson, Alexander, *The Fortress: The Great Siege of Przemyśl* Penguin, 2019

Chapter 6: The Test of Endurance

Becker, Annette, 'From the *Bulletin Internationale des Sociétés de la Croix Rouge* to the *International Review of the Red Cross*: The Great War as Revelator' *International Review of the Red Cross* 100, 907–9, 2019, pp. 97–113

Bekele, Shiferaw, Uoldelul Chelati Dirar, Alessandro Volterra and Massimo Zaccaria, eds, *The First World War from Tripoli to Addis Ababa (1911–1924)* Centre Français des Études Éthiopiennes, 2018

Bose, Sugata and Kris Manjapra, eds, *Cosmopolitan Thought Zones: South Asia and the Global Circulation of Ideas* Palgrave MacMillan, 2010

Cohen, Aaron J., 'Flowers of Evil: Media, Child Psychology and the Struggle for Russia's Future during the First World War' in James Martin, Robert Coles, eds, *Children and War: A Historical Anthology* New York University Press, 2002, pp. 38–49

Dal Lago, Enrico, Róisín Healy and Gearóid Barry, eds, *1916 in Global Context: An Anti Imperial Moment* Routledge, 2019

Fahrenthold, Stacy, 'Transnational Modes and Media: The Syrian Press in the *Mahjar* and Emigrant Activism during World War I' *Mashriq & Mahjar* 1, 1, 2013, pp. 30–54

Gram-Skjoldager, Karen, 'Denmark during the First World War: Neutral Policy, Economy and Culture' *Journal of Modern European History* 17, 2, 2019, pp. 234–50

Harper, Tim 'Singapore, 1915, and the Birth of the Asian Underground' *Modern Asian Studies* 47, 6, 2013, pp. 1782–811

Johnson, S. Marianne, Ian Isherwood, 'Gettysburg and the Great War' *War & Society* 36, 3, 2017, pp. 217–34

Jones, Heather, 'International or Transnational? Humanitarian Action during the First World War' *European Review of History* 16, 5, 2009, pp. 697–713

Kaiga, Sakiko, 'The Use of Force to Prevent War? The Bryce Group's "Proposal for the Avoidance of War" 1914–1915' *Journal of British Studies* 57, 2, 2018, pp. 308–32

Keene, Jennifer D., 'Americans Respond: Perspectives on the Global War, 1914–1917' *Geschichte und Gesellschaft* 40, 2, 2014, pp. 266–86

Liebau, Heike, 'Kaiser ki Jay (Long Live the Kaiser): Perceptions of World War I and the Socio-Religious Movement among the Oraons in Chota Nagpur, 1914–1916' in H. Liebau, K. Bromber, K. Lange, D. Hamzah, R. Ahiya, eds, *The World in World Wars* Brill, 2010, pp. 251–75

Moyd, Michelle, 'Ordeal and Opportunity: Ending the First World War in Africa' *Fletcher Forum of World Affairs* 43, 1, 2019, pp. 145–54

Neiberg, Michael, 'German Spies in New York!' *Military History* 31, 1, 2013, pp. 66–71

Nicolson, Beryl, 'On the Front Line in Someone Else's War: Mallakastër, Albania 1916–1918' *Region* 4, 2, 2015, pp. 247–63

Page, Melvin E., *The Chiwaya War: Malawians in the First World War* Westview, 2000

Piller, Elisabeth, 'American War Relief, Cultural Mobilization and the Myth of Impartial Humanitarianism 1914–1917' *Journal of the Gilded Age and Progressive Era* 17, 4, 2018, pp. 619–35

Ponce, Javier, 'Commerce Warfare in the East Central Atlantic during the First World War: German Submarines around the Canary Islands, 1916–1918' *Mariner's Mirror* 100, 3, 2014, pp. 335–48

Reeves, Caroline, 'Sovereignty and the Chinese Red Cross Society: The Differentiated Practice of International Law in Shandong, 1914–1916' *Journal of the History of International Law* 13, 2011, pp. 155–77

Salvado, Francisco Romero, *Spain: Between War and Revolution* Routledge, 1999

Singha, Radhika, *The Coolie's Great War: Indian Labour in a Global Conflict, 1914–1921* Oxford University Press, 2020

Tanielian, Melanie, 'Politics of Wartime Relief in Ottoman Beirut (1914–1918)' *First World War Studies* 5, 1, 2014, pp. 69–82

Wiel, Jérôme aan de, 'The Shots That Reverberated for a Long Time, 1916–1932: The Irish Revolution, the Bolsheviks and the European Left' *International History Review* 42, 1, 2020, pp. 195–213

Zaccaria, Massimo, 'Feeding the War: Canned Meat Production in the Horn of Africa and the Italian Front' in Shiferaw Bekele, Uoldelul Chelati Dirar, Alessandro Volterra, Massimo Zaccaria, eds, *The First World War from Tripoli to Addis Ababa* Centre Français des Études Éthiopiennes, 2018, np

Chapter 7: Revolutionary Warfare, 1917

Abbenhuis, Maartje, Neill Atkinson, Kingsley Baird, Gail Romano, eds, *The Myriad Faces of 1917: A Year of War and Revolution* Palgrave, 2018

Bessel, Richard, 'Revolution' in Jay Winter, ed., *Cambridge History of the First World War,* Volume 1, Cambridge University Press, 2014, pp. 126–44

Engel, Barbara Alpern, 'Not by Bread Alone: Subsistence Riots in Russia during World War I' *Journal of Modern History* 69, 4, 1997, pp. 696–721

Engelstein, Laura, *Russia in Flames: War, Revolution, Civil War 1914–1921* Oxford University Press, 2018

Fitzpatrick, Sheila, *The Russian Revolution* Oxford University Press, 1994

Gerwarth, Robert, *The Vanquished: Why the First World War Failed to End* Straus and Giroux, 2016

Guoqi, Xu, *Strangers on the Western Front: Chinese Workers in the Great War* Harvard University Press, 2011

Hemenway, Elizabeth Jones, 'Nicholas in Hell: Rewriting the Tsarist Narrative in the Revolutionary Skazki of 1917' *Russian Review* 60, 2, 2001, pp. 185–204

Holquist, Peter, 'Violent Russia, Deadly Marxism? Russia in the Epoch of Violence, 1905–21' *Kritika: Explorations in Russian and Eurasian History* 4, 3, 2003, pp. 627–52

Horne, John, ed., *State, Society and Mobilization in Europe during the First World War* Cambridge University Press, 1997

Lieven, Dominic, *Towards the Flame: Empire, War and the End of Tsarist Russia* Penguin, 2016

Linkhoeva, Tatiana, 'The Russian Revolution and the Emergence of Japanese Anticommunism' *Revolutionary Russia* 31, 2, 2018, pp. 261–78

Loveridge, Steven, 'What Should Daddy Do in the Great War? The Second Division Question and Conditional Commitment to New Zealand's War Effort, 1917–1918' *Journal of New Zealand Studies* 27, 2018, pp. 16–34

Lunn, Joe, 'Kande Kamara Speaks' in Melvin E. Page, ed., *Africa and the First World War* Macmillan, 1987, pp. 28–53

Ortaggi, Simonette, 'Italian Women during the Great War' in Gail Braybon, ed., *Evidence, History and the Great War* Berghahn, 2003, pp. 216–38

Retish, Aaron B., Matthew Rendle, 'Introduction from Lenin's Overcoat? The Global Impact of the Russian Revolution' *Revolutionary Russia* 31, 2, 2018, pp. 145–51

Sanborn, Joshua, *Drafting the Russian Nation: Military Conscription, Total War and Mass Politics 1905–1925* Northern Illinois University Press, 2003

Sanborn, Joshua, 'The Genesis of Russian Warlordism: Violence and Governance during the First World War and the Civil War' *Contemporary European History* 19, 3, 2010, pp. 195–213

Smith, Leonard V., 'Mutiny' in Jay Winter, ed., *Cambridge History of the First World War*, Volume 2, Cambridge University Press, 2014, pp. 196–217

Stevenson, David, 'Britain's Biggest Wartime Stoppage: The Origins of the Engineering Strike of May 1917' *History* 105, 365, 2020, pp. 268–90

Stockdale, Melissa Kirschke, *Mobilizing the Russian Nation: Patriotism and Citizenship in the First World War* Cambridge University Press, 2016

Werth, Nicolas, 'Russia 1917: The Soldiers' Revolution' *South Central Review* 34, 3, 2017, pp. 48–57

Yost, Franziska, 'Glory to the Russian Maximalists! Reactions to the Russian Revolution in Argentina and Brazil 1917–22' *Revolutionary Russia* 31, 2, 2018, pp. 247–60

Chapter 8: The End of Neutrality?

Abbenhuis, Maartje, 'Not Silent, nor Silenced: Neutrality and the First World War', in José-Leonardo Ruiz Sánchez, I. C. Olivero, Garcia Sanz C, eds, *Shaping Neutrality throughout the First World War* Editorial Universidad de Sevilla, 2016

Compagnon, Olivier, 'Latin America' in Jay Winter, ed., *The Cambridge History of the First World War*, Volume 1, Cambridge University Press, 2014, pp. 533–56

Coogan, John, 'Wilsononian Diplomacy in War and Peace' in Gordon Martel, ed., *American Foreign Relations Reconsidered 1890–1993* Routledge, 1994, pp. 71–89

Craft, Stephen G., 'Angling for an Invitation to Paris: China's Entry into the First World War' *International History Review* 16, 1, 1994, pp. 1–24

Dehne, Philip, 'Profiting Despite the Great War: Argentina's Grain Multinationals' in Andrew Smith, Simon Molan, Kevin D. Tennent, eds, *The Impact of the First World War on International Business* Routledge, 2017, pp. 67–86

Gillispie, William, 'Colonialism in Global Conflict: Liberia's Entry and Participation in World War One' *First World War Studies* 9, 1, 2018, pp. 111–29

Keene, Jennifer, 'A "Brutalizing" War? The USA after the First World War' *Journal of Contemporary History* 50, 1, 2015, pp. 78–99

Keene, Jennifer, 'Deeds Not Words: American Social Justice Movements and World War I' *Journal of the Gilded Age and Progressive Era* 17, 4, 2018, pp. 704–18

Krebs, Gerhard, 'German-Japanese-United States Mutual Perceptions and Diplomatic Initiatives over Mexico: New Perspectives on the Zimmerman Telegram' in Jan Schmidt, Katja Schmidtpott, eds, *The East Asian Dimension of the First World War* Campus Verlag, 2020, pp. 247–67

Neiberg, Michael, 'Blinking Eyes Began to Open: Legacies from America's Road to the Great War, 1914–1917' *Diplomatic History* 38, 4, 2014, pp. 801–12

Neiberg, Michael, *The Path to War: How the First World War Made Modern America* Oxford University Press, 2016

Raymond, Gregory V., 'War as Membership: International Society and Thailand's Participation in World War I' *Asian Studies Review* 43, 1, pp. 132–47

Rinke, Stefan H., *Latin America and the First World War*, trans. Christopher W Reid, Cambridge University Press, 2017

Sharp, Alan, 'The Genie That Would Not Go Back into the Bottle: National Self-Determination and the Legacy of the First World War and the Peace Settlement' in Seamus Dunn, T. G. Fraser, eds, *Europe and Ethnicity: World War I and Contemporary Ethnic Conflict* Routledge, 1996, pp. 9–28

Tato, María Inés, 'An Overseas Trench: Social Mobilization in Buenos Aires during the Great War' in M. Lakitsch, S. Reitmar-Juárez, K. Seidel, eds, *Bellicose Entanglements 1914: The Great War as a Global War* LIT Verlag, 2015, pp. 43–59

Tooze, Adam, *The Deluge: The Great War and the Remaking of the Global Order* Penguin, 2014

Zeiler, Thomas W., David K. Ekbladh, Benjamin C. Montoya, eds, *Beyond 1917: The United States and the Global Legacies of the Great War* Oxford University Press, 2017

Chapter 9: Peace-Making

Boak, Helen L., 'Women in the German Revolution' in G. Kets, J. Muldoon, eds, *The German Revolution and Political Theory* Springer, 2019, pp. 25–44

Dhabade, Rohan, *Something about Jallianwala Bagh and the Days of British Empire* Evince, 2019

Clavin, Patricia, 'The Austrian Hunger Crisis and the Genesis of International Organization after the First World War' *International Affairs* 90, 2, 2014, pp. 265–78

Clavin, Patrica, *Securing the World Economy: The Reinvention of the League of Nations* Oxford University Press, 2010

Gatrell, Peter, *The Making of the Modern Refugee* Oxford University Press, 2015

Gerwarth, Robert, ed., *War in Peace: Paramilitary Violence in Europe after the Great War* Oxford University Press, 2013

Guoqi, Xu, 'The Year 1919 and the Question of "What Is China?"' *International Politics* 55, 6, 2018, pp. 752–64

Horne, John, 'Defending Victory: Paramilitary Politics in France, 1918–1926: A Counter-Example' in Robert Gerwarth, ed., *War in Peace: Paramilitary Violence in Europe after the Great War* Oxford University Press, 2013, pp. 216–34

Lunn, Joe, 'France's Legacy to Demba Mboup? A Senenalese Griot and His Descendants Remember His Military Service during the First World War' in Santanu Das, ed., *Race, Empire and First World War Writing* Cambridge University Press, 2011, pp. 108–24

MacArthur-Seal, Daniel-Joseph, 'Intoxication and Imperialism: Nightlife in Occupied Istanbul, 1918–1923' *Comparative Studies of South Asia, Africa and the Middle East* 37, 2, 2017, pp. 299–313

Manela, Erez, *The Wilsonian Moment: Self-Determination and the International Origins of Anticolonial Nationalism* Oxford University Press, 2007

Marks, Sally, *The Illusion of Peace: International Relations in Europe 1918–1933* Palgrave MacMillan, 2003

Moyd, Michelle, 'Radical Potentials, Conservative Realities: African Veterans of the German Colonial Army in Post-World War I Tanganyika' *First World War Studies* 10, 1, 2019, pp. 88–107

Osborne Humphries, Mark, 'Paths of Infection: The First World War and the Origins of the 1918 Influenza Pandemic' *War in History* 21, 1, 2013, pp. 55–81

Rasmussen, Anne, 'The Spanish Flu' in Jay Winter, ed., *Cambridge History of the First World War,* Volume 3, Cambridge University Press, 2014, pp. 334–57

Rice, Geoffrey, *Black November: The 1918 Influenza Pandemic in New Zealand* Canterbury University Press, 2005

Sammartino, Annemarie H., *The Impossible Border: Germany and the East 1914–1922* Cornell University Press, 2010

Schmitt, Hans A., ed., *Neutral Europe between War and Revolution 1917–1923* University Press of Virginia, 1988

Stevenson, David, *With Our Backs to the Wall: Victory and Defeat in 1918* Harvard University Press, 2011

Tomkins, Sara M., 'The Influenza Epidemic of 1918–19 in Western Samoa' *Journal of Pacific History* 27, 2, 1992, pp. 181–97

INDEX

Abadan 63
Aborigines 54
Abyssinia (Ethiopia) 19, 55, 106
Adwa 18
Africa 8, 19, 30, 35, 36, 40–2, 45, 46,
    48, 50–5, 58, 66, 70, 78, 81–3, 92,
    98, 99, 101, 102, 106, 110, 129,
    130, 151, 164, 167
African Americans 6, 101
Africans 35, 42, 53, 78, 82, 88, 98,
    101, 102, 129, 130, 167
Aksakal, Mustafa 2
Albania 99
Alexander I (king of Greece) 152
Alsace Lorraine 58, 115
Amritsar Massacre (1919) 168–9
Amsterdam 63
Anglo-Sanussi War (1915–17) 106
anti-colonialism 18, 19, 21, 27, 58,
    130, 132, 133, 167
anti-Germanism 2, 31, 34, 41, 42, 47,
    83, 85–8, 92, 93, 136, 140
anti-semitism 86, 90, 91, 166
Antwerp 36, 40
Apollinaire, Guillaume 161
Arab Revolt (1916) 106
Arabia 73, 78, 106, 170
Arabian Gulf 73
Argentina 30, 36, 44, 70, 93, 125,
    135–7, 139, 146, 154
Arizona 140
Armenian genocide 91, 92, 94, 169,
    170
Armenians 36, 56, 91, 92, 94, 169,
    170
Armistice (1918) 12, 40, 117, 141,
    146, 157, 158, 160, 164, 169
Asia 6, 8, 15, 15, 23, 46, 48, 54–8, 66,
    72, 73, 82, 92, 98, 105, 115, 133,
    147, 150, 164, 170
Asquith, Herbert 113

Assyrians 56, 170
Atlantic Ocean 50, 55, 56, 66
atrocities 10, 11, 16–24, 30–8, 71, 77,
    82, 89–92, 105, 131, 136
Audoin-Rouzeau, Stéphane 81
Aulihan Uprising (1915–18) 106
Australia 52, 54, 59, 88, 104, 117,
    126, 162
Austria-Hungary 1, 9, 12, 17, 24, 25,
    29, 36, 45, 47, 50, 52, 55, 59, 63,
    64, 66, 67, 90, 94, 98–100, 103,
    113, 114, 117, 121, 123, 165
Azerbaijan 56

Baghdad 78, 94
Balakian, Grigorius 169
Balkan 9, 23–5, 28–30, 33, 36, 91,
    110, 152
Balkan Wars (1912–13) 9, 23–5,
    28–30, 33, 36
Baltic Sea 49, 51, 56, 74
Baltics 17, 49, 51, 56, 74, 91, 121
Bantu 83
Barbosa, Rui 111
Barcelona 126
Basra 63, 69, 77
Battle of Ctesiphon (1915) 77
Battle of the Marne (1914) 61
Battle of the Somme (1916) 98, 103
Becker, Annette 1, 11, 89, 111
Becker, Jean-Jacques 118, 130
Beijing 150
Belgium 9, 10, 16, 19, 29–43, 45, 46,
    49, 50, 52, 53, 55, 56, 59, 61, 66,
    70, 80, 88, 89, 92, 99, 101, 110,
    111, 113, 136, 151, 152, 160
Bethmann-Hollweg, Theobald von 31,
    41, 113
Bignami, Enrico 111
Binding, Rudolf 80
Black Sea 17, 56, 57, 72

blacklisting 70–3, 106, 107, 136, 145, 151, 154
Black Tom explosion (1916) 109, 140
blockades 17, 49–51, 63, 64, 67, 70, 73, 74, 81, 85, 106, 107, 111, 152–4
Blücher, Evelyn 102
Blue Book Report on the Natives of South-West Africa and their Treatment by Germany (1918) 42
Bolivia 136
Bolshevism 116–17, 122–5, 128–32, 149, 159, 165, 166 See also Communism
Bombay 71, 72
Borneo 73
Brazil 111, 125, 136, 146, 160
Brisbane 162
Britain, See Great Britain
British Expeditionary Force 61
Brooke, Rupert 36
Brusilov, Aleksei 91, 98
Brussels 17, 40
Bryce Group 36, 112
Bryce Report (1915) 36–7, 85
Buenos Aires 44, 70
Bulgaria 110
Burgfrieden 25, 54
Burkina Faso 129, 130
Burton, Antoinette 18

Cameroon 52, 98
Canada 55, 88, 104, 145
Cape Town 88
Caribbean 16, 51, 54, 69, 82, 145
Caribbean Sea 51
Carnegie Endowment for International Peace 24, 28, 33, 36, 143
Carnovale, Luigi 155
Caroline Islands 56
Carporetto 128
Catalonia 93, 105
Caucasus 57, 61, 80, 91, 120, 122, 170
Cendrars, Blaise 161
Central Africa 53, 98
Central Organisation for Durable Peace (CODP) 111, 112
Channel, See English Channel
charity 17, 33, 40, 111, 136, 141, 154

Chaudhuri, Jyotirmoy Pal 71
chemical warfare 80–1, 85, 168
Chemin des Dames 103
Chen Duxiu 38
Cherbourg 84
Chicago 99, 155
children 1, 31, 35, 38, 42, 71, 89, 94, 98, 99, 102, 103, 119, 138, 143, 152
Chile 48, 70, 154
China 3, 12, 16, 18, 38, 46, 47, 54, 57, 82, 94, 101, 105, 117, 132, 133, 137, 147–50, 152, 157, 172
Choson peninsula 19, 23 See also Korea
Christians 56, 57, 58, 91
Cicilia 170
civic cleansing 86, 90–1
civil war 2, 12, 27, 55, 109, 116, 118, 124, 126, 152, 154, 157, 162, 165, 166, 170
civilians 3, 5, 8, 9, 11, 23, 30, 31, 34, 35, 40, 42, 54, 58, 62, 64, 65, 74, 80, 81, 84, 85, 89–94, 98, 104, 105, 108, 111, 119, 122, 129, 144, 151, 160, 168
civilization 8, 19, 21, 23, 30, 31, 38, 39, 41–3, 46, 57, 82, 83, 113, 136, 148, 158
Clausewitz, Karl von 15
Clemenceau, George 5, 158
CODP, See Central Organisation for Durable Peace (CODP)
Colombia 43, 62, 68, 71
colonialism 18, 22, 30, 36, 41, 42, 58, 82, 89, 103, 129–33, 167, 169, 172
colonized communities 18, 54, 82, 106, 129, 172
Commission for the Relief of Belgium (CRB) 111
communism 112, 116, 122–3, 128, 166 See also Bolshevism
Concha, José Vincente 68
Congo 34, 55, 98
conscription 1, 6, 53, 54, 58, 64, 83, 100–4, 106, 116, 118, 126, 144
Constantine I (king of Greece) 152
Constantinople 71, 169
Constantinople Convention (1888) 71
contraband 10, 27, 49, 64, 66, 67, 70

Copenhagen 63
Costa Rica 136
CRB, *See* Commission for the Relief of Belgium (CRB)
Crimean Peninsula 17
Crimean War (1853–56) 17
Cuba 16, 69, 145

Damaraland Concession (1892) 41
Dardanelles 63, 73, 74, 110
Dar-es-Salaam 51
Daudet, Léon 2, 3, 5, 97, 100, 103
Declaration of London (1909–10) 10, 49–50, 63
Declaration of Paris (1856) 17
declaration of war 3, 10, 12, 24, 25, 28, 32, 43, 45–50, 53, 56, 57, 107, 110, 135, 136, 140–2, 150
Dehne, Philip 70
Delagoa Bay 110
demography 71, 101, 102, 164
Denmark 70
desertion 7, 77, 103, 121, 164
Deutsch-Asiatische Bank 71
Deutsche Gesellschaft für Völkerrecht 112
Diagne, Blaise 130
diplomatic relations 7, 8, 15, 17, 19, 22, 24, 25, 28, 43, 57, 65, 67, 92, 106, 112, 136–8, 140, 141, 145, 146, 148
diseases 73, 90–1, 99, 162, 164 *See also* Spanish flu
Dolchstoss myth 166
Dominican Republic 69, 145
Duan Qirui 148
Dublin 105
Duma 25, 119–20, 123
Dupuis, Emile 108
Durban 88
Dutch East Indies (Indonesia) 4, 54, 105, 117, 130–2, 154, 172

Easter Rising (1916) 104–5
economic warfare 10, 11, 17, 49, 51, 61–75, 78, 79, 98, 107, 139
economy 4, 6–8, 10, 11, 15–19, 21, 24, 25, 43, 44, 49, 50, 51, 54–7, 61–75, 80, 98, 101, 145, 151

Egypt 2, 59, 71, 102
SMS *Emden* 72
English Channel 51, 63, 66
Erzberger, Matthias 127, 166
Ethiopia, *See* Abyssinia
expansionism 16, 57, 69, 146, 147

fertilizers 98, 109, 130
Fiji 125
Finland 122
food 1, 7, 48, 61, 62, 64, 74, 77, 78, 81, 90, 98, 99, 102, 103, 106, 111, 116, 118, 119, 124, 126, 127, 131, 148, 165
food riots 48, 99, 126
forced labour 89, 100
France 2, 3, 5, 9, 10, 12, 17, 24, 26, 29–34, 37–45, 48, 50, 52, 58, 61, 69, 78, 80–2, 84, 86, 89, 92, 97, 99, 101, 103, 109, 113, 117, 124, 125, 129, 130, 139, 141, 147, 148, 150, 151, 155, 158, 160–2, 167
Franco-Prussian War (1870–1) 34
franc-tireurs 34
Franz Ferdinand (Archduke) 24
Franz Joseph (Kaiser) 113
free trade 10, 17, 22, 46, 48–51, 55, 63–7, 70, 72–5, 106, 117, 151, 154, 171
Freikorps 165–6
French West Africa 70, 82
Fried, Alfred 110
fuel 7, 61, 63, 68 *See also* oil

Galicia 90–2, 98, 121
Gallipoli 59, 63, 170
gas attacks, *See* chemical warfare
Gatrell, Peter 4
Geneva Convention 17, 111
genocide 11, 16, 41, 42, 58, 91–2, 169, 170
Germany 9, 10, 12, 16, 24, 26, 29–42, 45, 48–50, 58, 63, 64, 67, 69, 70, 78, 80, 81, 85–8, 93, 94, 98, 102, 103, 107, 110, 113, 122, 127, 136–40, 145, 146, 148, 151, 154, 164–6
Gerwarth, Robert 117
Gibraltar 88
Godsvrede 25

Goll, Yvon 115
Gorki, Maxime 122
Goschen, Edward 31
Graeffe, Constance 39
Grayzel, Susan 38
Great Britain 7, 10, 16, 21, 31, 40,
    43–59, 65, 69, 71–3, 88, 94, 101,
    103, 106, 112–14, 124, 125, 139
Greek Orthodox community 91, 170
Greene, Sidney 159
Guatemala 136, 145
Guilbeaux, Henri 110
Guinea 70
Gullace, Nicola 38, 86, 88
Guoqi, Xu 57, 148

Hague Conventions (1899, 1907) 10,
    17, 18, 22, 33, 66, 80, 89, 143
Hague Peace Conferences (1899, 1907)
    22, 143–4
Hague Conference (1915) 112, 164
Hahn, Albert 149, 153
Haile Selassi 55, 106
Haiti 69, 136, 145
Hamburg 63, 66
Hawai'i 16
Heinz, Friederich Wilhelm 165–6
Heligoland Bight 51
Herero 36, 41–2
Heymann, Lida Gustava 164–5
Hobhouse Report (1901) 36
Hollywood 93
Honduras 136
Hopps, Harry R. 32
Horne, John 8, 11, 34, 38, 81, 84
Hötzendorf, Franz Conrad von 90
humanitarian aid 17, 28, 40, 111, 141,
    154, 155, 171, 173
humanitarianism 7, 31, 75, 111, 138,
    142
hunger, See starvation
Hutu 55

ICRC, See Red Cross
imperialism 1, 16, 21, 53, 68, 115, 129,
    146, 168, 172
India 2, 6, 41, 54, 58, 59, 62, 72, 74,
    77–9, 83, 102, 105, 115, 117, 125,
    144, 168, 169

Indian Expeditionary Force 2, 63, 77, 82
Indian Ocean 56, 57, 66
indigenous communities 16, 42, 54, 58,
    88, 104, 106, 116, 117, 122, 129,
    132, 144, 172
Indo-China 54, 150, 167
Indonesia, See Dutch East Indies
inflation 47, 48, 68, 72, 73, 95, 98, 99,
    107, 118, 126, 131, 157
Inter-Allied Conference (1916) 106
Inter-American High Commission 68
International Committee of the Red
    Cross, See Red Cross
internationalism 23, 141, 142
inter-state warfare 6, 9, 15–19, 22, 24,
    27, 29, 30, 33, 110, 138, 141, 160,
    172, 173
Ireland 54, 58, 59, 64, 83–6, 104, 105,
    160
isolationism 85, 107, 141
Istanbul, See Constantinople
Italy 40, 55, 90, 99, 110, 117, 128,
    170, 172
Ivanovich, Matvei 119
Ivory Coast 70
Izmir 170

J.P. Morgan Company 69
Jaluit Atoll 56
Japan 1, 3, 8, 10, 12, 16, 18, 19, 22–4,
    26, 47–9, 56, 57, 62, 71–3, 94, 99,
    101, 115, 117, 124, 126, 132, 133,
    147, 148, 167, 172
Jaures, Jean 103
Jews 78, 90, 91, 166
jihad 57, 58, 91, 93, 104, 106
Johannesburg 88
Jordaan, L.J. 163

Kamara, Kande 129, 130
Kariko, Daniel 42
Kavalli River 70
Kazakhs 4, 105
Kemal, Mustafa 170
Kerensky, Alexander 120–3
Kitchener, Horatio Herbert 20, 21
Korea 16, 19, 23, 99, 117, 132, 133
Kramer, Alan 34, 38
Kuki 41

Kurdistan 170
Kurds 6, 18, 55–6, 91, 170
Kut al-Amara 77–9, 89

labour shortage 100–2
Lake Tanganyika 51
Landsdowne, Henry Charles Keith Petty-
    Fitzmaurice, Marquess of 113, 114
Latin America 18, 24, 39, 44, 48, 50,
    51, 55, 68–70, 93, 94, 98, 117,
    135–7, 145–7, 160
League of Nations 12, 112, 113, 135,
    141, 142, 146, 147, 151, 159, 171,
    172
League of Neutral Nations 111
League to Enforce Peace 112, 143
Lebanon 53, 73
Lemnos 59, 94
Lenin, Vladimir 110, 116, 122, 123,
    125, 129, 132, 133, 142, 168
Leonhard, Jörn 8, 99, 133, 137
Lettow-Vorbeck, Paul von 53
Liberia 16, 62, 70, 71, 137, 151, 152
Liebknecht, Karl 166
Liege 35, 40
Lifschütz, Alex 154, 155
Lima 48
Limburg Stirum, Johan van 131
limited war 8–10, 43, 52, 62, 171
Liverpool 84, 86
Lloyd George, David 113, 114
London 10, 46, 49, 50, 63, 86, 89, 114
Louvain 35, 40
Loveridge, Steven 127
loyalty 12, 54, 78, 79, 81–4, 88–90,
    92, 95, 99, 100, 110, 115, 117, 118,
    121, 122, 124–6, 129, 130, 133,
    145, 165, 166
Ludendorff, Erich 166
RMS *Lusitania* 37, 84–8
Luxembourg 9, 10, 16, 29, 30, 42, 43,
    45, 56, 89, 160
Luxemburg, Rosa 22, 166
Lyon 161

Macdonell, John 37, 38
Madagascar 72
Madras 72
Madrid 126

Malaka, Tan 132, 172
Malawi 99
Malaysia 54, 73, 104, 105
Mali 129, 130
malnutrition, *See* starvation
Manchuria 23, 57, 132, 147, 148
Manela, Erez 146
Maori 41, 54, 101, 168
Mariana Islands 56
Marshall Islands 56
Mathieu, Benath 154
Mboup, Dembo 167, 168
McMahon, Henry 71
Mediterranean Sea 51, 56, 57, 73, 94
Meiji government 16, 19, 22, 23, 132
Mesopotamia 57, 63, 77
Mexico 107, 109, 140
Meyer, Kathryn 46
Middle East 2, 6, 8, 36, 40, 41, 50,
    54, 55, 58, 66, 74, 80, 89, 91, 93,
    102, 104, 106, 116, 160, 164, 169,
    170
migrants 88, 89, 101, 115, 125, 135
Milan 128
military service, *See* conscription
Military Service Act (1916) 103
mobilization 8, 11, 12, 16, 27, 29, 33,
    39, 41, 46, 50, 53–5, 57, 62, 64, 72,
    74, 78, 79, 86, 91, 92, 101, 106,
    121–4, 127, 129, 144, 170
Moltke, Helmuth Johannes Ludwig
    von 50
Monger, David 92
Monrovia 151
Moscow 86, 121, 123
Moyd, Michelle 53, 130
Mukherji, Kalyan Kumar 77, 78, 81,
    82, 94
Munro, Thomas 25
Muslims 56–8, 91, 93, 104, 131, 169,
    170
Mussolini, Benito 128
mutiny 103–5, 124, 131, 164

Nabatiyya 53
Nama 41–2
Namibia, *See* South-West Africa
Nasiriyah 77
Neiberg, Michael 9, 12, 24, 107

The Netherlands 15, 25, 33, 37, 39, 40, 50, 53, 58, 62, 66, 67, 70, 85, 88, 99, 103, 111, 131, 132, 137, 143, 149, 152–4, 163, 172
Netherlands Oversea Trust Company (NOT) 70
neutrality 6–8, 10, 12, 15, 16, 27–31, 37, 45–7, 52, 55, 56, 62, 65, 88, 94, 97, 107, 109–11, 126, 131, 135–55, 171, 172
New Guinea 50, 52
New Mexico 107, 140
New York 84, 85, 109, 159
New Zealand 21, 40, 41, 52, 54, 59, 86, 88, 104, 117, 127, 162, 168
Ngati Porou 40–1
Nicaragua 136, 145
Nicholas II (Tsar) 25, 90, 116, 119, 123
Nigeria 48, 106
Noailles, Anna Comtesse Mathieu de 158
Nobel, Alfred 142
'non-whites' 20, 39, 41, 54, 83, 94, 130, 131, 167, 168
North Sea 51, 63, 64, 111, 140
Norway 106, 107, 112, 142
Noschke, Richard 89
Nyasaland 82, 83, 99

oil 48, 56, 63, 68, 69, 170 *See also* fuel
O'Mara, Pat 86, 88
Ortaggi, Simonette 128
Orthodox Greeks, *See* Greek Orthodox community
'Othering' 11, 84, 86, 88, 103, 112, 144, 166, 169
Ottoman Empire 1, 2, 10, 12, 17, 18, 23, 36, 37, 49, 53, 55, 57–9, 62–4, 67, 69, 72–4, 77–9, 91, 92, 95, 98, 100, 103, 104, 106, 114, 117, 121, 141, 152, 169–71

Pacific Ocean 51, 56, 57, 73, 94, 115
Pacific region 2, 8, 16, 46, 52, 55–7, 66, 72, 73, 82
pacifism 46, 84, 93, 110, 117, 124, 127, 142

Palestine 73, 102
Panama 68, 136, 138, 145
Panama Canal 55, 68, 69, 145
Papeete 51, 52
Paraguay 136
Pax Britannica 46
Perez Triana, Santiago 39
Persia 18, 56, 57, 63, 73, 164, 170
Peru 48, 136
Petrograd, *See* St. Petersburg
The Philippines 16, 23, 146
Pietermaritzburg 88
poison gas, *See* chemical warfare
poisoning 34, 80
Poland 91, 92, 99, 113, 127
Polesine 128
Port Said 62, 71, 72
ports 17, 48–52, 63, 71, 74, 126, 147, 151, 162
Portugal 93, 99, 110
Prazeres, Otto 160
Prior, Robin 99
propaganda 31, 37, 38, 42, 65, 67, 85, 86, 88, 92, 93, 104, 125, 145, 155
protests 22, 70, 100, 103, 105, 116, 117, 122, 125–8, 136, 150, 151
public opinion 24, 31, 37, 125, 136
Puerto Rico 16
Punin, Nicolai 119
Punjab 2, 83, 168

Qing empire 23, 147 See also China
Qurna 77

racialization 19, 23, 31, 39, 82, 91, 169
racism 19, 31, 36, 39, 41, 54, 82, 101, 129, 131, 167–9, 172, 173
Ramos, Juan P. 36
rape 31, 38, 39, 90, 91
'rape of Belgium' 10, 31, 38, 86, 144
Rasputin, Grigori 118
Rathenau, Walther 166
rationing 67, 68, 73, 95, 100
rebellion 18, 19, 21, 25, 36, 54, 58, 98, 104–6, 170
Red Cross 17, 33, 110, 111, 154
Red Sea 73
refugees 11, 23, 33, 36, 37, 39, 40, 66, 82, 88, 90, 101, 119, 162

Reichstag 25, 127
Rensberg, Nicolaas van 54
Renouvin, Pierre 65
revolutionary movements 5, 12, 18,
    22, 55, 100, 107, 110, 112, 115–33,
    154, 164, 168 *See also* Russian
    Revolutions
revolutions *See also* Russian
    Revolutions
Ritter, P.H. 53
Rolland, Romain 110
Romania 69, 92, 110, 113
Romanov government, *See* Tsarist
    regime
Roosevelt, Theodore 23, 146
Root, Elihu 143
Russia 12, 22, 25, 26, 49–51, 56, 57,
    74, 86, 90, 91, 94, 98, 99, 106,
    116–25, 132, 133, 139, 148, 149,
    172 *See also* Soviet Union
Russian Civil War (1917–23) 118, 124,
    162, 165
Russian Revolutions (1917) 1, 12, 74,
    116, 117, 120, 122, 124–33, 136,
    139, 140, 142, 146, 153
Russo-Japanese War (1904–5) 22, 23,
    118
Ruthenians 90, 91
Rwanda 4, 55

Saint-Amour, Paul K. 5
Saloniki 63, 94, 152
Samoa 16, 50, 52, 88, 89, 162, 164
Sao Paolo 126
Sarbadhikari, Sisir Prasad 94, 95
Sardinia 17
Sassun Report (1896) 36
Scandinavia 15, 50, 85, 142, 143, 154
Schaepdrijver, Sophie de 89
Schlieffen Plan 29, 34, 50
School Peace League 143, 144
Second Anglo-Boer War (1899–1902)
    36
Senegal 59, 117, 129, 130, 167
Serbia 9, 24, 25, 29, 36, 37, 47, 50, 63,
    90, 92
sexual violence, *See* rape
Shandong 148

Shanghai 46–8, 62, 71
shipping 47–51, 57, 63, 64, 66,
    67, 69–71, 73, 98, 104, 107,
    110, 139
shortages 48, 61, 68, 98–100, 104,
    109, 110, 126, 127, 131, 148, 165
Siam 54, 105, 137, 150–2
Siberia 91, 94, 147, 148
Singapore 54, 104, 105, 131
Singapore Mutiny (1916) 104, 105,
    131
Smolensk 118
smuggling 27, 67, 70
Sneevliet, Henk 131
Soiza Reilly, Juan José de 93
Sophie, Duchess of Hohenberg 24
South Africa 41, 42, 52, 54, 82, 83, 88,
    101
South-West Africa (Namibia) 41, 42,
    52
Soviet Union 1, 118, 167, 168, 172
soviets 119, 121–5, 127, 131, 165
Spain 16, 55, 93, 99, 101, 105, 109,
    117, 126, 161
Spanish flu 161–4 *See also* diseases
Spartacist uprising (1919) 166
Sri Lanka 88
St. Petersburg 119, 121–3
St. Petersburg Declaration (1868) 17
starvation 11, 64, 73, 77–9, 81, 85, 90,
    91, 99, 114, 119, 130, 152, 157,
    164, 169
state violence 6, 11, 15, 16, 19–22, 30,
    42, 79, 100, 130, 168
Stevenson, David 99
stock market 47
Stockton, C.H. 7, 17
Streets-Salter, Heather 54
strikes 19, 36, 73, 99, 107, 119, 125,
    126, 128
Struycken, A.A.H. 37, 38
Sudan 20, 21
Suez Canal 57, 63, 71, 72
Sun Yat-Sen 150
Sweden 56, 112, 142
Switzerland 16, 37, 50, 70, 85, 94, 99,
    110, 111, 115, 122, 155
Syria 8, 73

Tabora 55
Tagore, Rabindranath 115, 158, 168, 169
Tahiti 51, 52
Taiwan 16
Tanga 51
Tanzania 1, 66
Tata Iron and Steel Works 72
Tato, María Inés 136
telegraph cables 47, 50, 51, 70
Texas 140
Thomson-Urrutia Treaty (1914) 68
Togoland 52
Tokyo 47
total war 2, 4–8, 11, 12, 27, 41, 59, 61, 62, 64–6, 74, 77–81, 83, 84, 91, 93, 95, 97, 98, 100, 103, 111, 117, 118, 130, 133, 135, 140, 145, 161
Townshend, Charles 78
Treaty of Berlin (1885) 52
Treaty of Versailles (1919) 151
Trinidad 125
Trommler, Frank 86
Tsarist regime 22, 23, 25, 74, 90, 91, 100, 105, 116–23, 132, 172 *See also* Russia
Tsingtao 47, 56, 57, 71, 89, 94, 148
Turkestan 105
Turkey, *See* Ottoman Empire
Tutsi 55

U-boats 64, 66, 81, 84–6, 107, 136–40, 145, 146, 148
Ukraine 122, 127
unemployment 47, 48, 70, 98, 126
United Kingdom, *See* Great Britain
United States 1, 3, 6, 8, 12, 18–20, 23, 32, 37, 40, 46, 48, 49, 55–7, 62, 67–9, 75, 85, 93, 98, 101, 105, 107–9, 111, 115, 124, 126, 135–55, 161, 164, 167, 172
Uruguay 136

Vajiradvudh (king of Siam) 150, 151
Valdés, Ramón Maximiliano 138
Valparaiso 70
Vietnam 58, 101
Villa, Pancho 107, 109, 140
Vina del Mar 70
violence against civilians 3, 9, 11, 30, 31, 34, 35, 64, 78, 81, 85, 89–91, 93, 105, 108, 129, 151, 160, 168
Vistula 80
Vladivostok 72, 94
Volta Bani 117, 129–31
Vyborg 119

Wagogo 1, 2, 5, 99, 130, 164
war profiteering 38, 73, 74, 107
Washington DC 68
Watson, Alexander 91
Weihaiwei 47
Weimar Republic 165, 166
Wellington 88
Weseler, Hans 35
White Book on Belgium (1915) 42
Wilhelm II (Kaiser) 34, 58, 164, 165
Wilson, Trevor 4
Wilson, Woodrow 56, 57, 75, 107, 109, 112, 113, 133, 135, 137, 140–3, 145, 146, 148, 152, 158, 168, 170–2
Winnebago 144
Winter, Jay 12, 116
Wolfe, William Leon 145
women 31, 33, 35, 38, 42, 53, 58, 64, 65, 82, 91, 101, 112, 119, 128, 162, 164
Women's Peace Conference (1915) 112, 164

Ypres 32, 80, 81, 85

Zaanstroom 66
Zeebrugge 66
Ziemann, Benjamin 99
Zweig, Stefan 110